S. MICHELE

D0014464

Canale delle Fondamenta Nuove

Sal. Specchieri

Fond. Mendicanti

Fond. Nuove

Campo SS. Giovanni e Paolo

Campo S. Lorenzo

Campo Confraternita

Sal. S. Giustina

Fond. di S. Lorenzo

CASTELLO

Campo S. Zaccaria

Campo Bandiera e Moro

Fond. dell'Arsenale

Riva degli Schiavoni

Riva Ca di Dio

Riva dei Sette Martiri

Via Garibaldi

Viale Garibaldi

Fond. S. Giuseppe

Canale di S. Marco

Campo S. Giorgio

J. S. Giovanni

Giardini Pubblici

Giardini Pubblici

Viale Trento

Viale 24 Maggio

Campo Sportivo

Parco della Rimembranza

Viale Piave

Viale 4 Novembre

Viale Vittorio Veneto

VENICE

Art & Architecture

VENICE

Marion Kaminski

Frontispiece
View of the Rialto Bridge

Note:
Information regarding the location of works in museums and churches as well as
concerning opening times are subject to change.

© 2005 Tandem Verlag GmbH
KÖNEMANN is a trademark and an imprint of Tandem Verlag GmbH

Original Title: *Kunst & Architektur. Venedig*
ISBN 3-8331-1308-1

Art Direction: Peter Feierabend
Project Management: Ute Edda Hammer
Assistant: Jeannette Fentroß
Editing: Barbro Garenfeld
Layout: Anne-Claire Martin, Philine Rath
Graphics: Rolli Arts, Essen
Cartography: Astrid Fischer-Leitl, Múnich
Picture Research: Monika Bergmann

© 2005 for the English edition: Tandem Verlag GmbH
KÖNEMANN is a trademark and an imprint of Tandem Verlag GmbH

Translation from German: Mark Cole and Eithne McCarthy in association with Goodfellow & Egan
Editing: Kay Hyman in association with Goodfellow & Egan
Typesetting: Goodfellow & Egan
Project management: Jackie Dobbyne for Goodfellow & Egan
Project coordination: Kristin Zeier

Printed in Germany

ISBN 3-8331-1490-8

10 9 8 7 6 5 4 3 2 1
X IX VIII VII VI V IV III II I

Table of Contents

View of the Grand Canal

Detail of mosaic facade from San Marco

View from Campanile of the Frari church

Palazzi on the Grand Canal

View of Il Redentore

View of the facade from Fondamenta Gaspare Contarini at Madonna dell'Orto

San Giorgio Maggiore

View of the Lido

Facade of Santa Fosca, Torcello

View of nave from San Michele in Isola

View from Campanile of the Frari church

1300 years: a brief overview
From the beginnings to the end of the Republic

Goethe was reminded of a gigantic beaver lodge when he saw Venice for the first time on September 28, 1786. The jumble of waterways, paths, alleys, bridges and cul-de-sacs that make up Venice becomes understandable, however, only once you know how the city came into being.

Early history

The lagoon at the northwest edge of the Adriatic, which was known as Venetia as far back as Roman times, used to be larger than it is today. It was slowly silted up by the many rivers that flow here from the Alps into the Mediterranean. In the brackish water of the open lagoon, there were small, muddy islands and larger sandbanks (known as *lidi*). They were inhabited by fishermen and salt producers, and used as summer residences by wealthy Roman citizens.

The quiet, isolated life of the lagoon dwellers gradually changed during the 4th century, as increasing numbers of people from northern Italy settled here, fleeing the wars. The biggest wave of refugees came when Attila the Hun invaded Rome in 452–53. New cities such as Chioggia, Jesolo, and Torcello flourished, while, in the place where Venice would stand, the

first larger settlements started to develop in the region of Olivolo (today's Castello), around Rivo Alto (today's Rialto), and on various other pieces of high ground that emerged from the lagoon.

From the 6th century onwards, Venice was in the sphere of influence of the Ostrogoths, who ruled from Ravenna. With the death of King Theodoric in 526, however, their authority collapsed, and Venice fell under the rule of the Roman emperor, Justinian (482/3–565). The invasions of the Lombards in 568 succeeded in dismembering the Roman empire, and again new refugees flooded to the lagoon. Torcello and Malamocco evolved into major centers of trade and culture, and the population of the islands also started to grow.

For a while, each island remained a world unto itself. When, in 680, the Roman emperors finally withdrew to Constantinople, leaving northern Italy to the Lombards, Rome and a few other regions, including the exarchate (ecclesiastical state) of Ravenna, of which the Venetian lagoon was part, remained under the Roman emperors. The islands gradually developed. In addition to farming and fishing, trade (particularly in salt and fish) grew in importance. Because of the constant threat from the Lombards,

Vittore Carpaccio: Lion of St. Mark, 1516, oil on canvas, 130 x 368 cm, Doges' Palace, Venice. After the transfer of his relics in 828, St. Mark's symbol, the lion, was adopted as the symbol of Venice. On the open pages of the book lies the greeting with which an angel announced that Venice was the place where the saint would be most highly honored.

the inhabitants of the lagoon managed to persuade the Byzantine emperors in Constantinople to replace the military tribunes who were responsible for protecting it with a local *dux* (leader), who had greater decision-making powers. The first such *dux*, Paoluccio Anafesto, was chosen in 697.

But times were still difficult. When Charlemagne defeated the Lombards in 774, Venice became the object of a tug-of-war between Byzantium and the German emperors. Charlemagne's son Pepin attempted to invade the lagoon, but failed. This reconfirmed Byzantium's supremacy over the area. But after these perilous attacks the *duca*, or doge, withdrew further into the protected part of the lagoon, the Rivo Alto. Moving the military command post onto one of the islands of

the future Venice marked the beginning of the rise of this collection of tiny islands into a city-state and a major power in the Mediterranean.

It was not until the 13th century that the new city, which had grown out of numerous little island villages and townships, finally received the name of Venezia. More important to Venice's identity than the transfer of the seat of power to the island was the transfer (or translation) from Alexandria in 828 of the relics of St. Mark, in whose honor a church was immediately built. A legend about the saint promptly developed: while the Apostle was preaching in the lagoon, an angel appeared to him in his sleep and told him that the spot where the Basilica di San Marco now stands would be his final resting place and the location where he would be most greatly honored.

Francesco Bassano: Pope Alexander III Hands Over the Sword to Doge Sebastiano Ziani, 1577–85, Doges' Palace, Venice.
This 16th-century painting shows the ceremony by which, in 1177, the Pope recognized the doge for mediating the peace between Emperor Frederick Barbarossa and the Papacy. The Piazzetta depicted here is not that of the 12th century, however, but of the 16th century.

The rise of Venice

The new city gradually took shape. At the end of the 9th century, the fortifications stretched from the Riva degli Schiavoni, past San Giorgio, to the Punta della Dogana, and back to Santa Maria Zobenigo. Within this area the occasional wooden bridge crossed the many watercourses and swampy stretches. But the inhabited districts outside the fortifications could be reached only by boat. The roads within the city – save for a few main thoroughfares – did not connect the islands with each other, but were designed to serve their own separate communities. What unified the people of Venice was the patron saint of the city, defense requirements, and trading interests. With combined efforts they succeeded in bringing the entire Adriatic under Venetian control.

Again and again the Venetians had to put their successful navy at the service of Byzantium, which was suffering under the attacks of the Saracens. In return, the doges extracted greater trade privileges and more independence. In the power struggle between the capital, Constantinople, and its distant possession in Italy, the island city gradually prevailed. Even if Byzantine documents still described Venice as Byzantium's "eldest daughter," it became increasingly clear that the city was largely independent of the declining Byzantine Empire. The magnificent basilica built at the end of the 11th century in honor of St. Mark, patron saint of the city, was a clear expression of Venice's increasing power and wealth. In the 12th century Venice had trading posts throughout the eastern Mediterranean, and was a growing rival to Pisa and Genoa, Italy's other major sea-trading cities. They had a common enemy in the German emperors, who regarded themselves as the legitimate heirs to the Roman empire.

Theoretically, Venice belonged to Byzantium, however, and therefore stood apart from the struggles for independence between the other Italian cities and German imperial power. Although, after a great deal of hesitation, Venice finally joined the Lombard League, a federation of cities, the Venetians exercised such clever diplomacy that they were finally called as intermediaries between the German emperor and the Pope, who supported the city-states. In 1177 a peace treaty between Emperor Frederick Barbarossa, Pope Alexander III, and the city-states was signed in Venice, which gave the city on the lagoon its place among the Great Powers. It was only a matter of decades until Venice was freed from the now nominal rule of Byzantium.

Doge Enrico Dandolo (1192–1205) was, despite his great age and blindness, one of the most prominent figures in Venetian history. It was largely thanks to his skillful negotiations that the Crusaders who set off on the Fourth Crusade from the Lido on Venetian ships were persuaded to take Constantinople. The pretext for this was that a rightful heir to the throne had been denied his rights; however, the young man whom the Crusaders set on the throne in 1203, died in battle. In 1204 the Crusaders and the Venetians divided the Byzantine empire between themselves, but not before plundering the vast treasures of Constantinople. Not even the churches were spared. The Venetians carried countless works of art westwards to embellish the basilica of their patron saint.

Another benefit from the campaign was that they gained control over three-eighths or, as the Venetians put it, one quarter and a half, of the former Byzantine empire. Thus Venice controlled a tight chain of harbors throughout the eastern Mediterranean, and it was only a matter of time before Genoa, the other major trading power, would try to put a stop to Venice's expansion. Indeed, in 1261 the Genoese allied themselves with Byzantium and, with combined forces, they toppled the kingdom that the Crusaders had set up on Byzantine soil. This also affected the fate of Venice. The Venetians lost all the trading privileges they had enjoyed up until then, although, with their diplomatic skills, they managed to regain at least some of their earlier trading concessions.

But the Genoese did not let them off that easily. The fortunes of war swung back and forth: the two rivals fought for supremacy in the eastern Mediterranean for over 100 years. In 1378–79 it seemed that Genoa had finally succeeded in its ambition. The Venetian fleet suffered a crippling defeat, and the Genoese became masters of the Mediterranean. Now the Genoese, enlisting the help of the Austrians and also of the Carraras, the rulers of Padua, tried to destroy Venice itself. These attacks on the city have gone down in Venetian history as the Chioggia Wars. The Genoese and their allies succeeded in taking the city of Chioggia and thus making incursions into the lagoon.

But the Venetians did not give up. With incredible effort they built a new fleet, barricaded the entrance into the lagoon, and blocked off the Porto di Lido, which was the only route into the open sea. In addition, they reappointed as supreme commander Vittore Pisani, the man who had been beaten by the Genoese in 1378–79, and who had since been languishing in prison. On August 13, 1380, the Genoese were finally pushed back: the Republic of Venice had succeeded in staving off the greatest threat to its existence.

Venice was also subject to internal political crises, however. In 1310 Bajamonte Tiepolo had tried to overthrow the incumbent doge and to replace him on the throne. In 1355 Doge Marino Falier himself posed a much greater threat to the state when he tried to follow the examples of other Italian city-states by making himself the sole ruler of the city. But his conspiracy was betrayed, and was suppressed by the very craftsmen and arsenal workers on whom he had relied. On April 17, Falier was beheaded on the steps leading to the Doges' Palace, where he had been crowned.

Domenico Tintoretto: The Conquest of Constantinople, 1578–85, Doges' Palace, Venice

The Golden Age

Until the early 15th century, the Republic had looked, above all, to the sea: navigation and sea trade were the foundations of Venice's wealth. Conscious of their growing might, the Venetians then started to subjugate towns on the nearby mainland. Some, like the aged Doge Tomaso Mocenigo (in office 1414–23), warned the Venetians against getting involved with the mainland, advocating a return to their old source of power, the sea. But there were other voices too. And so, in 1423, Francesco Foscari was elected doge, and pursued a consistent policy of increasing Venice's mainland possessions.

Thus, by the middle of the 15th century, the Republic stretched from the river Po to the Alps, and to Istria and Dalmatia in the east. But the price was high. The conquests required great resources, and the whole of Europe looked on Venice's growth with suspicion. Venice's luck turned when, in 1453, the Turks overran Constantinople. In a short period of time, the economic foundation of Venice's wars of conquest, its flourishing trade in the East, was almost entirely wiped out. Although the Venetians were quick to make treaties with the new rulers of Constantinople, the situation was not the same as before. The Turks became a constant threat and the Republic's finances started to become exhausted. The doge and his heedless policy of expansion were blamed, so that in 1457 Francesco Foscari was forced to tender a humiliating resignation. He died two days after the election of his successor. During the 15th century the Venetians lost island after island and city after city in the eastern Mediterranean to the Turks.

The whole of Europe watched the losses of the hated Republic, which had grabbed more and more land in Italy, with satisfaction. In 1508 the Pope, Spain, the German

Empire, and France joined together in a League against Venice at Cambrai, which was later joined by the Dukes of Mantua, Ferrara, and Savoy. One year later the Venetian army suffered a decisive defeat, and Venice's might seemed to be broken.

The plague raged in the city, and, in 1509, the Pope excommunicated Venice. The Venetians fought on doggedly until finally they won a diplomatic victory. They managed to sow discord among their opponents and, thereby, split their ranks.

Jacopo de Barbari: Map of Venice, 1500, woodcut, Museo Correr, Venice.
In 1500, the Venetian Jacopo de Barbari had Anton Koberger of Nuremberg print a woodcut from his plan, which accurately portrayed every house in his native city.

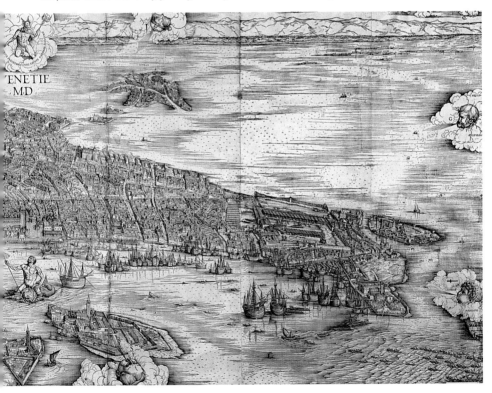

Lorenzo Bastiani: Doge Francesco Foscari, 2nd half of the 15th century, Museo Correr, Venice.

Gentile Bellini: Sultan Muhammad II, Conqueror of Constantinople, 1480, canvas, 70 x 52 cm, The National Gallery, London.

The Republic was on its last legs, but the war against the League of Cambrai ended without any loss of territory. For the last time, Venice was again at the peak of its power, but the times in which the city-state could play a major role in Europe were coming to an end. The cause was not so much the discovery by Christopher Columbus of a New World in 1492, and the subsequent development of new trade routes taken over by Spain and Portugal, as many may assume; Venice's volume of trade fell only very slowly during the 16th century. The reason was, in fact, the Venetian aristocracy's growing preference for investment in land rather than in risky overseas trade ventures.

The slow death of the Republic

European politics increasingly became an arena for the Great Powers, where small Italian city-states, even wealthy ones like Venice, lost in influence. The Venetian fleet's major victory over the Turks at the Battle of Lepanto in 1571 was more of a triumph for the king of Spain, who had been allocated the role of the protector of Christendom. Nonetheless, the Venetians succeeded in holding on to their independence. Their political system spared the city from falling completely under the influence of the Great Powers. This had happened to Florence which, by marrying members of its ruling family to the leading dynasties of Europe, was gradually absorbed into it.

The strict separation of Church and State in Venice meant that not even the Pope could hold great sway over the Republic. In 1607 Pope Paul V tried to give the Catholic Church greater power in Venice by laying the city under the interdict, i.e. banning all church rites. The Venetians, however, promptly banned the publication of the papal decree, and the Pope had to give in.

Luigi Querena: The Arrival in Venice of Napoleon's Troops, Museo del Risorgimento, Venice.

Another threat that, in the long run, the Venetians were unable to hold back, was the loss of their possessions in the Mediterranean to the Turks. Countless battles and changing fortunes finally forced Venice to give up everything it owned in the eastern Mediterranean. In 1669, after bloody battles, the fertile island of Crete was lost. Although the Venetians did manage, under the courageous Doge Francesco Morosini, to regain the Peloponnese some 14 years later, this was not a long-term victory. How insignificant Venice had become can be seen by the fact that, in the Peace of Passarowitz in 1718, Turkey and Austria decided Venice's fate without the Republic having a say.

During the 18th century, Venice's economic decline also became evident. When, in 1797, Napoleon forced the Great Council to end an independence dating back almost 1000 years, this was merely the fulfilment of an act that had been fore-seen much earlier. Some people did expect that the Habsburg empire would bring Venice to its knees, as it had long had its eye on the city, but it was not until Napoleon's defeat that Venice, along with the rest of northern Italy, was given to the Austrian empire.

Not long after this the Italians began their own struggle for independence. Although the Venetians played a heroic and tragic part, they were no longer able to influence the fate of their city. Prussia's defeat of Austria, in which the kingdom of Italy also took part, forced a referendum to be held: in 1866, 674,426 voters in Venice and the Veneto voted in favor of, and 69 against, joining the kingdom of Italy. The age of independence was thus over, and 1000 years of Venetian history were at an end.

Anonymous: Engraving based on a map from the 14th-century map of Venice, Museo Correr, Venice

The map shows east placed at the top (instead of north, as is usual today). The Doges' Palace can be seen clearly center right, surrounded by a wall.

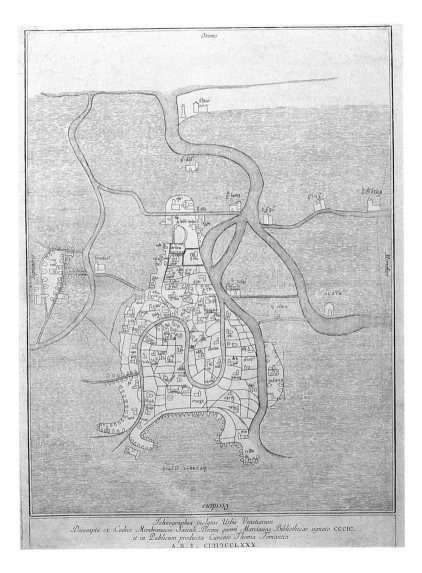

Oriens

Occidens

Meridies

Septentrio

Ichnographia inclytae Urbis Venetiarum
Desumpta ex Codice Membranaceo Saeculi Decimi quarti Marcianae Bibliothecae signato CCCIC.
et in Publicum producta Curante Thoma Temantia
A.R.S. CIƆIƆCCLXXX.

The streets of Venice

To this day rumor has it that there is no reliable street plan of Venice. Although this is untrue, the official map of Venice which gives every road, canal, and alley is so detailed that it is hardly conducive to an enjoyable walk around the city. However, the most important routes to the main buildings and museums are, in fact, very well signposted, so that anyone can get to the Piazza San Marco, the Rialto, the Accademia or the train station. The signs lead you safely through the maze of streets

Anonymous: Perspective view of Venice, oil on canvas, Museo Correr, Venice.

and canals, while at the same time giving the visitor the chance to see a large and important part of Venice. Even if you are in a hurry it is worth risking a small diversion and letting yourself be drawn into the maze of confusing and nameless alleys.

Roaming through the narrow streets of Venice brings you face to face with the charm of the city, although you may experience a slight sense of insecurity. The  bright sunlight falling at an angle from above into the narrow lanes, a dark, motionless canal, an open window with the smell of cooking wafting from it, dark narrow streets that suddenly open out into a small, forgotten square with a splendid palazzo – all this is as much a part of Venice as San Marco, the Doges' Palace or the palazzi along the Grand Canal. This makes Venice one of the easiest cities in the world in which to get lost, while being small enough to get across within two or three hours. If you get tired or hungry, there is always a vaporetto stop from which you can take a boat back to more familiar landmarks, which are usually no more than 15 minutes' walk away.

Decoding the different types of Venetian street names helps you to find your way around. Some streets are marked with the Italian word *calle*. However, it is more usual to come across *salizzada* (in other words, a main thoroughfare that was paved in the old days), *fondamenta* (a canalside path), or *ruga* (a path flanked by shops and workshops). *Ramo* is used to designate a small street connecting two large thoroughfares. As one of these thoroughfares could be a canal, it is not uncommon for the *ramo* to turn out to be a dead-end. A *sottoportego* is a path that goes underneath a building, while a *rio terra* is a former canal that has become a footpath.

Venice is divided into six districts, known as *sestiere* (from the Italian *sesto*, meaning one-sixth): San Marco in the center, Santa Croce and San Polo in the northwest, Cannaregio in the north, Dorsoduro in the west, Giudecca in the south, and Castello in the east. They are all self-contained districts, which have survived to this day thanks to the fact that Venice consists of numerous small islands. The pavements and bridges were built mainly to help people get around within a *sestiere*, while longer distances have always been covered by boat.

Appendix

Glossary

Albergo (It., hostel, shelter), in the context of the Venetian *scuole* (or confraternity buildings), the richly decorated assembly hall where the committee of the *scuola* met.

Al fresco (Italian "on the fresh"), fresco painting, wall painting on fresh wet plaster, the opposite of *secco* painting on dry plaster.

Allegory (Gk., *allegoria*: to allegorize or depict differently), the depiction of abstract concepts and ideas by physical entities, usually by means of human figures or scenes.

Al secco (Italian "on the dry"), secco painting, wall painting on dry plaster, the opposite of fresco painting on wet plaster.

Altarpiece (Lat., *altar*, sacrificial table), also known as an "altar panel," frequently used to decorate medieval altars. While gold or sculpted figures were originally used, later on paintings were also incorporated. The altarpiece could consist of a single painting or of several panels. It is often situated behind the altar, or is a retable attached to the rear of the altar. (See also Pala.)

Annunciation (Lat., *annunciare*, to announce), according to the Gospel of Luke (1, 26–38), the moment at which the Archangel Gabriel gave Mary the news that she would give birth to Christ. The Annunciation was one of the most widely depicted themes in medieval and Renaissance art.

Altarpiece

Antiquity (Fr., *antique*, ancient, from Latin *antiquus*, old), the Graeco-Roman period, beginning with the early Greek settlement in the 2nd millenium B.C. and ending in the West with the overthrow of the Roman emperor Romulus Augustulus (c. 475 A.D.), and in the East in 529 A.D. with the closure of Plato's Academy by the Emperor Justinian (482–565 A.D.).

Apostle (Gk., *apostolos*, messenger, protagonist), one of the Twelve Disciples whom Jesus selected from his large group of followers to continue his works and to preach the Gospel.

Apotheosis (from Gk., to deify, transfigure), elevation of a human being to divine status.

Apse (Lat., Gk., *hapsis*, connection, vaulting), a niche with a semicircular or polygonal base crowned with a half-dome over the location of the altar. When attached to the main hall or to the choir area reserved for the clergy, it is also known as the choir. Smaller side apses are often found in the ambulatory or the transept or side aisles.

Arcade (Fr., *arcade*, from Lat., *arcus*, bow, hunting weapon), an arch or a row of arches supported by columns.

Arch (Lat., *arcus*, bow), a vaulted load-bearing aperture in a wall, supported by pillars or columns. The highest point in an arch, with the keystone, is the crown. The height of the arch is the distance between the crown and the line on which the impost (the masonry between the wall, pillar or column and the arch) lies. The inner surface is called the intrados or soffit, while the front surface of the arch is called the extrados.

Architrave (Gk., *archein*, to commence, master, and Lat., *trabs*, beam), the main beam supported by uprights, e.g. columns, and which bears the weight of the superstructure. It may be divided into three horizontal sections.

Atrium (Lat., ante-room), the open forecourt of a church enclosed by an arcade or colonnaded walk on three or four sides sides, often with a well at the center. The term is also used for the vestibule of a church.

Attic (Lat., Atticus, Attic), a low, subdivided section built over the cornice of an order of columns or pilasters, which can also be used to conceal the roof covering. In Baroque buildings it is a half-height story with windows.

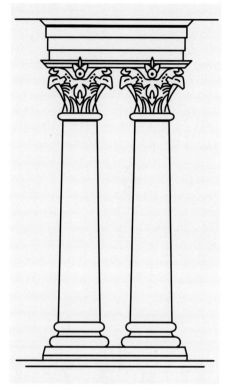

Two columns joined by an architrave

Attribute (Lat., *attributum*, addition), an object provided to identify a person in a work of art, or a symbol identifying the person, usually in relation to an event in that person's life.

Augustinian order, medieval mendicant order whose members observe rules derived from the writings of St. Augustine of Hippo (354–430 A.D.).

517

It was founded in 1256 and expanded in the 14th and 15th centuries following the congregation of church associations. As a result of the spread of Renaissance humanism, a philosophy based on the principles of true humanity, many supporters of the Early Reformation movement were members of the Augustinians, including its founding member Martin Luther (1483–1546). The order's main mission is in education.

Aureole (Lat., *aureolus*, golden, fine, favorite), a circle of light around the head or surrounding an entire person.

Bacino di S. Marco (It., (harbor) basin of San Marco), the bay in Venice, onto which the Piazzetta with the Doges' Palace opens, and which forms the mouth of the Grand Canal.

Baldachin (It., *baldacchino*), cloth canopy over a throne or a bed, or carried on poles during processions; in architecture a wood or stone decorative ceiling above a throne, bishop's throne, altar, catafalque (ceremonial funeral bier), or pulpit and statue. The name derives from the expensive silk, embroidered with gold thread, imported from Baghdad (Baldacco in Italian) and used for the first processional canopy in Italy.

Balustrade, a barrier or parapet made up of balusters (upright, often vase-shaped supports for a rail).

Baptistery (Latin and Greek *baptisterion* "bathing place," "swimming pool"), a separate usually octagonal centrally planned church building used for the sacrament of baptism. Baptisteries were often built on the west side of episcopal churches and dedicated to St. John the Baptist.

Baroque (Port., *barocco*, pebbles), a European style lasting from the end of Mannerism (c. 1590) to the beginning of the Rococo (c. 1725). The term originates from the work of goldsmiths, who used the term *barocco* to describe irregularly-shaped pearls.

Basilica (Gk., *stoa basilike*, king's hall), a church, usually facing east, with a nave and two or four lower side aisles. To this can be added a transept between the nave and the choir reserved for the clergy. Originally the basilica was an ancient Greek public building and a Roman market hall and law courts, after which it was an early Christian assembly hall. The term originates from the office of Archon Basileus, the supreme judge presiding in the market place of Athens.

Balustrade

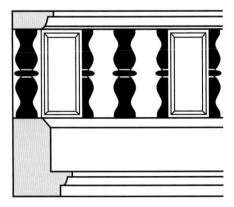

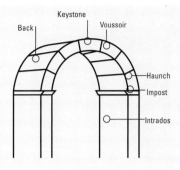

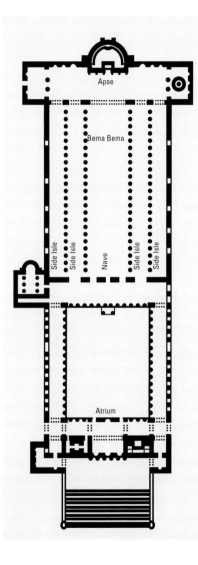

Bay, regular structural subdivision of a building, e.g. church. In Classical buildings the bays may be marked by the use of different architectural orders, vaults, roof-trusses, or beams.

Bessarion, John (c 1403–72), bishop of Nicaea, who became cardinal in 1439. He promoted the idea of a union of the Eastern and Western Churches at the Council of Florence in 1439 and, after this failed, became a vehement supporter of action against the Turks.

Biennale (Lat. *biennium*, *bis*, twice, and *annus*, year), the Venice Biennale is an international art exhibition, started in 1895, held every two years in the Giardini Publicci in Venice; since 1932 associated with international film festivals.

Bishop (Gk., *episkopos*, overseer), a high-placed church dignitary. In early Christianity the bishop was head of a community and later, as a successor to the Apostles, the ecclesiastical head of a bishopric or diocese. Bishops are devoted to teaching, the priesthood, and pastoral work; they wear a miter and a gold ring and carry a crozier.

Illumination

Bucintoro, the doge of Venice's ceremonial barge, or galley, which was rowed by 200 oarsmen. It was used to carry the doge into the open sea on Ascension Day so that he could throw into the water a ring symbolizing Venice's marriage to the sea.

Bust (Fr., *buste*, half-length portrait), a sculpture (usually set on a pedestal) depicting the head, shoulders, and upper chest.

Campanile (It., *campana*, bell), a free-standing church belltower.

Campo (It., field), the Venetian term for a city square, usually the forecourt of a church or a small area between palazzi, usually with one side opening onto a canal.

Capital (Lat., *capitulum*, little head), the head of a column or pillar. May be decorated with foliage, flowers, figures or a pattern.

Chapel (Middle Lat., *cappella*, small cloak), a small self-contained room in a church, or a smaller church without a priest for a particular purpose, e.g. baptism or burial. The name comes from a small room for prayer in the royal palace in Paris, where the cloak of St. Martin of Tours (316/17–397 A.D.) was kept from the 7th century onwards.

Cherubim (Hebr., sing. cherub), in the Old Testament, together with the seraphim, part of the upper hierarchy of the angels, and choirs in the celestial retinue. In the New Testament they are also part of Christ's guard of honor. There are two types of cherubim in Christian art: the tetramorph, which has a human, lion's, bull's, and eagle's head and eyes in its four wings; and the cherub angel, with a human face and four eyed wings. The two types are often also given six wings, thus making them indistinguishable from seraphim. The cherubim originate from early oriental winged beasts with human faces.

Choir (Lat., *chorus*, Gk., *choros*, round dance, group of singers and dancers), a usually elevated and differentiated area in a church reserved for prayers by the clergy or for choristers. Since Carolingian times it has described the extension of the nave after the crossing (where the nave and transepts meet), including the apse (a semicircular domed extension of the wall).

Choir screen, or rood screen, screen or wall that partitions off the part of the choir strictly reserved for song or prayer by the clergy. It is often painted or carved. (See also Iconostasis.)

Condottiere (It., leader), head of an army or mercenaries in 14th–15th century Italy.

Confraternity (Lat., *con*, with, *frater*, with), or brotherhood, from the Early Middle Ages, a Catholic society for common prayer, originally consisting only of monks and clergymen, but later also involving laymen. Its aim was to promote piety and love of one's neighbor.

Consiglio dei Dieci (It., Council of Ten), an influential political investigation committee set up in 1310 in Venice. Its members were temporarily elected from the Great Council, which was the parliament of the Venetian nobility.

Cornice, a strip set out from the wall which separates the horizontal sections of a building.

Courtesan (Fr., *courtisan* and It., *cortigiano*, courtier), lady of the court; mistress of distinguished and aristocratic gentlemen; fashionable, elegant prostitute.

Crossing, the area in a church where the nave crosses the transept.

Cruciform-domed basilica, a church whose main structure has a cruciform plan and is topped by one or more domes. The adjoining spaces may also have large or smaller domes (e.g. San Marco, Venice), or be covered

by tunnel vaults. The plan was developed in Byzantine church architecture and is widespread in Eastern Christianity.

Crypt (Lat., *crypta* and Gk., *krypte*, covered passage, vault), subterranean religious or burial

Campanile

521

Trefoil

area, usually below a church's choir, reserved for the clergy.

Cycle (Late Lat., *cyclus*, Gk., *kyklos*, circle), a series of works of art with a common theme.

Dante Alighieri (1265–1321), Italy's most illustrious writer. In 1302 he was banned from Florence, his native city, for political activity. His best-known work is *La Divina Commedia*, whose three main sections, *Inferno*, *Purgatorio,* and *Paradiso*, were written in the last ten years of his life in the Tuscan dialect.

Doge (It., Lat., *dux*, leader), the holder of the highest political office in Venice (697 A.D.–1797) and Genoa (1339–1797).

Dolce, Lodovico (1508-68), Venetian writer and art scholar. Among his works is the *Dialogo della Pittura intitolato l'Arentino*, containing the earliest surviving biography of Titian (1485/90 –1576).

Dome, a ceiling or roof vaulting a round, square, or polygonal room in regular curves. The square plan can merge into the round base of the dome in a number of ways: in the sail vault dome, the base of the dome forms an imaginary circle around the square plan; in the pendentive dome, an imaginary sail vault is cut off horizontally and the resulting circle topped with a hemispheric dome; the resulting spherical triangles are known as the "pendentives"; in the Bohemian cap, as with the sail vault, the vaulted area is smaller than the square of the plan.

Dominican Order (Lat., Ordo Fratrum Praedicatorum, Order of the Preaching Friars), a mendicant order founded by St. Dominic (1170– 1221) in Toulouse in 1216, sworn to spreading and defending the Gospel by preaching and teaching. In 1232 the Pope assigned the Dominicans with the conduct of the Inquisition, the church court which tried unbelievers.

Doric column, a vertical element of the Doric order of columns (Greek architectural system). Its features were: no base, sharp fluting, narrowing shaft, and uncarved capital with incised rings (anuli), rounded molding (echinus), and square surmounting slab (abacus).

Festoon, a sculpted decorative motif in the shape of a hanging garland of flowers, laurels, or fruit.

Franciscan Order (Lat., Ordo Fratrum Minorum, Order of the Lesser Brothers), a mendicant

Friezes

Antiquity:

Running dog wave

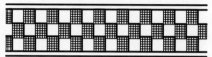

Chessboard

Meander

Notched

Crenellated

Round arch

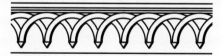

Cross arch

Romanesque:

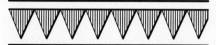

Sawtooth

Diamond band

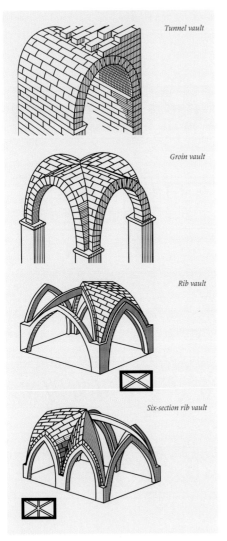

Tunnel vault

Groin vault

Rib vault

Six-section rib vault

order founded in 1209 (or 1223) by Francis of Assisi (1181/2–1226), which was sworn in particular to asceticism and poverty. The most fervent worshippers of the Virgin Mary in the Middle Ages, the Franciscans placed their order under the protection of the Madonna.

Fresco (It., fresh), a method of mural painting where the paint is applied onto wet plaster. As the plaster dries quickly, only the section of the wall which the painter can cover in one day is plastered at a time. Compared to secco (It., dry), where the painting is done on dry plaster, frescoes are much more durable, under favorable climatic conditions.

Frieze (Middle Lat., edge, fringe), a sculpted or painted horizontal decorative strip, used to decorate, divide, or restore a wall.

Gothic (It., *gotico*, barbaric, nonclassical), an architectural and artistic style of the Middle Ages originating in northern France in about 1150. It lasted there until ca. 1400, although it persisted elsewhere until the early 16th century. The term is derived from the Germanic tribe, the Goths. Specifically Gothic features in architecture include the pointed arch (which was broken in the crown) and the groin vault (two tunnel vaults of the same size crossing each other at right angles), and the external addition of flying buttresses (arches and piers to reinforce the walls in absorbing the pressure of the vaults and the roof). The overall impression of Gothic buildings is their upward motion, and their segmented walls and windows. The ultimate Gothic building was the cathedral. Sculpture is a particularly important part of the architecture,

Icon

characterized by depiction of natural forms and an idealized, usually elongated, depiction of bodies and robes. The main pictorial works in the Gothic style are panel paintings, illuminations, and stained glass.

Groin vault, two tunnel vaults of identical size crossed at right angles, the ceilings being semicircular or segmented. If its cross-sections are ribbed, then it is known as a rib vault.

Hall church (Greek *kyriakon* "that which belongs to the Lord"), a church whose nave and aisles are of the same height and have one roof, i.e. with no clerestory. Hall churches do not usually have a transept. They are a common feature in German Gothic architecture.

Heresy (Gk., *hairesis*, chosen way of thinking), originally, in antiquity, the choice of a certain field of knowledge; in Christian thinking it was belief that diverged from the ruling dogma.

High altar, the main or middle altar in a church, usually in front of or in the apse.

Icon (Gk., *eikon*, picture, depiction, likeness), a small portable painting of the Eastern Church. Forms and colors are strictly idealized. The cult-like worshipping of icons originated in the concept of the passing on, through the centuries, of an original likeness of Jesus, Mary, and the Saints.

Iconography (Gk., *eikon*, picture, and *graphein*, to describe), the teaching of the content, meaning, and symbolism of paintings, particularly in Christian art; it was originally the study of portraits in antiquity.

Iconostasis (Middle Gk., *eikon*, picture, and *stasion*, stand), a partition wall decorated with icons, which in the Greek Orthodox Church separates the church hall from the sanctuary. (See also Choir screen.)

Illumination, a hand-painted decorative illustration or picture in a manuscript.

Incrustation (Lat., *incrustare*, to cover with bark), a decorative covering of colored, polished stone,

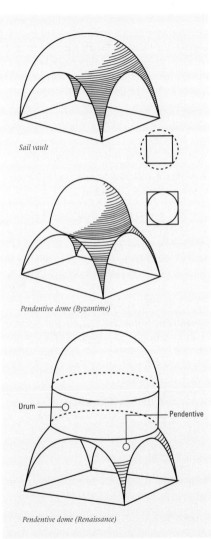

Sail vault

Pendentive dome (Byzantime)

Drum — Pendentive

Pendentive dome (Renaissance)

usually marble or porphyry slabs in a pattern on walls and floors; also of gemstones on metalwork.

Inquisition (Lat., *inquisitio*, investigation, study), the medieval Church's institution for the persecution of heresy and misdeeds. Papal inquisitors (preferably Dominican and Franciscan monks) were appointed from 1231. Pope Gregory IX (1227–41) in 1234 turned the Inquisition into a papal institution (Sanctum Officium), which later broadened its attention to other areas such as sorcery, witchcraft, and soothsaying.

Interior, artistic representation of the inside of a building or room.

Intrados, the vertical inner surface of a wall aperture, usually an arch, window, or portal.

Lantern (Latin *la(n)terna* and Greek *lamptera* "lamp"), a circular or polygonal structure pierced with windows rising above a dome or vault.

Latin cross (Latin crux), a cross in which the vertical part below the horizontal is longer than the other three parts. The most popular plan in medieval western churches.

League of Cambrai, an alliance against Venice formed from 1508 to 1510 between Pope Julius II (1443–1513), the Emperor Maximilian I (1459–1519), Ferdinand of Aragon (1452–1516), and Louis XII of France (1462–1515) and some Italian states.

Linear perspective (from medieval Latin *perspectiva (ars)* "science of optics"), representation of three-dimensional objects on a flat picture surface. Filippo Brunelleschi (1376–1446) developed a scientific and mathematical method of perspectivist representation in the early 15th century. For the observer, all parallel lines converge on a central vanishing point. A three-dimensional illusion is conveyed on the two-dimensional picture surface by means of the precise foreshortening and proportioning of the depicted objects, landscapes, figures, and buildings.

Liturgy (Greek *leitourgia* "public service," "worship of the gods"), in the Roman Catholic and Orthodox churches, the form according to which public religious worship is conducted.

Loggia (It.), open arcade or hall supported on columns or piers.

Madonna with the Cloak, painting of the Virgin Mary depicting her protecting believers with her cloak. The gesture of protection originated in the secular legal world, when a father took children "under his cloak" to legitimize or adopt them. Highly-placed people, particularly women, could give refuge to persecuted people "under their cloaks" and ask for mercy for them. This right to protect was transferred to Mary in these paintings.

Manuscript, a document written by hand. In the Middle Ages manuscripts were usually written in scriptoria (writing rooms) in monasteries, and often decorated with illuminated pictures and ornate initials.

Medallion (Fr., *médaillon*, large medal), a picture or a bas-relief in a round or oval frame.

Mendicant orders (Lat., *mendicare*, to beg), orders of monks or friars dedicated to an ascetic lifestyle and no ownership of property, which originated in the 13th century as a reaction to the growing secularization of the church. They were particularly devoted to spiritual care, teaching, and missionary work. The mendicant orders are the Franciscans, Capucins, Dominicans, Augustinians, and Carmelites.

Molo (It., mole), the canalside promenade in front of the Doges' Palace in Venice. On the other bank it is called the Riva degli Schiavoni.

Mosaic (Lat., *musaicum, musivum*, from Gk., *mousa*, muse, art, artistic activity), an ornamental or figurative decoration made up of multi-colored polished stones, stone fragments, or clay or glass pieces. In antiquity mosaics were usually used to decorate floors, but during the 5th and 6th centuries A.D., with the advent of glass mosaics, the technique reached its height in Italy (Rome and Ravenna), and was also applied to mural and ceiling decoration.

Narthex (Gk.), narrow ante-room of Early Christian and Early Byzantine basilicas.

Nave (Lat., ship), the elongated part of a church between the west end (facade) and the crossing (where the nave and the transept intersect) or the choir reserved for the clergy. The nave can be a single space or, as in a basilica, consist of several aisles.

Neoclassicism (Fr., *classique*, and Lat., *classicus*, of the highest rank), an architectural and artistic style from 1750 to 1840 based on classical antiquity (Greece in 5th–4th century B.C.).

Niche (Fr., niche), a semicircular, rectangular, or square recess in a wall, closed at the top.

Mosaic

Obelisk (Lat., *obeliscus* and Gk., *obeliskos*, small spit), a square stone column tapering towards the top and topped by a small pyramid. In Egypt it was the symbol of the sun god, and since the Renaissance it has been used for general and monumental ornamentation.

Ogee arch, or keel arch, an arch originating in c. 1300 made up of four arcs, in which the center points of two of the arcs are inside and the center point of the other two arcs are outside the arch, resulting in a curve which is first convex and then concave.

Pala (It., tablet), a painted or sculpted altar painting or ornament. (See also Altarpiece.)

Panel painting, a painting made on a piece of wood or, in smaller format, on copper. They first appeared in the 12th century, and were widespread before the introduction of canvas.

Pedestal, socle or substructure of a pier, column, or statue.

Pediment (prob. from Lat., *pyramid*), the classical gable surmounting a facade or wall, with straight sides or in curved segments, which was imitated in Renaissance, Baroque, and Neoclassical architecture. As with the original, it was open-bedded or open-topped so that the middle section was either non-existent or more (or less) prominent. The tympanum (i.e. the area enclosed by the pediment) can be decorated.

Pendant (Fr., hanging), a companion piece, a counterpart.

Pendentive (Fr., sail vault), the part of a vault in the shape of a curved triangle used to transfer a square ground plan to a dome.

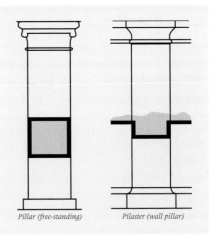

Pillar (free-standing)   *Pilaster (wall pillar)*

Pendentive dome, type of dome in which an imagined sail vault is cut off horizontally and the resulting circle vaulted by a hemispherical dome. The resulting triangles are known as pendentives.

Perspective (Middle Lat., *perspectiva (ars)*, (art) which sees through), the depiction of three-dimensional objects on a flat surface. It reproduces objects and figures in optical conditions as closely as possible to the way they would appear in reality.

Piano nobile (It.), the main story of a building, located over the first floor; the reception rooms were situated here.

Pier (from Latin *pila* "pillar"), vertical support with square, rectangular, or polygonal cross-section. It can be subdivided into a base (bottom), shaft (middle), and capital (top). Depending on the position and form, it is possible to make a distinction between freestanding, engaged, and corner piers and pier buttresses (pier on the exterior of a building which resists the thrust of a flying buttress).

Pietà (It., mercy, compassion, Lat., *pietas*, piety), a picture or statue of the Virgin Mary mourning the body of Christ in her arms.

Pietra d'Istria (It.), stone originating in Istria.

Pilaster (It., *pilastro*, from Lat., *pila*, pillar), a rectangular pillar with a base, shaft, and capital, usually set into a wall to subdivide it. Often fluted with vertical grooves.

Pillar (Lat., *pila*), or column, vertical support with a round, square, rectangular, or polygonal section. It can be divided into base, shaft, and capital, the characteristics of which determine to which Order (e.g. Doric, Ionic, Corinthian) its design belongs. Depending on the situation and design, it can be free-standing or form part of the walls or structure of the building.

Pointed arch, a characteristic element of the vertically oriented Gothic architectural style. In contrast to the Romanesque round arch, it is broken and pointed at its crown.

Polychrome (Greek *poly* "many" and *chroma* "color"), multi-colored. The opposite of mono-chrome (single color).

Pietà

Polyptych (from Gk., *polyptychos*, with many folds), an altarpiece (painted or sculpted) made up of several panels and with more than two wings. Suitable for depicting a variety of different themes. Also: diptych, with two panels; triptych, with three panels.

Portal (Middle Lat., *portale*, ante-room), a decorative entrance to a building. The model for the Western portal is the Roman triumphal arch (a free-standing arch built to honor a general).

Portico (Lat., *porticus*, passage of columns, hall), a usually open porch supported by columns of pillars, before the main entrance of a building. Often features a pediment.

Presbytery (Gk., *presbyterion*, council of elders), a raised area at the altar end of the nave reserved for the clergy (see also Choir.)

Procurators' Offices (It., Procuratie), palazzi containing the headquarters of the procurators on the Piazza San Marco in Venice. The Old Procurators' Offices were built in 1414–1520, while the New Procurator's Offices were built on the south side in 1528–1640.

Quadratura (Middle Lat., dividing into four, Lat., *quadrare*, make rectangular), painting of architectural elements on the walls and ceilings to give an illusion of greater space.

Quadriga (Lat., from *quattuor*, four, and *iugum*, yoke), a set of four horses in chariot harness. In architecture quadrigas started to appear as decorative elements on buildings in the 4th century B.C.

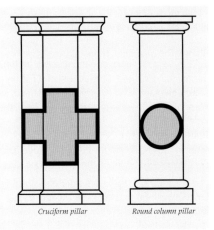

Cruciform pillar   *Round column pillar*

Quatrefoil (Lat., *tres*, three, *folium*, leaf), decorative motif in Gothic art of four identical circular cutouts in clover formation.

Quattrocento (Italian "four hundred"), Italian for the 15th century.

Radiography (from Latin *radius* "beam," and Greek *graphien* "write," "draw"), x-ray test. In painting, scientific method for analyzing paintings used specifically to reveal overpaintings and additions.

Refectory (Middle Lat., *refectorium*, Lat., *reficere*, to recreate), dining hall in a monastery.

Relics (Lat., *reliquiae*, remains), the corpse or part of the corpse of a specially revered saint, or an item which belonged to them.

Relief (from Lat., *relevare*, to raise), a picture raised by carving or molding. Depending on their shallowness they are known as bas-reliefs, half-reliefs (or mezzorelievos), and high reliefs.

Renaissance (Fr., It., *rinascimento*, rebirth), the cultural and stylistic age originating in Italy during the 15th and 16th centuries. (The late phase, between 1530 and 1600, is also known as Mannerism.) The description stems from the term *renascita* (rebirth) coined in 1550 by Giorgio Vasari (1511–74), who initially used it to refer to the passing of medieval art. Humanism developed the model of the *uomo universale*, that is, a human being fully developed both intellectually and physically, a reference to the classical model of a new image of man, the world, and nature as they existed in the physical world. This resulted in the promotion of painting and sculpture from crafts to creative arts, giving the artist a higher social status and a greater self-awareness. Art and science were inter-linked and started to influence each other, e.g. in the mathematical calculation of perspective or in anatomical knowledge. Architecture was based on the theories of Vitruvius (c. 84 B.C.), and was characterized by the use of ancient structural elements and the emergence of a specific architecture for palaces and homes. The typical architectural design was a centralized building with main axes of equal length.

Replica (French *réplique* "reply," "repeat," "imitate"), an exact copy of a work of art executed by the artist or his studio.

Retable (Fr., from Lat., *retabulus,* back wall), a carved or painted altarpiece fixed behind or at the back of the altar.

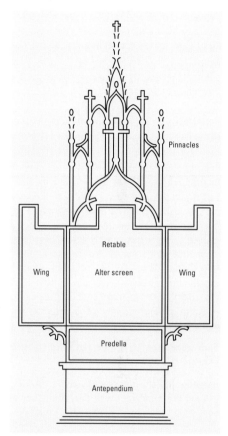

Pinnacles

Retable

Wing   Alter screen   Wing

Predella

Antependium

Rib, a prominent band-like, often shaped, reinforcement of a groin (edge section) of a vault. Between the ribs are the non-load-bearing cells.

Rococo (Fr., *rocaille*, boulders, grotto, shell-work), style in European art and architecture between 1720/30 and 1770/80. It was characterized by a style of ornamentation which emphasized levity, movement, detail and lighter colors.

Romanesque (It., Romanus, Roman), a term introduced in France in the first third of the 19th century to describe the forms of ancient Roman architecture (arch, pillar, column, vault) used in early medieval building in the West. It covers the period from around 1000 A.D. (in France; in Germany and Britain from the mid-11th century) until, in some areas, the mid-13th century. In central France it was superseded by Early Gothic in the mid-12th century, in England around 1200. The style was everywhere influenced by national features and stylistic elements. Romanesque architecture developed most fully in Burgundy, Normandy, northern Italy, and Tuscany. It affected church architecture above all, typically consisting of the addition of individual structural elements and the clear interplay of cylindrical and cubic forms.

Roof cornice, projecting molded horizontal strip between the wall and the roof.

Rotunda (Italian *rotonda*, "round"), building shaped like a cylinder with a central, circular plan. Also a cylindrical room within a building.

Rustication (Lat., *rusticus*, rustic), masonry finished on the exterior only with roughly hewn stone rectangles.

Sacristy (Middle Lat., *sacristia*, from *sacer*, sacred, holy), a small room in a church where priests prepare and put on their robes, and various liturgical objects are kept.

Sannazaro, Jacopo (1456–1530), Italian poet, whose novel *Arcadia* was the first European pastoral novel based on ancient, classical pastoral poetry.

Sarcophagus (Gk., meat eater), a richly ornamented wooden, metal, clay, or stone coffin.

Scapular (Middle Lat., *scapulare*, shoulder garment), part of the vestments of some monastic orders, e.g. Benedictines or Dominicans, consisting of two long strips of cloth covering the chest and back of the monks, and worn over the main garment.

Schism (Greek *skhisma* "cleft"), the formal separation of a church into two churches or secession of a group owing to doctrinal and other differences. The period between 1378–1417 when the western church was divided by the reign of two popes in Rome and Avignon is known as the Great Western Schism.

Scholasticism (from Latin *scholasticus* "belonging to school"), medieval system of theology and philosophy based on Aristotelian logic, the dogmatic exegesis of Holy Scripture and the writings of early Christian Fathers.

Scorcio (Italian "foreshortening"), in painting and graphics an extreme perspectivist reduction of a depicted object.

Scuola (It., school), an association originating in the medieval penitent and apprentices' fraternities, usually consisting of members of the same ethnic or trade group. Scuola is also the Venetian term for a Jewish synagogue.

Madonna with the Cloak

Secular building/architecture, building used for worldly, non-religious purposes. The opposite of religious building/architecture.

Sepulchre (Lat., *sepulcrum*, tomb), elaborate, often independent structure for the interment of a human corpse, for example funerary chapel, mausoleum. Many tombs and monuments are found in churches and cloisters.

Serenissima (It., abbreviation of "La Serenissima Repubblica Venezia," "The Most Serene Republic of Venice"), a term used since the Middle Ages to describe the magnificence and the dignity of the city on the lagoon, and which exemplifies the pronounced Venetian sense of self-worth.

Sfumato, (from Italian *sfumare* "to cover in smoke"), painting technique generally ascribed to Leonardo da Vinci (1452–1519) whereby tones and colors are allowed to shade gradually into one another, producing softened outlines or hazy forms.

Signoria (Italian "lordship"), from the late Middle Ages, the ruling council or government in Italian towns and cities. Usually presided over by a single family.

Spandrel, a three-sided area. The spandrel of an arch can result from arches framed by a square. Hanging spandrels consist of spherical triangles where domes are transferred from a square ground plan to the circle of the dome.

Still life (from Dutch *still-leven*), also known as *nature morte* (French) and *natura morta* (Italian), visual representation of artistically arranged inanimate objects, e.g. flowers, fruit, books, vessels, and dead animals. Still life emerged as an independent genre in the 14th century and reached its zenith in 17th-century Dutch painting.

Tambour, also drum (Arabic *tanbur* "drum"), cylindrical architectural element that carries a dome or cupola. It is usually pierced with windows and is used to raise the height of the space.

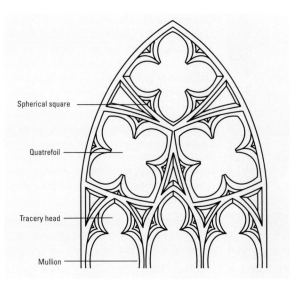

Spherical square

Quatrefoil

Tracery head

Mullion

by many layers of parallel lines. The color differences between wet and dry tempera make it difficult to add a similar tone when painting later.

Temple facade, in classical architecture, a structure or portico attached to or separate from a building, consisting usually of columns supporting a pediment.

Tenebrists (from It., *tenebre*, "gloom, darkness"), name given to a group of Late Baroque artists who adhered to the technique of chiaroscuro (light-dark) painting.

Terraferma (Lat., firm land), that area of the North Italian mainland that was part of Venice at the height of its power.

Tabernacle (Lat. *tabernaculum*, small tent, small hut), an ornamental surround in architecture made up of columns and a pitched roof, mainly designed for statues, situated for instance on Gothic flying buttresses (pillars built on the outside of the building to absorb the thrust of the vaults and the weight of the roof). Also, shrine where the Communion host is kept.

Tempera (Lat., *temperare*, "mix correctly, measure"), a painting technique in which the pigments (colored powder) are mixed with a binding medium of egg, lime, or casein (the protein making up the bulk of milk). The paint dries quicker than with oil painting, making "wet-on-wet" painting impossible. For this reason fine shading and merging is carried out

Thermal window (after the Thermae, i.e. Baths, of Diocletian in Rome), a type of window introduced to church architecture in Venice and the Veneto, mainly by Andrea Palladio (1508–80). It was based on classical models consisting of a semicircular lunette divided into three panes by two thin pillars.

Tondo (It., "round"), a circular painting or relief.

Tracery, in Gothic architecture, geometrical ornamentation, traced with compasses, used to subdivide large windows, and later also to segment gables, walls, and other surfaces.

Transfiguration (Lat., *transfigurare*, transform), the glorious transformation of Christ before the three Apostles and its depiction in art.

Trefoil (Lat., *tres*, three, *folium*, leaf), a decorative motif used in Gothic art, consisting of three identical cloverleaf-shaped curves.

Triumphal arch (Lat., *triumphus*, triumphal procession), free-stand-ing arch originating in the 2nd century B.C. bearing passages in honor of an emperor or general.

Volute with an Ionic capital

Tunnel vault (Middle Lat., *tunna*, barrel), a form of ceiling with a semicircular or segment of a circle section; occasionally the section is pointed or parabolic.

Tympanum (Gk., drumskin, tambourine), area of an arch above a portal or enclosed by a pediment.

Vanishing point, in linear perspective, the central point at which parallel lines converge in an image.

Vault, (Lat., *volvere,* to turn), a curved ceiling, usually constructed of wedge-shaped stones. Unlike domes, vaults are also found over rectangular rooms. Abutments such as walls or columns absorb the pressure and thrust of the arch.

Vedutista, (It., *veduta*, view, prospect), landscape painter of works characterized by strictly realistic depictions of landscapes or townscapes. These paintings contrast with *vedute ideate*, consisting of imagined landscapes or townscapes depicting imaginary buildings.

Virtues (Lat., *virtus*, virtue), the four Platonic virtues adopted by Christian ethics: Temperantia (moderation), Fortitudo (courage, strength), Prudentia (wisdom), and Justitia (justice). Pope Gregory the Great (540–604 A.D.) added to these the three divine theological virtues: Fides (faith), Spes (hope), and Caritas (love). These seven became the basis for the development of the Christian system of cardinal virtues in the High Middle Ages.

Volute (Lat., *voluta*, snail, rolled), a spiral scroll-like ornament and building element. It is particularly widely used on Ionic capitals and on pediments, as well as at the joints between horizontal and vertical structural elements.

Votive painting (Lat., *votivus*, praised, honored), a painting dedicated to God or to a saint as a token of gratitude or in support of a prayer made or heard.

S. Secondo

S. Georgio dalega

S. Biagio Catoldo

S. Marco

f Rom
or Cha
and s

etian
Cyp

Assu
8

pp: t
05

ce.
Ro

Be
hist
volg

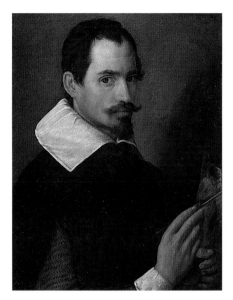

Francesco Bassano

Basaiti, Marco (ca. 1470 Venice – after 1530), possibly came from a Greek or Albanian family. His work appears stylistically heterogeneous, always leaning towards the leading Venetian masters of his time, and the influence of Alvise Vivarini, Giovanni Bellini, and Cima da Conegliano can clearly be seen. After 1500, the influence of Giorgione and the artists of Lombardy becomes apparent. Along with altarpieces, we still have many of hisportraits. Basaiti's figures, with their severe, distant poses, often seem a little wooden, although he did produce some atmospheric landscapes.

Bassano, Francesco (1549 Bassano – 1592 Venice) was trained in the studio of his father, Jacopo Bassano (1510/15 – 1592). He moved to Venice in 1578, but continued to collaborate occasionally with his father and his brothers, Gerolamo (1566–1621), Giambattista (1553–1613), and Leandro (1557–1622). Stylistically, therefore, it is not always easy to tell their work apart. Francesco Bassano's paintings often contain many figures, and his light brushwork shows the influence of Tintoretto and late Titian. The almost magical lighting effects created by the way the paint was applied and by the use of color make the paintings of the Bassano studio some of the most interesting Venetian works of the late 16th century. With its genre-style depictions of rural scenes, which nonetheless retain a Biblical theme, the work of Bassano and his sons has an unmistakable character.

Bella, Gabriel (1730 Venice – 1799 Venice). Bella's paintings reveal only modest artistic talent. Nevertheless, he received several large commissions as a decorator. His work achieved outstanding significance due to a series of paintings for the Giustiniani family depicting scenes of Venetian life. Around 70 of these pictures survive today, most of which are in the Querini Stampalia Museum in Venice.

Bellini, Gentile (ca. 1429 Venice – 1507 Venice) was trained by his father, the artist Jacopo Bellini, whose studio he later took over. From 1466 he received official commissions from the city of Venice, and was sent to Constantinople on a diplomatic mission from 1479 to 1481. Bellini's paintings are typical of a training in perspective composition, and are characterized by a serenity of line surrounding areas of delicate color. His narrative style, full of realism and nonchalant vigor, and his inventorial eye make life in the lagoon city come alive, and it is in this that the artist's great significance for the development of Venetian *vedute* and panoramas is to be found.

Bellini, Giovanni (ca. 1430 Venice – 1516 Venice), the younger brother of Gentile Bellini, was one of Venice's most famous artists. Trained by his father, Jacopo, and also influenced by his brother-in-law Mantegna, he worked primarily in his home city, where he ran his own studio. Taking the work of Mantegna and Netherlandish methods (introduced into Venetian art by Antonello da Messina) as his starting point, Bellini developed his own way of handling light and natural ambience. He used only bright, warm colors in his paintings, and employed stylistic techniques which created an atmospheric integration of forms, figures, and space.

Bombelli, Sebastiano (1635 Udine – 1719 Venice) was trained in the studio of his father, Valentino Bombelli, and was certainly in Venice after 1660. He first came to prominence with copies of paintings by Tintoretto and Veronese, which became very popular, particularly in France. Around 1664–65 he worked in Bologna in the studio of Guercino, who, in his youth, had achieved his own fame with fake Titians. Later, it was Bombelli's portraits which attracted great attention throughout Europe, and he became one of the most sought-after artists for portraits of top European nobility.

Boschetti, Lorenzo (1709 – definitely present in Venice in 1772), an architect, was probably a pupil of Giuseppe Massari. His most important work, the Palazzo Venier dei Leoni in Venice, is unfinished. A study revealing his intentions is in the Museo Correr.

Bregno, Antonio (15th century, Venice) was the brother of the architect and sculptor Paolo Bregno. Antonio Bregno may be the Maestro Antonio di Rigezzo da Como who worked on the Doges' Palace in 1425–26 as assistant to Matteo Raverti. Later, he often worked with the Paduan sculptor Antonio Rizzo and, stylistically, it is not always possible to tell their work apart. Since 1777, the tomb of Doge Francesco Foscari has been ascribed to Antonio and his brother Paolo Bregno. It is presumed on stylistic grounds that the creator of the Foscari tomb was also involved with the Arco Foscari, and likewise created the *Fortitudo* on the Porta della Carta, both in the Doges' Palace. The style of these works shows an evident affinity with contemporary Venetian painting, and is particularly influenced by Andrea Mantegna.

Bregno, Paolo (15th century, Venice), also called Paolo da Como, was the brother of the sculptor Antonio Bregno, and likewise came from Righeggia on Lake Lugano. He may be the Maestro Paolo mentioned in Venetian records, who, in 1459, was Proto (i.e. chief architect) to the Procurators of San Marco, and thus responsible for numerous civic buildings, including San Marco. A certain Paolo inzignero della Signoria was also mentioned, together with Bartolomeo Buon, in connection with the construction of the Ca' del Duca.

Buon (Bon), Bartolomeo (ca. 1400 Venice – ca.1464–67 Venice) ran a studio with his father, their work encompassing architecture and sculpture in equal measure. Bartolomeo's oeuvre has still not been fully reconstructed. Documentary evidence exists for his collaboration on the Ca' d'Oro and the commission for the Porta della Carta in the Doges' Palace (signed by Bartolomeo), which father and son accepted in 1438. The figures on the portal are the work of other sculptors, however, and it seems that he often passed on commissions for sculptures to other artists. His style is characterized by the transition from Late Gothic to Renaissance. His Ca' del Duca on the Grand Canal was the first building in Venice to combine traditional motifs with the forms of the Renaissance.

Buon (Bon), Giovanni (ca. 1360 Venice – 1443 Venice) was the father of Bartolomeo Buon. In many documents, he appears principally as a building contractor and supplier of stone. Together with his son Bartolomeo, he ran probably one of the largest, if not *the* largest, builders' workshop in Venice in the first half of the 15th century. The extent to which he himself was active as an architect and sculptor is disputed, and it is possible that he simply acted as the manager.

Cadorin, Ludovico (1824 Venice – 1892 Venice) was one of the most influential architects and interior decorators in 19th century Venice. His name is linked with historicism, which sought to design buildings in a historical style appropriate to their function. With his interiors based on motifs from previous eras, Cadorin created a new and unmistakable style.

Calendario, Filippo (before 1315 Venice – 1355 Venice). An architect and sculptor, Calendario worked from 1341 on the construction of the Sala del Maggior Consiglio and the redesign of the west and south facades of the Doges' Palace. Calendario's sculpture is captivating, displaying craftsmanship of extraordinary quality and an accurate eye for nature, along with a psychological sensitivity and a delight in narrative. History remembers this wealthy master builder (he owned several ships) for his participation in Doge Marino Falier's conspiracy to set himself up as autocrat of Venice. Calendario was executed as a co-conspirator.

Campagna, Girolamo (ca. 1548–49 Verona – 1625 Venice) was the most important sculptor in Venice ca. 1600. He was a pupil of Danese Cattaneo. His first stylistic influences were the tranquil forms in his teacher's work, and Jacopo Sansovino. Increasingly, however, he also drew on the potent and eloquent forms of Michelangelo. The search for intensity of spiritual expression led to a disagreement with Tintoretto and to his vision of the physical ideal, which also leaned towards Michelangelo. The effect of Campagna's figures lies mostly in the impression created by the piece as a whole. Psychological formulations encompassing the facial expression were far from his mind.

Canaletto (1697 Venice – 1768 Venice), real name Giovanni Antonio Canal, learned scenery (stage) painting from his father. In 1719, he went on a study tour to Rome. He gained further inspiration from Pannini, and above all from Luca Carlevarijs, the painter of *vedute*, or views. Underlying his painting is a trained use of perspective and accurate observation of nature. Thus, his topographical views of Venice capture the beauty of the architecture and combine it with the reproduction of light and ambience, bringing genre-style scenes to life. Canaletto, who from 1746 to 1753 primarily worked in England, helped Venetian *veduta* painting to spread and flourish beyond the borders of Italy.

Candi, Giovanni (? Venice – after 9 August 1506 Venice) was the son of a carpenter from Spilimbergo. He, too, took up this craft, and is documented as being responsible for woodwork in the Scuola Grande di San Marco. Aside from carpentry, he also worked from time to time as an architect. The design of the Palazzo dei Rettori in Belluno is ascribed to him. His principal work is the spiral staircase in the Palazzo Contarini in Venice.

Canova, Antonio (1757 Possagno, Treviso – 1822 Venice) grew up in modest surroundings in the care of his grandfather. He was taken on at the studio of the sculptor Giuseppe Torretti when he was 11, and later studied at the Venetian Academy of Art under the brothers Michelangelo and Gregorio Morlaiter. With the proceeds from his first successes in Venice he financed a trip to Rome, where he studied the ancient world. From there he visited the most recent excavations at Paestum, Pompeii, and Herculaneum. This encounter with the sculpture of antiquity proved to be a defining experience. Canova, who was highly regarded in both Venice and Rome, settled down in Rome. He not only worked as a sculptor, increasingly admired throughout Europe, but also became involved in politics. In 1814, he managed to win back for Italy numerous works of art which had been seized by Napoleon. Antonio Canova is considered the most important sculptor of the 19th century. For his contemporaries throughout Europe and North America, his figures – drawing on his knowledge of antiquity, and therefore cool, noble, but at the same time sensual with their silky, polished marble – were the embodiment of art and beauty. Today, they are still considered the undisputed zenith of Neoclassicism.

Carpaccio, Vittore (ca. 1455–65 Venice? – ca. 1525–26 Venice) is an important representative of the Renaissance in Venice. He worked in the studio of Gentile Bellini, whose pupil he probably was, and decorated the interior of the Doges' Palace together with Giovanni Bellini. Aside from these two artists, he was also inspired by Antonello da Messina. In his works, Carpaccio combined faithful representation of subjects handed down by legend with images of his own invention. Although his "additive" method of story-telling still bound him to the Early Renaissance, he also adopted new

Canaletto: Veduta of Venice

innovations with his brightly lit architectural landscapes and accomplished perspective composition. Carpaccio produced cycles of paintings for the *scuole*, the confraternities of Venice, as well as numerous single works with religious subjects.

Carriera, Rosalba Giovanna (1675 Venice – 1757 Venice) was highly regarded by her contemporaries, primarily as a portrait artist. She was trained by Giuseppe Diamantini and Antonio Balestra, but was also inspired by her brother-in-law, Giovanni Antonio Pellegrini. She started out painting miniature portraits, but later turned to larger formats, concentrating on pastels, and was the first to perfect the new technique of drawing with chalks, which enabled artists to work in a quick and spontaneous way. This brought her great success, and her commissions included many from the royal courts of Europe. In addition, she was admitted to Rome's Accademia San Luca in 1705, and to the Académie Royale de la Peinture during her stay in Paris in 1720. Rosalba Giovanna Carriera was forced to give up painting in 1746, due to an eye ailment, but she had a lasting influence on French pastel painting.

de Chirico, Giorgio (1888 Volos, Greece – 1978 Rome) was born in Greece, the son of Italian parents. He began his study of painting in Athens, continuing in Munich after his family moved there in 1906. From 1910 he lived alternately in Paris and Italy. De Chirico first leaned towards turn-of-the-century German painting, but subsequently changed his style to depictions of an exaggerated, mysterious dreamworld. These paintings had a great

Rosalba Giovanna Carriera

influence on the Surrealists. In the 1920s, townscapes constructed with strict adherence to the rules of perspective predominated, although the extreme clarity of their composition, the simple shapes in bright colors, and the stark, heavy shadows were still reminiscent of dream images.

Cima da Conegliano (ca. 1459 Conegliano – ca. 1517–18 Conegliano), originally Giovanni Battista Cima, was possibly trained under Bartolomeo Montagna in Vicenza and Alvise Vivarini. He was also influenced by the work of Antonello da Messina, and later by Titian and Giorgione. In 1492, he went to Venice, and was active there until 1516. He was quick to find his own style, which was thematically and graphically allied to the work of Bellini. Characteristic of his balanced compositions are a tender, peaceful atmosphere, full of feeling, and accurate observations of nature. In the main his subjects were religious, primarily Madonnas, although he did take some secular themes.

Codussi, Mauro (ca.1440–45 Lenna, Valle Brembana, Bergamo – before 23 April 1504 Venice) may have been trained in Lombardy, and remained a citizen of Bergamo throughout his life. However, the only remaining evidence of his activities is in Venice. Codussi was the most important architect of the Early Renaissance. He was the first to articulate the forms of the Florentine Renaissance, with its rounded arches and stone-clad facades, on a consistent basis. At the same time, though, he also called upon the old Venetian architectural forms, such as the cruciform-domed basilica. In the 15th century, these were not seen as a medieval so much as a Byzantine bequest, and thus as classical. This made them a suitable model for the new, classically oriented architecture. Codussi was familiar with Florentine themes, particularly the work of Leon Battista Albertis, but developed them further to create his own style of architectural expression, permeated with traditional Venetian elements.

Colonna, Gerolamo Mengozzi (ca. 1688 Ferrara – ca. 1766 Verona?), also known as Mingozzi, was a pupil of the quadratura artists (architectural painters) Francesco Scala and Antonio Ferrari. Instead of people, Mingozzi likewise created the complex, architectural perspectives which were an important feature of 17th and 18th century decoration. He worked all over northern Italy (in Turin, Brescia, and Udine), but primarily in Venice, where he often collaborated with Giovanni Battista Tiepolo.

Donatello (1386 Florence – 1466 Florence), real name Donato di Niccolò di Betto Bardi, was probably taught by Lorenzo Ghiberti and Nanni di Banco in Florence. He worked primarily in his home city, but also in Siena, Rome, Padua, and elsewhere in Italy. Donatello is considered the greatest sculptor of the 15th century. No other artist matched his extensive work for variety and innovation. In his early period, he principally created standing figures in marble. From the 1420s, however, he worked mainly on bronze sculptures.

Dyck, Anthony van (1599 Antwerp – 1641 London) is the most important Flemish painter after Rubens. At just 11 years old he was studying under Hendrik van Balen, and running his own studio from 1615. From 1617 to 1620, he worked in the studio of Rubens, who lauded him as his most talented pupil. He then went traveling, first to London, and from 1621 to 1627 to Italy, where he particularly admired the works of Titian, Giorgione, and the Bologna School. Upon his return, he became court painter to Archduchess Isabella, Stadtholder of the Netherlands, and, in 1632, entered the service of Charles I of England. Profoundly influenced by Italian art, van Dyck developed the genre of representative portraits of nobility which became the model for Western portraiture, especially in England.

Anthony van Dyck

Eyck, Jan van (ca. 1390 Maaseyck nr. Maastricht – 1441 Bruges) worked as court painter to Prince Johann of Bavaria, Count of Holland, around 1422, then entered the service of Philip the Good, Duke of Burgundy, in Lille, in 1425. After many trips to Spain and Portugal, he finally settled in Bruges. Van Eyck's novel understanding of the graphical depiction of reality had an enormous influence on European art. He showed the human figure as a space-consuming body and captured even the smallest detail of nature. Continuing the development of oil painting, moreover, he achieved a hitherto unknown intensity of light and depth of color.

Fortuny y Madrazo, Mariano (1871 Granada – 1949 Venice) aroused the enthusiasm of fashion-conscious women in the early 20th century with his creations. He was the son of the painter Mariano Fortuny y Carbò (1836–74), who became one of the most famous Spanish artists of the 19th century with his lavish salon paintings, amassing a considerable fortune. His son did not follow in his footsteps, however, despite his training as a painter. Instead, he turned to design and fashion, where he, too, earned "artist" status with his painted and printed cloth.

Ernst, Max (1891 Brühl nr. Cologne – 1976 Paris) began by studying classical philology, philosophy, psychology, and the history of art. However, he soon gained close artist friends, and began his own artistic activities. Working first in Germany, then France, he was forced to flee to America to escape the Nazis. Max Ernst was the most significant representative of Surrealism. Realistic elements in his works are always fractured by confusing alienation effects which reveal a deeper significance. Ernst was continually inventing new methods of applying paint in order to increase the expressivity of his pictures and at the same time facilitate new levels of meaning.

Francesco di Giorgio, (1439 Siena – 1501 Siena), also known as Francesco di Giorgio Martini, was a painter, sculptor, architect, art theoretician, and fortress builder. Although initially trained as a painter in Siena, his most significant contribution was to the fields of architecture and the theory of art.

Fumiani, Giovanni Antonio (ca. 1645 Venice – 1710 Venice) was a pupil of Domenico Ambrogi, with whom he was in Bologna certainly as early as 1666. In 1668 he returned to Venice, where he produced a signed altarpiece. From 1684 until shortly before his death he devoted himself to his principal work, the grandiose oil-on-canvas ceiling painting of San Pantalon. Its complex structural perspective is reminiscent of similar works in Rome. Fumiani attempted to surpass these, however, with his heavy use of figures and elegant management of light which allows the colors to shine with varying shades.

Gambello, Antonio (died after 1479, in Venice), who is also documented as Antonio di Marco and Antonio di San Zaccaria, worked from 1458 as an architect and possibly as a stonemason, and was also involved with the construction of San Giobbe and Santa Chiara on Murano. However, he was unable to finish his main work, San Zaccaria, and it is precisely this which reveals his particular formal style, since Gambello's style is markedly different from that of his successor, Codussi. Like Codussi, Gambello also combined Gothic motifs and Renaissance elements, but his architectural ideas were articulated in relief, rather than in the round.

Giambono, Michele (ca. 1390 Venice – after 1462 Venice) was very probably a pupil of Jacobello del Fiore, and is considered the last significant exponent of Gothic painting in Venice. Even so, he did not lean towards the "soft" style as completely as his teacher. Giambono's works are characterized by a wildly magnificent feast of color and form, which gives his paintings an air of the sumptuous and the fantastic. Thus, his style has often been called Gothic Baroque.

Gian Giacomo de' Grigi (before 1530 Venice? – 1572 Venice) was the son of Guglielmo de' Grigi, and his work as an architect and chief architect is evident throughout the 16th century. Among other projects, he supervised work on the Scuola di San Rocco and the Scuola San Giorgio Maggiore. For his chief work, the Palazzo Papadopoli, he must be considered a solid, although not one of the outstanding, architects of his time.

Giorgione (ca. 1477 Castelfranco Veneto – 1510 Venice), real name Giorgio da Castelfranco, was an important painter of the Venetian High Renaissance. Along with his younger friend Titian, it is likely he was trained in the studio of Giovanni Bellini. Probably taking the work of Carpaccio, Antonello da Messina, Leonardo da Vinci, and the Netherlandish painters as his starting point, Giorgione developed a style which subsequently made an important contribution to the art of painting. He increasingly abandoned outlining in favor of color transitions, thus fixing the appearance of objects in the foreground. This enabled him to show figures moving freely in space and to portray the atmosphere evoked by the landscape.

Giotto di Bondone (ca. 1267? Colle di Vespignano nr. Florence – 1337 Florence) was one of the most influential artists in Western culture. As a painter and architect he is strongly linked with Cimabue, and was possibly his pupil. After 1292 he worked in Assisi, then in Rome, Padua, Naples, Milan, and finally Florence, where he was appointed Master of Works of the Cathedral in 1334. Giotto made a complete break with the Byzantine tradition, not least because he was strongly influenced by the Gothic plastic arts of France. He rediscovered the concept of the human figure as something substantial, three-dimensional, and, at the same time, monumental, thus inventing a new formal style with which to depict sacred events. His figures in drapery are shown interacting with the landscapes and interiors as though the narrative were a reality in which the viewer can participate.

Giovanni d'Alemagna (? – before 9 June 1450 Padua), was probably a German painter who

Francesco Guardi: Veduta of Venice

became a resident of Padua or of Murano at the beginning of the 15th century. With one exception, signatures show his surviving works to have been produced in collaboration with his brother-in-law, Antonio Vivarini. With its precise execution and obvious interest in decorative details, Giovanni's style is reminiscent of the Cologne School of painting. In its concern with the plasticity and solidity of its figures, however, it already marks the transition from the Gothic to the Early Renaissance era. Giovanni and Antonio Vivarini were the first to unify the individual picture panels of a Gothic altarpiece into a single picture, thereby paving the way for the so-called Sacra Conversazione (picture of the Virgin Mary with saints). They are considered the founders of the Murano School, which became the second most important studio of 15th century Venice, after that of the Bellinis.

Guardi, Francesco (1712 Venice – 1793 Venice) is the principal exponent of Venetian *veduta* painting. He was trained by his brother Giovanni Antonio and worked in his studio until 1747. Subsequently working as a master in his own right, he was admitted to the Academy of Painting in 1784. At first, Guardi primarily painted altarpieces, but later concentrated on atmospheric city views influenced by Canaletto and Michele Marieschi. For the sake of pictorial effect, however, he did not always stick to topographical fact. He also produced scenes depicting Venice's magnificent festive occasions and containing many figures.

Guardi, Giovanni Antonio (1699 Vienna – 1760 Venice) was initially trained by his father,

Domenico. After his father's early death, his main influences were Piazzetta and Sebastiano Ricci. Along with his possibly more famous younger brother Francesco, Giovanni Antonio Guardi was one of the most interesting artists of the nascent Venetian Rococo. His paintings are captivating, with their light, vibrant, but highly delicate colors, reminiscent of the work of his brother-in-law, Gian Battista Tiepolo.

Guariento (definitely alive in 1338 – 1365 Padua) was one of the most influential artists of the 14th century in Padua and Venice. Taking Giotto as his initial model, he increasingly incorporated the soft, sweeping forms of the International Gothic style. Guariento's influence was crucial in leading Venetian painters to turn away from the Byzantine tradition and finally seek out an affiliation with the Gothic style flourishing in the rest of Europe.

Guglielmo de' Grigi (before 1500 Alzano, Bergamo – before 1530 Venice?), also known as dei Grigi or Bergamasco, came from a widely branching family of architects and stone-masons from Bergamo. His buildings are typical of the richly ornamented style of Lombard architecture, which was extraordinarily popular with Venetian patrons at the beginning of the 16th century because it combined the forms of the Renaissance with characteristic Gothic extravagance.

Heintz the Younger, Joseph (ca. 1600 Augsburg – after 1678 Venice) was trained in Augsburg by his stepfather, Matthias Gondelach and, by 1625, was working in Venice. He made a name for himself in Italy, primarily with his frightening paintings of ghostly figures in the style of Hieronymus Bosch. However, he also painted altarpieces, as well as landscapes and townscapes, full of figures. The latter make him an interesting forerunner of the Venetian *veduta* artists of the 18th century.

Jacobello del Fiore (ca. 1370 Venice – 1439 Venice) was originally shaped by the Byzantine tradition, but quickly moved towards the so-called "soft" style of Late Gothic which was flourishing all over Europe. The greatest influence on him during this change in style was Gentile da Fabriano. Jacobello is one of a group of Late Gothic Venetian painters who, in the elegant and delicate coloration of their work and their attempt to use color to portray light, created the special relationship with color for which Venetian painting of the 15th and 16th centuries is famous.

Lombardo, Pietro (ca. 1435 Carona – 1515 Venice) worked in Padua during the 1560s, after which he moved to Venice. He was the progenitor of a family of architects and sculptors who had a decisive impact on Venetian art at the end of the 15th and the beginning of the 16th century. As an architect, he was an exponent of the typical, richly decorated Lombard style, which he perfected and then propagated through his large studio in Venice. The elegant, ornamental forms of his buildings are enchanting, both in their execution and their inventiveness. It was in Lombardo's tombs and monuments that the Venetian Renaissance first found full expression.

Lombardo, Sante (1504 Venice – 1560 Venice) was the grandson of Pietro and son of Tullio Lombardo. Trained in the family studio, he was primarily an architect. Whether he also worked as a sculptor is disputed. His formal repertoire was still reminiscent of the Venetian Early Renaissance and the buildings of Mauro Codussi and Pietro Lombardo. In the interplay of these forms, however, his work already showed the monumentality of the High Renaissance.

Lombardo, Tullio (ca. 1233 Venice – 1532 Venice) was the son of Pietro Lombardo. He was trained by his father and continued to run the family studio with his younger brother Antonio after their father's death. Like his father, Tullio worked both as an architect and as a sculptor. Although the previous generation of sculptors had already turned towards the classical world, Tullio brought a completely new quality to that model. His figures are distinguished by an idealization of form which, although influenced by classical figures in drapery, nonetheless had its foundation in accurate anatomical observation.

Longhena, Baldassare (1598 Venice – 1682 Venice) is the most significant architect of the Venetian Baroque. Although influenced by Vincenzo Scamozzi, Jacopo Sansovino, and Andrea Palladio, he was successful in reinterpreting the classical formal repertoire of the Renaissance. His chief work, the church of Santa Maria della Salute, displays his virtuosity, with its intersecting spaces and a facade of individual prospects visually held together by the mighty dome. Unlike many of his con- temporaries, Longhena did not lean towards the Roman Baroque, developing instead his own Venetian style.

Longhi, Pietro (1702 Venice – 1785 Venice) initially received instruction from Antonio Balestra. He went to Bologna in 1719 and completed his training under Crespi, who encouraged him in an intensive study of nature and of genre themes. He returned to Venice in 1730, becoming a member of the Academy in 1756. Longhi became famous for his small-scale satirical pictures, which portrayed the private and public lives of the Venetian nobility with a subtle and gentle humor. He also produced portraits and religious or historical paintings.

Lotto, Lorenzo (ca. 1480 Venice – 1556 Loreto, Marches), whose activities can be verified from 1503, was an important intermediary between the Venetian Old Masters and the later Baroque art of Upper Italy. He traveled a great deal and, among other places, worked in Treviso, Recanati, Bergamo, Venice, and Ancona. Lotto was one of the most sensitive and highly individual artists of his day. Initially influenced by the work of Giovanni Bellini and Antonella de Messina, he was later drawn to Giorgione, Titian, and Raphael. This led him to develop an eye for the precise depiction of fabrics, the portrayal of figures in motion, and the unusual use of color. In addition, Lotto occasionally reaches an extremely heightened level of drama and expressiveness.

Maccaruzzi, Bernardo (died 1798 in Venice), also known as Bernardino Maccarucci, was a student of the architect Giorgio Massari, with whom he frequently worked. His buildings, like the facade of the church of San Rocco (which was influenced by the adjacent Scuola di San Rocco) or the facade of the Accademia, following a design by Massari, are in a moderate, clear, Late Baroque style, typical of Venetian architecture at the end of the 18th century.

Andrea Mantegna

Mantegna, Andrea (1431 Carturo island, Padua – 1506 Mantua) was one of the most important artists of the Early Renaissance. In 1441 he went to Padua to study with Squarcione, which made him familiar with classical art. The sculpture of Donatello and the painting of Andrea del Castagno and Jacopo Bellini had a decisive influence. Working independently from 1448, he soon became a well-known painter and in 1460 was summoned to the Gonzaga court in Mantua. Mantegna's works are distinguished by the anatomically correct portrayal of the figures, precise delineation of details, and expertly constructed perspective. These innovations influenced, in particular, Gentile and Giovanni Bellini, and, through Mantegna's highly developed engravings, reached the artistic world of Northern Europe.

Mariano, Sebastiano (from Lugano, worked in Venice at the end of the 15th/beginning of the 16th century; died before 1518) is mainly known from documents. One definite work, the rebuilding of the choir of Santa Maria del Carmine, shows him to be a skillful intermediary between the Gothic church style and the new vocabulary of the Renaissance, which his choir expresssed.

Marini, Marino (1901 Pistoia – 1980 Viareggio) studied painting and sculpture at the Academy of Arts in Florence from 1917. From 1929 to 1940, he taught at the Villa Reale art school in Monza. In 1940, he became professor of sculpture at the Brera Academy in Milan. Marini made frequent trips to Paris, where he met avant-garde artists such as Kandinsky, Maillol, Braque, and Picasso. He also lived for a while in England, the Netherlands, Germany, Greece, and the USA. In 1952, he won the Grand Prize for Plastic Arts at the Venice Biennale and, in 1962, his first retrospective exhibition took place in Zurich. His work includes portraits and standing figures, especially horses and their riders.

Massari, Giorgio (active in Venice in the first half of the 18th century) was the leading Venetian architect of the 18th century. Influenced by Palladio and Longhena, he continued their tradition of a moderate, calm, Baroque architectural style. His creativity, however, did not match that of his predecessors.

Meyring, Heinrich (active in Venice at the end of the 17th century), also known as Enrico or Arrigo Merengo, came from northern Europe. Nothing is known of his training. He was one of the most sought-after sculptors in late 17th century Venice. His works decorate numerous facades and altars.

Morleiter, Giovanni Maria (1699 Niederdorf, Pustertal – 1781 Venice), also known as Johannes Maria Morleiter or Morleitner, was a sculptor and ivory carver. With Heinrich Meyring, he belongs to the group of Baroque sculptors who came from northern Europe to try their luck in wealthy Venice, where no native sculptors were having great success. Morleiter's style was even more conventional than Meyring's.

Padovano, Lauro (confirmed end of the 15th/beginning of the 16th century in Venice and Rome), also known as Laurino de Sancto Johanne de Padova, was in the first rank of miniature painters. In 1482, he enjoyed an exceptional reputation. With other painters he was called to Rome to admire the newly completed frescoes in the Sistine Chapel. He was strongly influenced by Giovanni Bellini and occasionally worked with him. Despite their strong colors, Lauro's works do not have the mysterious glow of those of Bellini.

Palladio, Andrea (1508 Padua – 1580 Vicenza), also known as Andrea di Pietro, was given the name Palladio by his first patron, the humanist Giangiorgio Trissino from Vincenza. The young Palladio started out as a stonemason but Trissino suggested that he become an architect. He enabled Palladio, then in his 40s, to make several trips to Rome, where he made a thorough study of classical architecture. Palladio not only practiced architecture but also wrote two books, one on Roman antiquities (1554), and the other the highly influential *I quattro libri dell' architettura* (*Four Books on Architecture*) (1570). He is as famous for the latter as for his buildings. These are distinguished by a felicitous relationship with classical architectural style, which Palladio accommodated with the artistic style of his own time, Mannerism. Palladio's buildings are seen as the pinnacle of Renaissance architecture and a model for countless buildings up to the 19th century. English architecture in particular shows his influence.

Palma il Giovane, Jacopo (ca. 1548–50 Venice – 1628 Venice), real name Jacopo Nigreti or Negreti, was the son of the artist Antonio Negreti and the grandson of Jacopo Negreti the Elder. The latter had already been attributed with the nickname Palma, which also passed to his grandson Jacopo. The two artists are differentiated using "Vecchio" (the Elder) and "Giovane" (the Younger). After time spent in Parma (from 1564) and Rome (1567), Palma il Giovane returned to live in Venice from 1573–74. In addition to his father, artists who influenced the young Jacopo before then can only be deduced from his post-1573–74 paintings. Titian,

Jacopo Palma il Giovane

Veronese, and Tintoretto were among his role models, as were Michelangelo and Federico and Taddeo Zuccaro. Palma's painting marked the transition from Renaissance to Baroque in Venice.

Palma il Vecchio, Jacopo (1480 Serina nr. Bergamo – 1528 Venice), real name Jacopo d'Antonio Negreti, went to Venice in the late 1490s, where he studied under Francesco di Simone da Santacroce. He then probably worked in the workshop of Giovanni Bellini. Palma il Vecchio, whose painting was heavily influenced by the work of Giorgione and the young Titian, was one of the foremost Venetian artists of the High Renaissance. Well-balanced compositions, an avoidance of dramatic themes, and a luminous, enamel-like coloring to convey harmony, are characteristic of his works.

Parodi, (Giacomo) Filippo (1630 Genoa – 1702 Genoa) began his career when very young as a woodcarver. From 1655 to 1661, he worked in the workshop of Gian Lorenzo Bernini, the most significant sculptor of the time in Rome. On his return to Genoa, Parodi immediately came to prominence. He not only worked in his native city, but, between 1667 and 1699, in both Venice and Padua as well. He is to be distinguished from his mentor Bernini through more detailed surface treatment, which gave less of a classical impression. He adopted his finely creased drapery from Puget.

Piazzetta, Giovanni Battista (1682 Venice – 1754 Venice) was the son of the woodcarver and sculptor Giacomo Piazzetta. After initially receiving instruction from his father, he then continued his training in Venice with Antonio Molinari and then, from 1703, he trained in Bologna, where he was particularly influenced by the genre painting of Giuseppe Maria Crespis. From 1711, he was permanently resident in Venice. Considered, along with his younger colleague and rival, Giovanni Battista Tiepolo, to be the most sought-after church painter of18th century Venice, Piazzetta also painted portraits as well as genre paintings and book illustrations.

Picasso, Pablo (1881 Malaga – 1973 Mougins, Côte d'Azur) was the most influential artist of the 20th century. The young Picasso received his artist's training in Barcelona and Madrid. Between 1900 and 1902, he journeyed to Paris, where he eventually settled in 1904. His *Les Demoiselles d'Avignon* from 1907, with its two-dimensionally distorted female nudes, is considered the first Cubist painting. It marks the final break with Naturalist tradition, which had dominated art since the 13th century. Initially Picasso developed Cubism along with Georges Braque, but was then inspired by other stylistic developments. Alongside painting, he also took up sculpture from 1905–06, and worked for the theater as well. He was also a fine graphic artist and a prolific book illustrator.

Raphael

Pollock, Jackson (1912 Cody, Wyoming – 1956 New York) was the leading figure in the movement known as Abstract Expressionism and one of the most influential North American artists in the 20th century. He studied under Thomas Hart at the Art Students League, where he was influenced by Hart's restless style. His late works, the so-called Drip Paintings, in which Pollock allowed color to run in a thin stream onto the canvas, were of the greatest importance for the development of what became known as Action Painting.

Pordenone (ca. 1483 Pordenone – 1539 Ferrara), real name Giovanni Antonio de' Sacchis, worked predominantly in Venice and the northeastern Veneto. Trained under Cima de Conegliano and Bartolomeo Montagna, Pordenone then developed his own style in Rome under the influence of Raphael and Michelangelo. His work is characterized by powerful figures full of pathos.

Raphael (1483 Urbino – 1520 Rome), real name Raffaello Santi, received his first artistic training from his father, the artist and poet Giovanni Santi. Around 1500, he joined the workshop of Pietro Perugino in Perugia. In 1540, he traveled to Florence, where he studied ancient and contemporary art. In 1508, Pope Julius II summoned Raphael to Rome. He worked there from 1509, principally on the frescoes for the Vatican's private apartments. After the death of Bramante, he was appointed clerk of works of St. Peter's. In 1515, he took on the role of directing all excavations of Roman antiquities in Rome. Raphael is considered the most important artist of the High Renaissance. His famous altarpieces, sensitive paintings of the

Madonna, and portraits, but also his large-scale wall frescoes, with their enormous detail, are characterized by formal clarity and a sense of deeply felt natural expression.

Raverti, Matteo (active in Milan 1389–1409, in Venice 1418–34), possibly received his training as a stonemason at Milan Cathedral, where he worked for some time before going to Venice in the second decade of the 15th century. Together with the workshop of Giovanni and Bartolomeo Buon, he worked on the Ca' d'Oro. Parts of the facade of San Marco and the portal of Santi Giovanni e Paolo are attributed to him because of the particularly fine stonework.

Ricci, Marco (1676 Belluno – 1730 Venice) was the nephew of Sebastiano Ricci, from whom he also probably received his first training in Venice. The influence of the Dutch landscape artist Antonio Tempesta, real name Pieter Mulier the Younger (ca. 1637 Haarlem - 1701 Milan), who was working in Venice, can also be detected. In 1708 he accepted an invitation to work as a theater artist in England. (He was, in addition, active in this field in Venice.) The clear architectural landscapes which he created for the theater, and which he also produced as paintings, were an important starting point for, among others, Canaletto. Particularly charming are Ricci's coastal scenes with their wide views in finely blended tones.

Ricci, Sebastiano (1659 Belluno – 1734 Venice), went to Venice as a young man, where he first received tutelage from Sebastiano Mazzoni and Federico Cervelli. From the late 1670s he worked at Giovanni Giuseppe dal Sole's workshop in Bologna. Sponsored by Duke Ranuccio II

Sebastiano Ricci

Farnese, Ricci received numerous commissions in Piacenza and Rome, where he lived for a number of years. In 1694, he went to Florence and, between 1696 and 1698, he worked in Milan. It is probably there that he got to know Magnasco. Thereafter, Ricci was again primarily based in Venice, but he spent long periods in Vienna (1701–03), Florence (1706–07) and London (1712–16). The paintings of this important Viennese Rococo artist are remarkable for their decoratively illusionist language of form, fullness of movement, and light palette.

Rizzo, Antonio (ca. 1430–35 Verona? – 1499–1500 Cesena or Foligno?) was first recorded in Venice in 1457. He worked for a time in the Certosa in Pavia, but then continued his career as an architect and sculptor and, from 1483, as clerk of works at the Doges' Palace in Venice. His rise ended in 1498, when he was accused of embezzlement, and had to flee the city. His best-known works are the signed statues of Adam and Eve on the Arco Foscari of the Doges' Palace. Here Gothic body proportions combine with the influences of both classical sculpture and the Florentine Renaissance with its exact observation of the human body.

Rossi, Domenico (1678 Morcote nr. Lugano – 1742 Venice) was one of the most important Venetian architects of the first half of the 18th century. Like his contemporaries, he based his work on that of Palladio, but accorded a stronger effect of light and shadow to the individual motifs of his buildings and, in so doing, brought them a Baroque flavor while losing nothing of their Classicism. With the opulent interior decoration of the Venetian Jesuit church, he took a completely different path. The splendid marble encrustation, which simulates rich material decoration, is a masterly example of Baroque illusionism.

Sansovino, Jacopo (1486 Florence – 1570 Venice), real name Jacopo Tatti, took the name of a mentor, the Florentine sculptor Andrea Sansovino. He went with the latter to Rome in 1505, where the young Jacopo marveled above all at the work of Raphael and Bramante. From 1511 to 1518, he was in Florence again and then returned to Rome, where he worked as a respected sculptor until 1527, when Charles V's troops plundered the city. He fled to Venice, which thereafter became his artistic home. With Sansovino's arrival, Venice discovered the current Roman trends in architecture and sculpture. He went on, though, to expand upon the experience he had gained in Rome and developed a specifically Venetian form, which was also affected by local traditions and his dealings with local artists, especially Titian.

Savoldo, (Giovan) Girolamo (ca. 1480–85 Brescia – after 1548 Brescia?) is first known as having been in Parma in 1506. From the 1520s he worked principally in the Veneto. Together with Lombard and Northern European influences, his style was above all influenced by contact with Venetian artists such as Cima da Conegliano, Giorgione and Lorenzo Lotto. Savoldo's work is significant for its clarity and the beauty of its colors. His landscapes, with their often powerful shades, and the unusual combination of dark green and blue with a trace of lilac, are reminiscent of those of Lorenzo Lotto. Savoldo dedicated all his attention to gleaming, shimmering materials.

Scalfarotto, Giovanni Antonio (ca. 1690 Venice – 1764 Venice) was, prior to 1612, chief architect at the Arsenal. Thereafter, he made a mark for himself with churches and monastery buildings. His main work, the church San Simeon Piccolo on the Grand Canal, illustrates how much the architect modeled his work on that of his greatest influence, Andrea Palladio. As early as the 1720s and 1730s, he anticipated tendencies that were to characterize Venetian architecture at the end of that century. It was in this that he also influenced his nephew and pupil, Tomaso Temanza.

Scamozzi, Vincenzo (1552 Vicenza – 1616 Venice) worked as an architect and engineer, but is significant for his theoretical writings. He was trained by his father, Domenico Scamozzi, who was also an architect, and by Jacopo Sansovino. He broadened his horizons through traveling to Rome, Florence, and Naples, but also to Poland and France. His greatest influence, and a figure who inspired Scamozzi throughout his life, was the architect Andrea Palladio. The completion of building projects left unfinished by Palladio has often been ascribed to him. His own main work was the New Procurators' Offices in Venice. In 1615, he published the treatise *Idea della Architettura universale*, which further increased his exceptional reputation with his contemporaries.

Scarpa, Carlo (1906 Venice – 1978 Sendai, Japan) was the most significant Venetian architect of the 20th century. His work, which transforms the material concrete, often with great imagination but always with strength and abstraction, are to be seen throughout Venice, for instance at the University or in the Palazzo Querini Stampalia. Scarpa's interest was not primarily the structure as such, but rather the space which he recreated and presented through his architecture. Scarpa influenced young architects throughout the whole of Europe with his style, which always found new and hitherto unknown solutions for traditional construction tasks.

Scarpagnino, Lo (ca. 1465–70 Milan – 1549 Venice), real name Antonio Abbondi (also Abondio), was one of the Lombard architects who dominated Venetian architecture at the beginning of the 16th century. As chief architect of the government buildings authority, he constructed numerous public buildings and produced expert reports on the work of his colleagues. From 1527, he was often to work with Jacopo Sansovino, but remained largely uninfluenced by the style of the latter. Lo Scarpagnino was, however, heavily influenced by the forms of the late 15th century. Even though he himself can only be regarded as an average architect, he did pave the way, with his simple, reduced constructions, for later developments in Venetian Renaissance architecture.

Sebastiano del Piombo (ca. 1485 Venice – 1547 Rome), real name Sebastiano Luciani, but known as Viniziano, trained in Venice, as did Vasari, first with Giovanni Bellini and then with Giorgione, whose painting had a strong influence on the young artist. In 1511 Sebastiano went to Rome, where he remained until his death, apart from one year spent in Venice, 1528–29. His style was influenced by Raphael and Michelangelo and characterized by monumentalism as well as a powerful formal style.

Spavento, Giorgio (active in Venice at the end of the 15th century – ca. 1509 Venice) was the successor of the more important Mauro Codussi as the chief architect of the Procurators of San Marco. In this capacity, he designed the sacristy of San Marco and the new construction of the Campanile, struck by lightning in 1489. With the church of San Salvatore, which was actually completed by Tullio Lombardo, he showed that, although he was heavily influenced by the forms of Codussi, he had developed them in relation to the

Jacopo Tintoretto

monumentalism of the individual structural components and therefore one step closer to the High Renaissance.

Tiepolo, Giovanni Battista (1696 Venice – 1770 Madrid) studied with Gregorio Lazzarini and was already working independently as an artist in 1717 in Venice, where he received important commissions for the decoration of churches and the palazzi of noble families. From 1756 to 1758, he assumed the post of president of the Venetian Academy. Tiepolo's fame spread across the whole of Europe and brought him commissions from, among others, the royal courts of France, Russia, and England. From 1762, he was in the employ of the Spanish court

of Charles III. Tiepolo's art marks the zenith of Italian painting in the 18th century. **Tintoretto,** Domenico (1560 Venice – 1620 Venice), real name Domenico Robusti, together with his brothers and sisters, took over both the workshop and nickname of his father, Jacopo Tintoretto, who had abandoned the real family surname long before. He also continued the work of his father in terms of style, but never attained the latter's artistic quality.

Tintoretto, Jacopo (1518 Venice – 1594 Venice), real name Jacopo Robusti, was first recorded as an independent artist in Venice in 1539. It is not known under which master he received his training, but Titian, Andrea Schiavone, and Paris Bordone, among others, have all been suggested. In 1547, he began, with the *Last Supper* (in the church of San Marcuola) and *St. Mark Rescuing a Slave* (in the Accademia), a series of commissions, mainly in Venice. Important works include the decoration, between 1564 and 1588, of the Scuola di San Rocco and the state commissions for the Doges' Palace, as well as the Gonzaga Cycle created for the Ducal Palace in Mantua. Tintoretto is considered the most important representative of Venetian Mannerism.

Titian (ca. 1490 Pieve di Cadore – 1576 Venice), real name Tiziano Vecellio, is considered the most important Venetian artist of the 16th century. No reliable information has been found as to his date of birth and early creative years. The Venetian mosaicist Sebastiano Zuccato, and Gentile and Giovanni Bellini are considered to have been his mentors. In 1508–09, Titian painted the frescoes of the Fondaco dei Tedeschi in Venice, along with Giorgione. Then, in 1510–11, followed the frescoes in the Scuola del Santo in Padua. From 1515, he worked for the families Este, Gonzaga, Farnese, and Rovere, amongst others, and for King François I of France. In 1533, he became the court artist of the Emperor Charles V, and he received the Order of the Golden Fleece. In 1545–46, he worked for Pope Paul III in Rome. In his later years, Titian was almost exclusively in the service of King Philip II of Spain.

Veneziano, Paolo (before 1333 Venice – before 1362 Venice) was the most interesting artist of the 14th century in Venice. Although occasionally in his early work an interest in Naturalism can be detected, he followed, like older Venetian artists, Byzantine art. He did not adopt Byzantine models slavishly, however. The enamel-like colors of his materials, richly decorated with gold, and an unconventional use of light and shadow are characteristic of Paolo's luxurious style.

Veronese, Paolo (1528 Verona – 1588 Venice), real name Paolo Caliari, probably studied with Antonio Badile in Verona and went, in 1553, to Venice, where he stayed until his death, apart from a sojourn in Rome in 1560–61. From 1553, he worked on the Sala del Consiglio dei Dieci in the Doges' Palace and between ca. 1555 and 1570 he worked on the decoration of the church of San Sebastiano. In ca. 1561–62, i.e. after his return from Rome, he produced the famous frescoes in the Villa Barbaro in Maser near Treviso. Along with Titian and Tintoretto, this multitalented artist made up the trio of great Venetian artists of the 16th century. His work, classed as Late Renaissance, consisted of ceiling frescoes, altarpieces, paintings of

Titian

mythological subjects, and portraits. After his death his brother Benedetto and his sons Carlo and Gabriel continued the workshop.

Vittoria, Alessandro (1525 Trento – 1608 Venice) joined the workshop of Jacopo Sansovino in Venice in 1543. From the 1550s he worked independently as a sculptor in Venice and in the Veneto. Alongside Sansovino, he is the most important Venetian sculptor of the 16th century. His figures, with their great sense of movement, tend towards the Baroque, but he found no worthy successor in Venice.

Vivarini, Alvise (ca. 1445 Venice – ca. 1504 Venice), the product of an artistic family, the members of which are recorded as having been mainly in Venice in the 15th and 16th centuries. Alvise was the son of Antonio Vivarini (ca. 1415 – ca. 1480), who is considered to have been the founder of what became known as the School of Murano. He was also the nephew of Bartolomeo Vivarini, in whose workshop he was probably trained. Alvise's most important commission, the decoration of the Sala del Maggior Consiglio in the Doges' Palace, which is also considered to be the main work of the School of Murano, was destroyed by fire in 1577. In terms of style, Vivarini's early work is related to that of his uncle and of Andrea Mantegna. After 1480, his work became more delicate, the forms calmer and more balanced. During this period he was heavily influenced by Giovanni Bellini.

Vivarini, Antonio (ca. 1415 Murano – ca. 1486 Murano) was the head of what was, after the Bellinis, the second most important artistic family in Venice in the 15th century. His work marks the passage from the soft forms of the Gothic to the Naturalism of the Renaissance. More so, however, than his contemporary, Jacopo Bellini, who worked intensively with the new style, Vivarini stayed loyal to the Gothic. However, he expanded his stylistic range, especially in terms of the representation of figures, with a new fullness of figure far removed from the Gothic.

Vivarini, Bartolomeo (ca. 1430 Murano – after 1490 Murano) was the younger brother of Antonio Vivarini of Murano, as well as the uncle and probable teacher of Alvise Vivarini. From 1450, he had a workshop partnership with his brother Antonio. In contrast to the latter's rather traditional work, which drew from the Late Gothic and the Early Renaissance, Bartolomeo's work is notable for its extreme attention to detail, sharp contors and drapery, and powerful colors. Also characteristic is the delight in the representation of decorative elements, above all evident in his flower arrangements and fruit garlands. His work represents the passage from the Early to the Late Renaissance.

Paolo Veronese

Venetian buildings

Fondaco dei Turchi (13th c., largely renovated during the 19th c.)

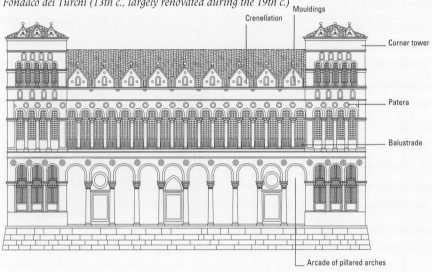

Crenellation
Mouldings
Corner tower
Patera
Balustrade
Arcade of pillared arches

Secular architecture

Fondaco dei Turchi

It is despite the fact that the Fondaco dei Turchi was restored with a certain element of imagination during the 19th century – or precisely because of this – that it has all the forms typical of the architecture of the palazzi of Venice of the 13th century. These include the dignified round arch, the crenellation, ornaments with round mouldings, and pateras, which often had petals and a relief in the center. However, it should be borne in mind that building had a slightly different form in the 13th century.

Ca' d'Oro

The Ca' d'Oro, richly decorated with pointed arches, marble, and open-work tracery, shows how long Gothic forms were retained in Venetian palazzo architecture. The facades of the Gothic palazzi clearly reveal the interior arrangement of the rooms. Loggias or rows of windows on the second and third floors indicate reception rooms; individual windows at the side indicate private apartments.

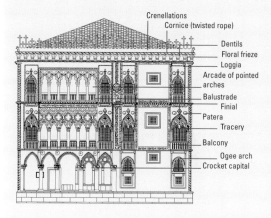

Ca' d'Oro, started 1421

Crenellations
Cornice (twisted rope)
Dentils
Floral frieze
Loggia
Arcade of pointed arches
Balustrade
Finial
Patera
Tracery
Balcony
Ogee arch
Crocket capital

Ca' Pesaro

The Ca' Pesaro contains a number of different styles of architecture current from 16th–18th centuries. The first floor, with its rustication, is presented as a kind of base for the floors above it with their large, arched windows and forward-set columns.

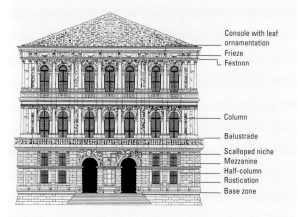

Ca' Pesaro, 1628–1710

Console with leaf ornamentation
Frieze
Festoon
Column
Balustrade
Scalloped niche
Mezzanine
Half-column
Rustication
Base zone

Ecclesiastical buildings

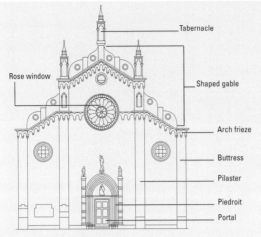

Santa Maria Gloriosa dei Frari, 1340–1443

- Tabernacle
- Rose window
- Shaped gable
- Arch frieze
- Buttress
- Pilaster
- Piedroit
- Portal

Santa Maria Gloriosa dei Frari
This church has the simple brick facade typical of Gothic churches until the mid-15th century, with ornamentation of white Istrian stone.

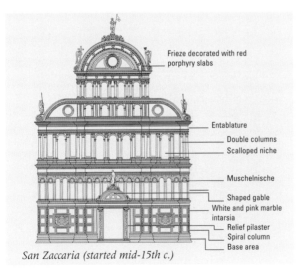

San Zaccaria (started mid-15th c.)

- Frieze decorated with red porphyry slabs
- Entablature
- Double columns
- Scalloped niche
- Muschelnische
- Shaped gable
- White and pink marble intarsia
- Relief pilaster
- Spiral column
- Base area

San Zaccaria
San Zaccaria was the first Venetian church to have a Renaissance facade: this is typified by its stone cladding, the use of round arches, scalloped niches, and the visual balancing out of horizontal and vertical elements.

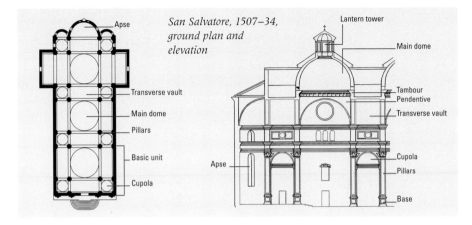

San Salvatore, 1507–34, ground plan and elevation

Apse

Transverse vault

Main dome

Pillars

Basic unit

Cupola

Apse

Lantern tower

Main dome

Tambour
Pendentive

Transverse vault

Cupola

Pillars

Base

San Salvatore

During the Renaissance, the Venetian architects re-adopted the cruciform-domed church plan of Byzantine times, a tradition which had deep roots in Venice. This type of church consists of a central unit of a dome set on pillars, to which other elements can be added at random.

Il Redentore

The temple-style fronts, as employed by Palladio for Il Redentore, borrow from Greek and Roman temples. During the Renaissance and Baroque periods they were frequently used for churches.

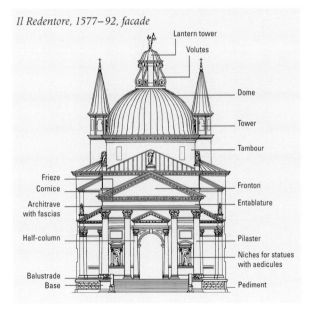

Il Redentore, 1577–92, facade

Lantern tower

Volutes

Dome

Tower

Tambour

Frieze
Cornice

Architrave
with fascias

Half-column

Balustrade
Base

Fronton

Entablature

Pilaster

Niches for statues
with aedicules

Pediment

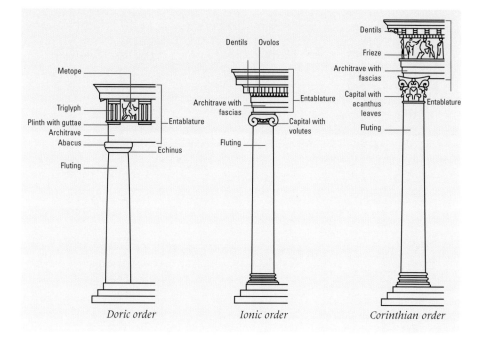

Labels for Doric order: Metope, Triglyph, Plinth with guttae, Architrave, Abacus, Fluting, Entablature, Echinus

Labels for Ionic order: Dentils, Ovolos, Architrave with fascias, Entablature, Capital with volutes, Fluting

Labels for Corinthian order: Dentils, Frieze, Architrave with fascias, Capital with acanthus leaves, Entablature, Fluting

Doric order　　*Ionic order*　　*Corinthian order*

Orders

The ancient orders played an important role in the way columns were built during the Renaissance and Baroque periods. (An order is a column together with its capital and entablature.) There are three main orders of columns: Ionic, Doric, and Corinthian. During the Renaissance they were used hierarchically: the slim Corinthian order was considered the most luxurious, followed by the Ionic and Doric orders.

Domes

The many domes used in Venetian religious architecture until the modern age traced their origins back to Venice's Byzantine roots. In the early period, such as with San Marco, they were direct borrowings from Byzantine originals. During the Renaissance they referred back to the putative antique precursors of the Venetian architectural tradition.

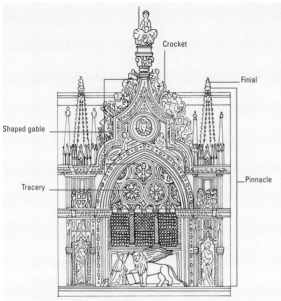

Crocket

Finial

Shaped gable

Pinnacle

Tracery

Steno Loggia of the Doges' Palace

Steno Loggia

The Steno Loggia is named after Doge Michele Steno, who had it added to the waterfront facade of the Doges' Palace in 1404. The loggia, embellished by the Dalle Masegne brothers, richly decorated with Gothic forms, indicates, on the building's facade, the assembly hall of the Venetian aristocratic parliament, the Sala del Maggior Consiglio.

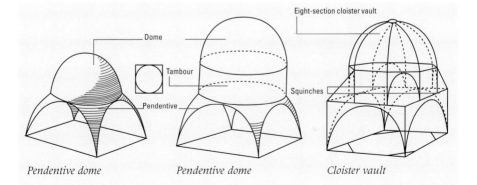

Dome

Eight-section cloister vault

Tambour

Squinches

Pendentive

Pendentive dome   *Pendentive dome*   *Cloister vault*

References and further reading

Arslan, Edoardo: *Venezia gotica*; Milan 1986

Barovier Mentasti, Rosa: *Il vetro veneziano*; Milan 1982

Bassi, Elena: *Architettura del Sei e Settecento a Venezia*; Naples 1962

Bassi, Elena: *Palazzi di Venezia*; Venice 1976

Benzoni, Gino (editor): *I Dogi*; Milan 1982

Brusatin, Manlio and **Pavanello,** Giuseppe: *Il teatro La Fenice*; Venice 1987

Chambers, David: *The Imperial Age of Venice 1380–1580*; London 1970

Concina, Ennio: *Le chiese di Venezia*; Udine 1995

Cooperman, Bernhard D. and **Curiel**, Roberta: *Il Ghetto di Venezia*; Venice 1990

Dazzi, Manlio and **Merkel,** Ettore: *Catalogo della Pinacoteca della Fondazione Scientifica Querini Stampalia*; Venice 1979

Demus, Otto: *The Church of San Marco in Venice. History, Architecture, Sculpture*; Washington 1960

Demus, Otto: *The Mosaics of San Marco in Venice*; Chicago, London 1984

Di Martino, Enzo: *La Biennale di Venezia. Cento anni di arte e cultura*; Milan 1995

Die Pferde von San Marco; Berlin 1982

Dorigo, Wladimiro: *Venezia Origini*; Milan 1983

Dorigo, Wladimiro: "I mosaici medievali di San Marco nella storia della basilica," in: *San Marco*; Milan 1990

Finlay, Robert G.: *Politics in Renaissance Venice*; New Brunswick 1980

Flint, Lucy, **Childs,** Elisabeth C. and **Messer,** Thomas M.: *La collezione Peggy Guggenheim*; Washington 1983

Fontana, Gianjacopo and **Moro,** Marco: *Venezia monumentale. I Palazzi*; Venice 1967

Forssman, Erik: *Venice in der Kunst und im Kunsturteil des 19. Jahrhunderts*; Stockholm 1971

Fortini Brown, Patricia: *Venetian Narrative Painting in the Age of Carpaccio*; New Haven, London 1988

Franzoi, Umberto and **di Stefano,** Dina: *Le chiese di Venezia*; Venice 1976

Goethe, Johann Wolfgang von: *Tagebuch der italienischen Reise*; Frankfurt am Main 1976

Goffen, Rona: *Piety and Patronage in Renaissance Venice. Bellini, Titian and the Fransciscans*; New Haven, London 1989

Goffen, Rona: *Il Tesoro di San Marco. I, La Pala d'Oro*; Venice 1994

Hahnloser, Hans R.: *Il Tesoro di San Marco*; Florence 1965–1971

Hale, John R.: *Renaissance Venice*; London 1973

Howard, Deborah: *Jacopo Sansovino. Architecture and Patronage in Renaissance Venice*; New Haven, London 1976

Howard, Deborah: *The Architectural History of Venice*; London 1980

Humfrey, Peter: *The Altarpiece in Renaissance Venice*; New Haven, London 1993

Huse, Norbert and **Wolters,** Wolfgang: *Venice, Die Kunst der Renaissance*; Munich 1986

Kretschmayr, Heinrich: *Geschichte von Venice*; Gotha 1905–Stuttgart 1934

Lane, Frederic C.: Venice. *A Maritime Republic*; Baltimore, London 1973

Mangini, Nicola: *I teatri di Venezia*; Milan 1974

Mariacher, Giovanni: *Il Museo Vetrario di Murano*; Milan 1970

Martineau, Jane and **Hope,** Charles (editors): *The Genius of Venice*, exhibition catalog; London 1983

Martineau, Jane and **Robinson,** A. (editors): *The Glory of Venice*; New Haven, London 1994

Miani, Mariapia, **Resdini,** Daniele, and **Lamon,** Francesca: *L'arte dei maestri vetrai di Murano*; Treviso 1984

Nepi Scirè, Giovanni: *Gallerie dell' Accademia*; Venice 1991

Norwich, John Julius: *A History of Venice*; New York 1982

Ongania, Ferdinando: *Le Vere da Pozzo in Venezia*; Venice 1911

Perocco, Guido and **Salvadori,** Antonio: *Civiltà di Venezia*; Venice 1973–76

Pallucchini, Rodolfo: *La pittura veneziana del Settecento*; Venice, Rome 1960

Pallucchini, Rodolfo: *La pittura veneziana del Trecento*; Venice, Rome 1964

Pallucchini, Rodolfo: *La pittura veneziana del Seicento*; Milan 1981

Pavanello, Giuseppe and **Romanelli,** Giandomenico (editors): *Venezia nell'Ottocento. Immagini e mito,* exhibition catalog; Milan 1983

Pignatti, Terisio: *Il Museo Correr di Venezia. Dipinti, del XVII e XVIII secolo*; Venice 1960

Pignatti, Terisio: *Le scuole di Venezia*; Milan 1981

Planiscig, P. Leo: *Venezianische Bildhauer der Renaissance*; Vienna 1921

Pullan, Brian: *Rich and Poor in Renaissance Venice*; Oxford 1971

Romanelli, Giandomenico: *Venezia Ottocento*; Rome 1977

Romanelli, Giandomenico (editor): *Venice, Kunst und Architektur*; Cologne 1997 (Italian edition Udine 1997)

Rosand, David: *Painting in Cinquecento Venice*: Titian, Veronese, Tintoretto; New Haven, London 1982

Rowdon, Maurice: *The Fall of Venice*; London 1970

Ruskin, John: *The Stones of Venice*; London 1851–53

San Marco: *I mosaici, la storia, l'illuminazione*; Milan 1990

Semenzato, Camillo: *La scultura veneta del Seicento e del Settecento*; Venice 1966

Tafuri, Manfredo: *Venezia e il Rinascimento*; Turin 1985

Tamassia Mazzarotto, Bianca: *Le feste veneziane, i giochi popolari, le ceremonie religiose e di governo*; Florence 1982 (2nd edition)

Tassini, Giuseppe: *Feste e Spettacoli. Divertimenti e Piaceri degli antichi Veneziani*; Venice, Castelfranco Veneto 1961 (2nd edition)

Timofiewitsch, Wladimir: *Girolamo Campagna, Studien zur venezianischen Plastik um das Jahr 1600*; Munich 1972

Toesca, Paolo: *Il Trecento*; Turin 1951

Trincanato, Egle Renata: *Venezia minore*; Venice 1948 (reprinted, Venice 1977)

Wolters, Wolfgang: *La scultura veneziana gotica (1300–1460)*; Venice 1976

Wolters, Wolfgang: *Der Bilderschmuck des Dogenpalastes*; Wiesbaden 1983

Index

Grand Canal

Bend at the Ca' Foscari from the west

The Grand Canal, which meanders through the entire city like a river, is the city's life line, its main thoroughfare and promenade rolled into one. In the olden days, trading ships sailed right up to the Rialto to discharge their goods – spices, silk, jewels, and furs. Wealthy Venetian families built their palaces overlooking the Grand Canal. In Venice, these palazzi simply go by the name of *ca'* (a typically Venetian abbreviation of *casa*). An unwritten code of honor ensured that nobody built their house further out into the canal than their neighbors, or was too lavish with architectural ornamentation. This centuries-old tradition is what gives the city its sense of uniformity, retained to this day. A trip along the Grand Canal gives visitors a unique insight into the development of Venetian architecture over the last 500 years.

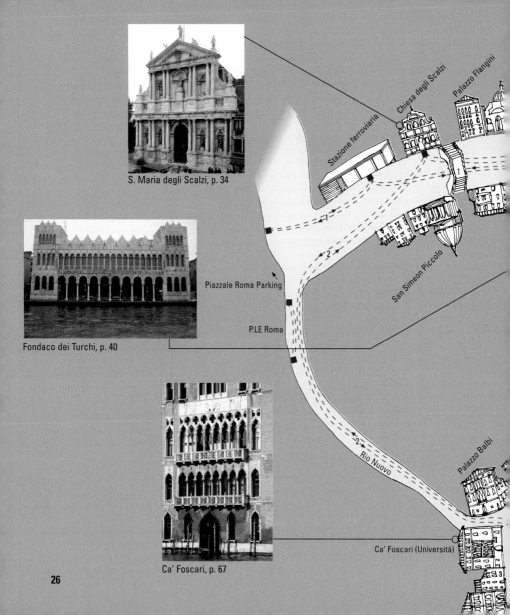

S. Maria degli Scalzi, p. 34

Fondaco dei Turchi, p. 40

Ca' Foscari, p. 67

Stazione ferroviaria

Chiesa degli Scalzi

Palazzo Flangini

San Simeon Piccolo

Piazzale Roma Parking

P.LE Roma

Rio Nuovo

Palazzo Balbi

Ca' Foscari (Università)

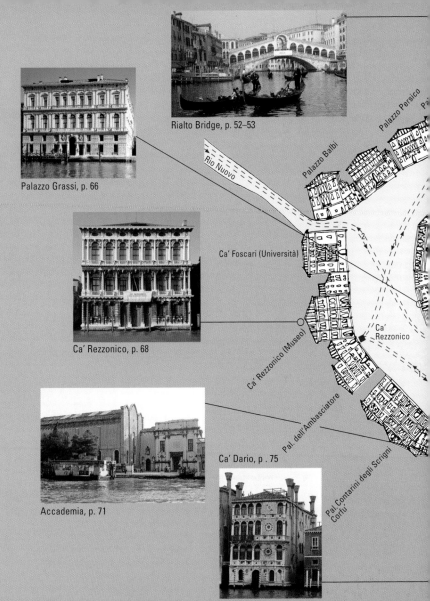

Rialto Bridge, p. 52–53

Palazzo Grassi, p. 66

Ca' Rezzonico, p. 68

Accademia, p. 71

Ca' Foscari (Università)

Rio Nuovo

Palazzo Balbi

Palazzo Persico

Ca' Rezzonico (Museo)

Ca' Rezzonico

Pal. dell'Ambasciatore

Ca' Dario, p . 75

Pal. Contarini degli Scrigni Corfù

Palazzo Donà
Palazzo Pisani
Pal. Papadopoli
Rialto
S. Silvestro
Rialto
Palazzo Dolfin-Manin
S. Tomà
S. Angelo
Palazzi Mocenigo
Pal. Corner-Spinelli
Palazzo Grimani
Pal. Contarini dalle Figure
Pal. Moro-Lin
Pal. Grassi (Museo)
Palazzo Giustinian-Lolin
Pal. Cavalli-Franchetti
Pal. Corner Ca' Grande
Pal. Hotel Gritti
Pal. Manolessi-Ferro
Pal. Contarini-Fasan
Palazzi Barozzi-Emo
Palazzo Giustinian
S. M. del Giglio
Accademia
La Salute
Gallerie dell'Accademia
Pal. Contarini dal Zaffo Manzoni
Pal. Venier dei Leoni
Palazzo Dario
S. Maria della Salute
Dogana

30

Piazza San Marco, pp. 86-87

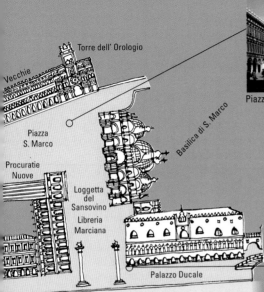

Torre dell' Orologio

Vecchie

Piazza
S. Marco

Basilica di S. Marco

Procuratie
Nuove

Loggetta
del
Sansovino

Libreria
Marciana

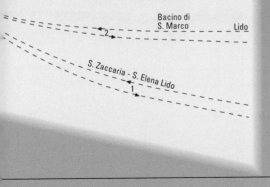

Palazzo Ducale

Doges' Palace, p. 128

Bacino di
S. Marco — — — — Lido

2

S. Zaccaria - S. Elena Lido

1

Santa Maria della Salute, p. 76

Bend at the Ca' Foscari from the east

A ride along Venice's main thoroughfare, whether you take a gondola, a private boat, or a vaporetto – one of the larger water buses – is one of the most memorable experiences of a visit to the city. It is the best way to experience the unique atmosphere created by the water, the sky, and the architecture.

Until the 19th century only one bridge spanned the canal at the Rialto. Today there is also the wooden bridge at the Accademia and a second stone bridge by the train station. The lack of bridges has never been a problem for the Venetians. In the old days, the majority of traffic consisted of gondolas or small boats of similar form. Thus canals were more important than streets, which tended to be there for getting around within a small district, which usually centered around a church. In addition, there is still to this day a perfectly adequate substitute for bridges, the *traghetti*, or gondola ferries, that for a small fee row you, standing up, across the canal. The *traghetti* give visitors a good opportunity to get a feel for real Venetian life.

disuse. The Carmelite monks commissioned the design from Baldassare Longhena in 1654, and it was built in 1656–72.

Giuseppe Sardi completed the church's rich marble facade in 1680. The sculptures are attributed to Bernardo Falcone. The building costs for the poor friars' church were met by Count Gerolamo Cavazza.

San Simeone Piccolo (Santi Simeone e Giuda)

Despite its name, this small ("piccolo") church is by no means smaller than San Simeone Grande, which is somewhat further to the north. The name refers rather to the Apostle Simon, while San Simeone Grande is named after Simon the prophet. San Simeone Piccolo was founded during the 9th century, though the present late Baroque circular building, with its bright green dome and tall classical facade, dates from the 18th century. It was built by Giovanni Scalfarotto in 1718–38 as a copy of the Pantheon in Rome.

Santa Maria degli Scalzi (Santa Maria di Nazareth)

The church of the barefooted Carmelite friars is one of Venice's finest Baroque churches. It is called "Scalzi" (barefoot) by the Venetians, while the original name of Santa Maria di Nazareth has fallen into

San Geremia, Palazzo Labia

A church dedicated to the prophet Jeremiah stood on this spot as far back as the 11th century. The campanile is one of the oldest surviving belltowers in Venice, and was probably built during the 12th century. The current church dates back to the 18th century. Building commenced in 1753 according to a design drawn up by Carlo Corbellini. The facades, after being destroyed in a fire caused by Austrian

bombs in 1848, were redesigned in 1871. Next to the campanile of San Geremia, the side facade of the Palazzo Labia, which was built in 1750 by Alessandro Tremignon, can be seen.

The extremely wealthy Labia family, which had just purchased its way into the Venetian aristocracy, was one of the few families able to afford to build such a costly new residence in the 18th century, a period during which Venice's wealth was on the decline. The palazzo also features some magnificent frescoes by

Giovanni Battista Tiepolo (see pp. 368–71), particularly in the ballroom.

San Marcuola
(Santi Ermagora e Fortunato)

The name of this church is a typically Venetian combination of the two first names, Hermagoras and Fortunatus, of the two martyrs from Aquilea, to whom the church is dedicated. As is the case with many other Venetian churches, the facade, built in 1728–36 by Giorgio Massari, remained unfinished. The single-naved interior is simple, yet more elegant than the rather forbidding exterior suggests. It is certainly well worth a brief visit. In addition to the Baroque altars with sculptures by Giovanni Maria Morleiter, a painting of the *Last Supper* by Tintoretto (1547) is particularly noteworthy.

Palazzo Vendramin-Calergi

Mauro Codussi, who was the first architect to express in Venice the architectural idiom of the Renaissance in its purest form, built this fine palazzo around 1500. After his death in 1504, the artistically significant building was completed by the Lombardi. The facade illustrates the typically Venetian device of dividing the windows into groups (one at either end and three together in the middle).

In place of the pointed arch, which was still common in the 15th century, Codussi fitted the two windows into a round arch. He then topped these with a round oculus in the spandrel above them. The rich ornamentation of the windows recalls the Gothic pointed windows of the earlier palazzi without copying their form. The same applies to the colorful porphyry and marble panels, as well as to the reliefs that Codussi added to the pilasters beside the windows and to the upper architrave.

The two long horizontals which separate the stories from one another and top off the upper window section, together with the vertical elements, give the building its harmonious, completed look. The *piano nobile* on the second floor is emphasized by an additional protruding floor, forming a balcony. This was the palazzo where Richard Wagner died on February 13, 1883. Today the building is occupied by the city casino, although it is only used in winter; in summer the casino on the Lido is open.

Deposito del Megio

This 15th-century former granary is a simple brick building, the Lion of St. Mark showing that it belonged to the city. The Venetian Republic kept several granaries of this kind in order to guarantee the populace a minimum supply of food at reasonable prices.

Fondaco dei Turchi

During the course of the 17th century this palazzo became the headquarters of the Turkish merchants in the city. It had been built in the 13th century in the Venetian-Roman style as the residence of the Da Pesaro family. In the 14th century it must have been one of the most imposing buildings in the city, as the Senate frequently used it to accommodate visiting dignitaries. In 1621, it leased the building out to Turkish traders. Parts of the original structure that have survived are among the oldest remnants of a stone residential building to be found in Venice.

After the end of the Republic the Fondaco dei Turchi fell into gradual disrepair. Between 1858 and 1869 it was radically restored, although modern experts do not consider this work to have been particularly successful. Today it houses the Museo di Storia Naturale with its interesting exhibition of animal and plant life from the lagoon.

San Stae (San Eustachio)

The Venetians typically abbreviate the name of this church dedicated to St. Eustace to "Stae." In 1709 a tender was held for the design of the facade, which had remained unfinished. Of the 12 entrants, Domenico Rossi was selected as master builder.

During the 19th century the facade was criticized as "top-heavy." This was because it was built like a temple, with a large pediment supported by three-quarter length columns on high bases, which makes the broken pediment over the main portal look awkward. Today, because of its good acoustics, the church is used for concerts. Inside are paintings by Tiepolo and Piazzetta.

Giovanni Battista Piazzetta: Martyrdom of St. James the Great, 1722
Oil on canvas, 165 x 138 cm

Piazzetta was one of the "tenebrists," whose paintings consisted of figures executed in dark, brownish shades. He was one of the great masters of the style. Worth noting is the skillful way in which the saint's shirt has been painted, glowing pure white, even though it is mixed in with many dark tones. The extreme highlighting makes the figures look fragmented. The opposition of dark and light sections emphasizes the drama of this horrific scene.

Giovanni Battista Tiepolo:
Martyrdom of St. Bartholomew, 1722–23
Oil on canvas, 167 x 139 cm

In 1722, 12 Venetian artists were invited to decorate San Stae, each one painting the martyrdom of one of the Apostles. The church is thus a gallery of the artists who enjoyed the greatest renown in Venice in the early 18th century.

An interesting point is that the 26-year-old Tiepolo was the only young artist selected among much older colleagues. With his bright colors, Tiepolo adds jarring accents, for example, the broken red of the executioner's pants, and the dark blue cloth that appears between the soldier's thigh and the saint's shoulder. The reddish hue of the pants intensifies the glow of the blue.

If we compare St. Bartholomew's bright loincloth with St. James' white shirt in Piazzetta's painting, we can see that Tiepolo worked with colored shadows (here light blue and lilac). Another striking aspect of this painting is the plasticity of the hands. The saint's right hand seems to reach out to the viewer. Both these hands are masterpieces of perspective, which Tiepolo achieves purely through his rendition of color.

Ca' Pesaro

Between 1558 and 1628 the Pesaro family purchased three adjacent palazzi, which were demolished in 1628. In the same year, they assigned to Baldassare Longhena the construction of a single large home on the site. By the time of his death in 1682, it had only reached the first story. The building was finally completed

in 1710 by Antonio Gaspari. Even while being built, the new Palazzo Pesaro was regarded as vulgar and ostentatious, and thus not proper for an aristocratic Venetian family. It is easy to see that these criticisms had their roots in more than just envy when you compare this palazzo with the many others along the Grand Canal. It has housed the Museo d'Arte Moderna since 1902. In the early part of the 20th century, the resourceful curators of the museum succeeded in adding various interesting accents to the building. While the artists showing in the Venice Biennale were selected by a generally conservative jury, the Ca' Pesaro exhibited definitive items of modern art. Today, works by artists such as Vedova, de Chirico, Miró, Grosz, Klee, Klimt, Arp, and Calder are on display here. The palazzo also houses the Museo d'Arte Orientale, with its rich collection of 17–19th century Japanese art.

could tell the branches of their families and their corresponding palazzi apart. This imposing building was begun in 1724 by Domenico Rossi. The facade illustrates the expressive yet severely structured and symmetrical idiom of Rossi, who was one of Venice's most talented 18th century architects. Today the palazzo houses the archives of the Venice Biennale, and a substantial library on contemporary art.

Palazzo Corner della Regina

Caterina Cornaro (1454–1510) cannot have commissioned this Baroque palazzo, since it was built more than 200 years after her death, but she was born in the building which preceded it. The branch of the Cornaro, or Corner, family from which the later queen (*regina*) of Cyprus was descended is named after her. There are indeed numerous Cornaro palazzi around the city.

Naming palazzi in honor of famous family members was one of the ways in which Venetian nobility

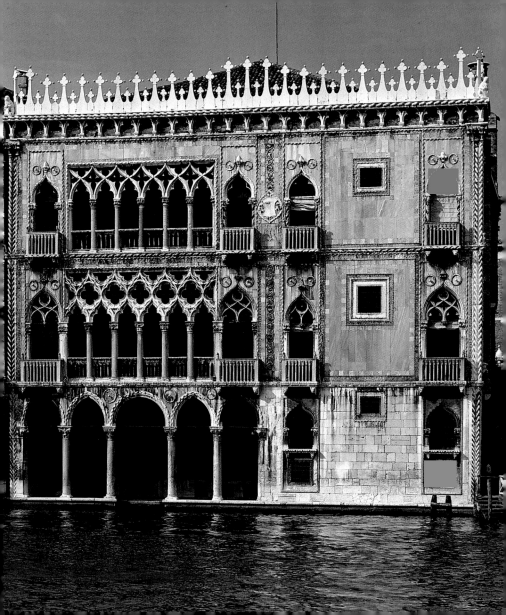

Ca' d'Oro

Even without its gilded and red and blue painted exterior, the "House of Gold" is one of the finest examples of the imaginative late Gothic style that was still current in Venice long after Florence had adopted the strict forms of the early Renaissance.

Marino Contarini had this palazzo built in 1421. The fine stone carvings were executed by Matteo Raverti among others. Raverti was probably responsible for the arcades on the second floor, which reflect the forms of the Doges' Palace.

In 1840, a Russian prince gave the Ca' d'Oro to the famous dancer Maria Taglioni, who showed little understanding of the artistic significance of this romantic and expensive gift. Count Giorgio Fanchetti, who acquired the building in 1894, removed Taglioni's inappropriate additions, and, in 1905, donated the palazzo, together with its valuable art collection, to the Italian state.

Pescheria (fish market)

Venice's fish market has stood on this site since the 14th century. The neo-Gothic market hall was built in 1907, to designs not by an architect, but by the painter Cesare Laurenti.

Fabbriche Nuove

Originally, this elongated building housed Venice's commercial authorities. It was built in 1552–55 by Jacopo Sansovino, who managed to use basic means to achieve a simple, economical style for an important city department.

The Fabbriche Nuove used to house the magistrate responsible for controlling trade on the Rialto. Venice's large marketplace is still situated on the side facing the Rialto. But it is no longer a place where loans are agreed upon and luxury goods traded, as was the case in Sansovino's time: today the Venetians go there to buy everyday goods.

That the Fabbriche Nuove, built as a utilitarian building during the High Renaissance, is still perfectly suited to its original purpose can be seen by the fact that major Venetian government offices, including various legal authorities, continue to be accommodated there. It is worth remembering, however, when admiring their fine situation on the Grand Canal directly opposite the picturesque Rialto market, that in the past, the main complaints of its occupants were the market rats, which were constantly burrowing into the brickwork.

Palazzo dei Camerlenghi

This palazzo, right beside the Rialto, once housed the three Venetian Lords of the Exchequer and other offices. The prison on the ground floor was reserved for tax evaders. To fight this crime there were numerous letter boxes for anonymous denouncements. The palazzo, which is angled slightly to accommodate the bend in the canal, was built under Doge Andrea Gritti in 1525–28. The architect, probably Guglielmo Bergamasco, did not face conditions as strict as those for the Fondaco dei Tedeschi, which lies opposite. The rich ornamentation underlines the significance of this important office, as almost all of Venice's income came from duties and taxes on merchandise.

Fondaco dei Tedeschi

The facade of the Fondaco is distinguished from the other early 16th-century buildings on the Grand Canal by its simplicity. The Venetian Senate, which funded rebuilding after a disastrous fire in 1505, forbade any marble decoration on the German merchants' headquarters. Instead, the external walls of the Renaissance building were covered with frescoes by Giorgione and the young Titian, which made it look just as remarkable as any amount of architectural ornamentation.

For Titian, who, unlike the already renowned Giorgione, was commissioned to paint the more accessible landward side of the building, this marked the beginning of his unprecedented career. Remains of the frescoes, which unfortunately have largely been eroded by the maritime climate, can today be seen in the Ca' d'Oro.

The word *fondaco* derives from the Arabic *funduk*, which means both inn and shop. German merchants were already in possession of such a combined accommodation and storage institution in Venice in 1228. This meant they could easily be reached, and customs formalities could be completed on the spot. Only Venice's most important trading partners were granted this kind of privilege. Today the building houses the central post office, so that taking a look inside presents no problem.

The Rialto Bridge

The structure which today is one of the symbols of Venice was for a long time a simple wooden bridge over the Grand Canal. In the 15th century, there was a drawbridge which was raised to allow sailing ships to enter the canal. In 1524, the first designs were made for a stone bridge, which was not finally built until 60 years later. The intention was to make the bridge a unique architectural symbol. What made the architect's job particularly hard was the difficult foundation work involved. The planning dragged on almost throughout the entire 16th century. All the famous architects of the period drafted designs, including Sansovino, Scamozzi, Palladio, and even the great Michelangelo.

The contract for a high-arched bridge with shops along it finally went to Antonio da Ponte in 1588. Da Ponte was not a particularly prominent architect of his time, but was rather a *proto*, or master builder, for the Magistrato al Sal, who was responsible for Venice's numerous public buildings. Da Ponte worked there in his capacity as hydraulic engineer, and it was perhaps his experience in this sphere that was decisive in winning him the commission. His design became a reality in just three years. The faces of the bridge depict in relief the city's patron saints, Theodore and Mark.

Palazzo Grimani

This monumental and ornate palazzo (built 1541–75), with its powerful configuration, almost looks like an alien entity among the dainty neighboring buildings inspired by Venetian Gothic. It is the work of the architect Michele Sanmicheli of Verona. He tried to distance his design as much as possible from the usual schemes for Venetian palazzi.

The central section of the building merges with the rest. Only the single columns between the three central windows indicate that the windows are connected. Double columns frame the other windows. When the light is right, the facade seems almost to be in two layers: the front layer formed by the prominently profiled columns and pilasters, and the wall area behind them.

The size of the windows, which were large by Venetian standards, even gave rise to a legend. The house was said to have been built by a jilted lover who was not wealthy enough for his beloved or her family, and decided to make the windows on his new home larger than the main door to his former lover's house.

Although untrue, the legend does show that the building was so unusual that even ordinary people had to look for some explanation.

In 1559, at the time of Sanmicheli's death, only the lower story was completed, and the *piano nobile* had been started, so that probably only the lower stories were built exactly to his plan. The flatter, more compressed top story was by Giangiacomo de' Grigi. The building was only finally completed under the supervision of Antonio Rusconi in 1575.

Palazzo Papadopoli

This High Renaissance palazzo was built in the mid-16th century by Giangiacomo de' Grigi, son and collaborator of the more renowned Gugliemo de' Grigi of Bergamo. His clients were the Coccina family, also from Bergamo. The simplicity of this design distinguished Grigi from the older Lombard architects, who were greatly prized for their sumptuous building techniques. Only the main axis is accentuated with large arched windows and columns. Also noteworthy are the two obelisks on the palazzo roof.

Paulo Veronese:
The Madonna of the House of Coccina, 1571
Oil on canvas, 164 x 416 cm
Gemäldegalerie Alte Meister, Dresden

Veronese's painting *The Madonna of the House of Coccina* (or Cuccina) is a portrait of the Papadopoli family, which commissioned the palazzo, at the time of its construction.

Today in Dresden, it shows the entire family kneeling before the Madonna and, together with the *Adoration of the Magi*, *Wedding at Cana*, and *Christ Carrying the Cross* of the same size, it decorated the *sala* of the palazzo.

The Madonna is surrounded by an angel, St. John the Baptist, and St. Jerome. The family is accompanied by figures representing the virtues of Faith, Hope, and Charity. Faith, symbolized by a figure in white drapery, is touching the hand of Zuanantonio, the head of the family. Hope and Charity stand behind him. Further to the left are his brothers Alvise (standing) and Antonio (kneeling), with his wife Zuana and his daughter Marietta; his other children are also included. The recently built family home is in the background. On the far right, a young nursemaid is bringing in the latest addition to the family, Zuanbattista.

Palazzi and other residences

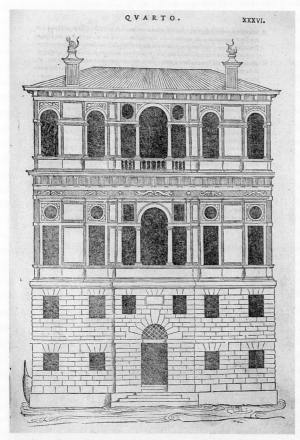
QVARTO.   XXXVI.

Woodcut of a typical Venetian palazzo (from Sebastiano Serlio, Regoli Generali di Architettura, Venice, 1537, p.156)

Venice has only one real piazza, the Piazza San Marco, and only one palace, the Doges' Palace. All of the other palazzi are called in the Venetian dialect simply *ca'*, which is a truncated form of *casa* (house).

In his description of the uniform construction of the Venetian palazzi, the architect Sebastiano Serlio (c. 1475–1554) expressed great admiration for the modesty of the Venetian nobility. Indeed, Venice, when compared with other major cities like Rome, Milan, and Florence, has a large number of not excessively large but nonetheless richly decorated houses, with almost the same building style, a style which had already taken shape by the 13th century.

The facade reveals a great deal about the interior allocation of the rooms. On the second floor, which is the *piano nobile*, are the main reception rooms of the house, where visitors were received

The Ca' da Mosto, one of the oldest palazzi on the Grand Canal (additional stories were added during the 17th century).

Ca' da Mosto (detail). The two lower stories date from the late 12th or early 13th century.

or parties were held. From the outside, the largest room, the *sala* or the *portego*, is marked by a wide, demarcated row of windows. Some palazzi feature another room of this kind on the third floor, again accentuated by means of grouping windows together. These reception rooms are flanked by the narrower living rooms, which can easily be distinguished from the central windows by the way they have been set off. This gives Venetian facades a sense of rhythm. Sometimes smaller rows of windows

Palazzo Bembo on the Grand Canal, with a typical 15th-century facade. Parts of the palazzo, however, are even older.

are visible between the first floor and the second floor, or immediately below the roof. These are known as the mezzanine floors, intermediate floors which are not as high as the others. They were used for storage, service rooms, and, as they were easier to heat, served as accommodation and offices during the colder winter months.

Its exterior can also reveal a palazzo's age. The earliest facades were smoothly plastered or were of plain brick and had tall, frequently stilted, round arches, often framed with decorative elements. Occasionally these very old facades were also decorated with *patere*, small tablets with bas-reliefs, originally from Byzantium. In the Gothic period, during the 14th century, the pointed arch became a characteristic element. It often appeared in the specifically Venetian form of an ogee arch, reminiscent of the section of a ship's keel or a donkey's back. Some experts believe this shape to be derived from oriental influence. Other ornamental motifs such as open-work tracery complete the Gothic facade. In the late 15th century sumptuous stone inlays were added, harking back to examples from the 13th century. A style featuring columns and natural stone facing finally took over in the 16th century, although the facing may have been painted rather than genuine stone. Painted facades in general played a very important role in Venetian architecture, though today almost nothing remains of these.

The characteristic palazzo design with its typical spatial subdivisions was also retained on more modest houses. Even in very small two-story houses, the main living areas are on

the second floor, and these usually have broad window sections in the center. These structures were almost all built on piles that had to be driven down through the water and silt into solid ground. This meant that the materials used for houses had to be extremely light. This applied not just to palazzi and private houses, but also to the many apartment houses that were built by wealthy individuals and by

Gothic tracery of the Ca' Foscari (detail), mid-15th century, modeled on the Doges' Palace.

Palazzo Dario on the Grand Canal, 2nd half of the 15th century.

the *scuole* and other institutions. Many of these apartments were allocated free to people who needed them. Others were built for speculative purposes to rent out. The buildings were often grouped around a common inner yard with a well or with a passage on either side. They were residential complexes and could be locked at night to protect their inhabitants. Each apartment usually had its own entrance. Even when they were small and situated on the third or fourth floor, common corridors were avoided as much as possible. Many of these apartment blocks have been preserved over the centuries. Even today, the visitor is astonished by the clever division of space and the relatively good quality of life which these early housing projects offered to the residents of Venice.

Palazzo Dolfin-Manin on the Grand Canal, built in 1536–74 from a design by Jacopo Sansovino.

The Marinarezza, housing for workers at the Arsenal in Castello, 15th century (extended in the 17th century).

Palazzo Corner-Spinelli

This palazzo is one of the most interesting structures of the Early Venetian Renaissance (1490–1510). The architect Mauro Codussi combined the clear forms of the Renaissance with the liveliness of the Gothic facade. Antique motifs were transformed into more gentle structures. The first floor, which consisted of store-rooms, with its flat rustication and small windows, has the effect of a pedestal on which the richly decorated

upper floors stand. The double (biforate) windows are topped by a single common arch. Codussi fitted the resulting spandrels with looped apertures reminiscent of the Gothic style, but which in Gothic architecture were used to frame additional details like foil ornaments, whereas here they are used independently. The colored stone decorations are throwbacks to marble inlays of the 13th century. The beautiful and highly prominent fleur-de-lys balconies below the side windows on the *piano nobile* are one of Codussi's more unusual ideas, and give additional vibrancy to the facade. This was the only time he used them.

Palazzo Contarini delle Figure

This Renaissance palazzo, built in the first half of the 16th century, was possibly begun by Giorgio Spavento, and was completed by Antonio Abbondio (known as Scarpagnino). It acquired the name "delle Figure" from the two (albeit not easily discernible and artistically unremarkable) caryatids that support the balcony over the main entrance. But some form of description was needed to distinguish this Contarini palazzo from the 21 others that this world-renowned family possessed.

Ca' Foscari

Francesco Foscari, the most prominent doge of the 15th century, commissioned this impressive palazzo, which was commenced in 1452. The windows outside the main reception rooms on the third floor are structured in the same way as the wing of the Doges' Palace that was built under Foscari's supervision. Perhaps this was meant to indicate Foscari's position as doge and the fact that he had ordered the extension of the Doges' Palace. Ornamentation of this kind is also to be found on other contemporary palazzi, however. It has been suggested that the Venetian nobility used it to demonstrate their connection with the seat of power in Venice, for the doge was not the sole ruler in the Doges' Palace: it was also the place of assembly for the Great Council, from which all government offices were filled, and to which only the nobility had access. Simply to say that the pointed arch retained its popularity over such a long time because the Venetians in particular had a liking for it is an oversimplification. The frieze over the third floor also has two putti holding the Foscari coat of arms.

Palazzo Grassi

The building of this palazzo was started in 1749 for the Grassi family of Bologna, whose wealth had enabled it to be accepted into the Venetian aristocracy in 1718. Shortly afterwards, the family commissioned the magnificent Baroque building to be built. Although the facade seems fairly monolithic, it is typically Venetian in that the middle windows are grouped together, while the outside windows are set apart by double pilasters. Today the palazzo is the property of the Fiat company, which uses it for exhibitions.

Ca' Rezzonico

This fine Baroque palazzo was built in the middle of the 17th century for the Bon family by Baldassare Longhena, who was the leading architect in Venice of the period.

Due to insurmountable financial difficulties and the sudden death of the heir, the building was not raised above the *piano nobile* level. It was another century before the palazzo came into the possession of the Rezzonico family, who financed the continued construction of the building by the architect Giorgio Massai from 1750 onwards.

The wall, which is completely obscured by the half-columns, the sculpted protruding capitals, the festoons over the window, and the small double columns supporting the window arches, gives rise to a powerful play of light and shadow, which obscures the surface and firmly defines the building as a creation in the Baroque style.

Today, the building houses the Museo del Settecento Veneziano (see p. 273). As a public building visitors have the opportunity to see the Rezzonico family's extravagant interior decoration of the palazzo.

Palazzo Giustinian

The Palazzo Giustinian actually consists of two buildings, both constructed during the mid-15th century and, like the adjacent Ca' Foscari, both striking examples of adherence to the gentle, decorative forms of the Venetian Gothic. The building's distinct facade, centered around a main window axis, with two identical sections to either side of the main water gate, shows that this is in fact two palazzi. In the Palazzo Giustinian Richard Wagner composed the second act of *Tristan and Isolde* in the winter of 1858–59.

Ca' del Duca

Today there are two palazzi on the site where the Corner family commissioned a palazzo from Bartolomeo Buon in the mid-15th century. In 1461, the family sold the newly commenced construction to Francesco Sforza, Duke of Milan, who wanted a magnificent residence in Venice. His palazzo was never finished, however, but was demolished at a very early stage.

At the right edge of the building one can see a few remnants of the original building with its light stone, which contrasts with the other plastered sections. These show that the palazzo planned in the mid-15th century was intended to incorporate unmistakable Renaissance forms, and thus, had it been completed, may have turned Venetian architectural development in a completely different direction for palazzi.

Gallerie dell'Accademia

The Accademia was housed in a former *scuola*, the Scuola Grande della Carità, which belonged to the Santa Maria della Carità church and the convent of the same name. The name "Accademia" indicates the beginnings of the important collection of paintings which originated in the art academy founded in 1750.

The academy building's facade, where today's museum entrance is located, was built by Bernardo Maccaruzzi in around 1760 to plans by Giorgio Massari. Napoleon turned the private academy into an official art university, and added the neighboring buildings to it. Works of art from churches and cloisters disbanded in Napoleon's time, as well as numerous private donations, increased the gallery's collection, which has been open to the public since 1807.

The Accademia is one of the most important art collections in Italy, and provides visitors with an excellent overview of Venetian painting from the 13th to the late 18th century (see also p. 310).

Casino delle Rose
(Cassetta Rossa)

This small red house, which is quite unlike the other magnificent palazzi of the area, built out to the waterfront, was the workshop of Antonio Canova (1757–1822), the most prominent Venetian sculptor of the 18th and early 19th century. Even during his lifetime his works enjoyed wide admiration.

During the First World War, the Casino was the home of the eccentric and controversial poet and politician Gabriele d'Annunzio (1863–1938).

Palazzo Venier dei Leoni (Peggy Guggenheim Collection)

The Palazzo Venier dei Leoni, so called because of the lion's heads in the base of the building's frontage, was never completed. A wooden model by the architect Lorenzo Boschetti, today in the Museo Correr, shows what a sumptuous home the Venier family had intended for the site in 1749. As was so often the case, financial difficulties meant that the construction had to be halted, however,

unlike other buildings, the construction of this one was never continued.

In this century the strange, unfinished palazzo was acquired as a modest home for the eccentric American, Peggy Guggenheim (1889–1979). The wealthy art collector and patron of modern art spent the last 30 years of her life in Venice. Her major collection of modern art is today open to the public in a museum run by the Solomon R. Guggenheim Foundation, under a bequest made by Peggy Guggenheim's uncle (see p. 334).

them the appearance of arcades, can only be part of the Venetian tradition. The purpose of the windows is less to emphasize the bulk of the building than to break up the walls. In the 17th and 18th centuries several palazzi, for example the Palazzo Pisano and the Ca' Rezzonico, followed this model.

Ca' Dario

Henry James likened this palazzo to a house of cards that would collapse at the slightest touch. Actually, even with its leaning facade, its marble inlays make it one of the prettiest palazzi in Venice. This crooked palazzo was built around 1487 for Giovanni Dario (whose name was carved into the first floor). The master builder was Pietro Lombardo. Marble cladding, previously fashionable during the 13th century, again grew in popularity with the Lombardi family, who had come to Venice from Lombardy. Such facades were very expensive and thus were a sure indication of wealth.

Ca' Grande

In 1533, following a disastrous fire, Jacopo Cornaro, a nephew of the queen of Cyprus, had the original building reconstructed by Jacopo Sansovino. Because of its vast dimensions, the Venetians called it the Ca' Grande. With his rusticated first floor and the Ionic and Corinthian columns on the two upper floors, Sansovino was borrowing the High Renaissance forms of Tuscany and Rome. However, the upper floors, with their numerous windows, which almost give

Santa Maria della Salute

At only 33 years of age, Baldassare Longhena was commissioned to build this church, erected as a token of gratitude to the Virgin Mary for the end of the plague of 1629–30. It was consecrated in 1687.

The prominent building with its domes, visible from afar, is an important architectural landmark opposite the Doges' Palace and the Piazzetta. It is particularly striking for the visitors approaching the Piazza San Marco by water from the east, when you can see the Doges' Palace and the islands of both San Giorgio and Santa Maria della Salute all at the same time.

Massive spiral volutes with sculptures lead from the tall lower story to the dome, giving the church its unique appearance. The interior has been even more tightly structured than the exterior. The expansive central area beneath the dome is surrounded by chapels which are visible from the outside as two-story porches.

Titian: Pentecost, 1545
Oil on canvas, 570 x 260 cm

The painting of the Apostles receiving the gift of the Holy Spirit comes, like five of Titian's other masterpieces which are now in this church, from the Santa Spirito monastery in Isola, which was dissolved in the 17th century.

Titian: St. Mark with SS. Cosmas, Damian, Roch, and Sebastian, c. 1510
Oil on canvas, 218 x 149 cm

Like the Santa Maria della Salute, this painting was commissioned to mark the end of a plague, and was created for the Augustinian choristers of the Santo Spirito in Isola. It is one of Titian's earliest known works, and can be dated to 1510, when the plague ended. The voluminous figures in their bright garments are reminiscent of those of his teacher, Giovanni Bellini. The elegant nude figure of St. Sebastian, with its skillfully painted white cloth, shows the talent of the young painter. The prayer to St. Mark for an end to the plague has been effectively represented. The two holy physicians Cosmas and Damian, on the left, introduce the scene: the former is looking beseechingly at the patron saint of the city. Both physicians are pointing to the plague scars which St. Roch is displaying on the right. St. Roch and St. Sebastian, who is pierced by arrows, were the saints most frequently appealed to for delivery from the plague.

Titian: Sacrifice of Abraham, 1542–44
Oil on canvas, 328 x 282 cm

This sacrificial scene was part of a sumptuous carved ceiling decoration which again originated in Santo Spirito in Isola. The ceiling, which was designed by Jacopo Sansovino, has not survived. Only Titian's canvas paintings were moved to the sacristy of Santa Maria della Salute in 1656.

In addition to the sacrifice of Abraham, they also depict Cain and Abel, and David and Goliath. The decorations include eight smaller circular pictures of the four Evangelists and the four Church Fathers.

Even contemporaries of Titian marveled at the skillful way this upward view was treated. Titian made his job even more difficult by showing the figures in motion, which required perfect mastery of an extremely short perspective.

The sacrifice of Abraham had been regarded since the Middle Ages as the prefiguration, i.e. the Old Testament prediction, of Christ's sacrificial death. Titian captures perfectly the drama of the scene. The young Isaac is already kneeling on the altar. His father is pressing his son's head down with a heavy hand, his knife in the other. The boy shows no fear: he trusts his father just as his father trusts God. Just at this moment an angel with fluttering garments descends from heaven. Crying in alarm, he grabs the knife and thus averts the death of the boy.

Dogana da Mar

The entrance to the Grand Canal when you approach from the Piazza San Marco is bounded on the right by the elongated building of the Dogana da Mar, the maritime customs office. This plain, squat building was erected by Giuseppe Benoni in 1677–82. The Bacino di San Marco, i.e. the area of water before the Doges' Palace, with the Piazzetta on one side and San Giorgio Maggiore and the Giudecca on the other, was once one of Europe's busiest ports. Sailing ships carrying sought-after goods from all over the world anchored here to be unloaded and obtain customs clearance. The large customs office with its huge store rooms still bears witness to its former glory, even if it is difficult to imagine the place bustling with activity as it used to.

Where formerly there had been a watchtower to guard against foreign invasion – which was never needed – the top of the Dogana is now embellished with a golden globe. Two Atlases bear the globe aloft, with a weather vane in the form of the goddess Fortuna standing on it with a steering oar in her hand. Not only does she indicate the direction of the wind, but also clearly shows arriving and departing ships the unpredictability of fate. The sculpture is by Bernardo Falcone.

Sestiere San Marco

San Marco

The seat of political power in Venice was located in the Sestiere San Marco, in the area around the Piazza San Marco, with the Basilica and the Doges' Palace. In the Middle Ages it was the real heart of the city, surrounded by a wooden fortified wall. There is enough in this district for a visitor interested in the history of Venice to spend several days examining the historically and artistically significant buildings. The administrative center of the city also consisted of the official residences and offices, the Mint, the Library, the granaries, and the prison. Numerous merchants had their premises on the Piazza San Marco and the Piazzetta. Until the 16th century, bakers, butchers and other tradesmen offered their wares here, until moves were made to attract shops selling luxury foods and jewelry, which were more in keeping with the exclusive nature of the government district. Little has changed to this day. The San Marco district has the finest hotels and international and Venetian luxury goods shops, inviting the visitor to explore the narrow alleys where they are situated.

Museo Fortuny (interior), p. 207

Santo Stefano (interior), p. 203

San Moisè, p. 200

Other sights:
1 The Doges' Palace   2 Piazzetta   3 Piazza San Marco   4 Libreria/Biblioteca Marciana   5 Campanile di San Marco and Loggetta   6 Café Florian   7 Museo Civico Correr   8 New Procurators' Offices   9 Napoleonic Wing   10 Old Procurators' Offices   11 Teatro La Fenice   12 San Salvatore

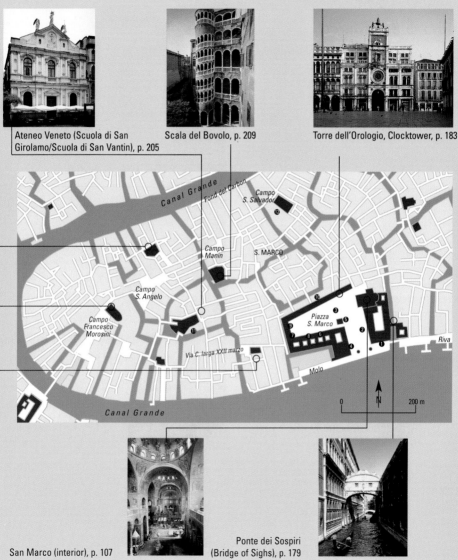

Ateneo Veneto (Scuola di San Girolamo/Scuola di San Vantin), p. 205

Scala del Bovolo, p. 209

Torre dell'Orologio, Clocktower, p. 183

Canal Grande

Fond. del Carbon

Campo S. Salvador

⑫

Campo Manin

S. MARCO

Campo S. Angelo

Campo Francesco Morosini

Via C. larga XXII marzo

⑩

⑨ ⑦ ⑧ ⑥ ⑤

Piazza S. Marco

⑪

②

④

①

Molo

Riva

Canal Grande

0   200 m

N

San Marco (interior), p. 107

Ponte dei Sospiri (Bridge of Sighs), p. 179

Piazza San Marco

There is only one piazza in Venice, and that is St. Mark's Square, which leads into the Piazzetta in front of the Doges' Palace on the lagoon. All the city's other squares are known as *campi*. This distinction may originally have arisen from the square in front of San Marco and the ruler's palace being paved, unlike the other squares in the city. Later the word piazza came to designate the area used for public festivals and ceremonies.

The Piazza San Marco was the focal point in Venice where rich and poor alike celebrated their city and their state with processions, parades, and reception ceremonies for foreign dignitaries. This did not, however, deter the practical, business-minded Venetians from using it as a market on other days. To describe the Piazza San Marco as "Europe's finest salon," as Napoleon did, was at the time of the Serene Republic hardly an overstatement. To this day the square is one of the main gathering places of Venice, and is crowded with visitors. Only early in the morning or in the evening, when the day's tourists have gone, is it possible to admire it in its sheer vastness.

San Marco

The Basilica di San Marco dominates the entire eastern side of the square. Since its construction in around 830, it has belonged to the Doges' Palace. The present building is the result of the third rebuilding, which was completed in 1060. It was not until Venice lost her independence in 1807 that the Basilica became the seat of a bishop. What San Marco reflects above all is not so much the might and wealth of the Church as the splendor and history of the city-state of Venice. With its cupolas and turrets, its multicolored marble columns, mosaics sparkling with gold, and the floral finials of its arches, its sculptures and colorful marble incrustations, San Marco gives the impression of an expensive jewelry box. At first sight the building seems to have little in common with the towering, sharply delineated facades of the European Romanesque and Gothic styles, which were constructed contemporaneously with San Marco, between the 11th and 13th centuries. The exterior of San Marco is the result of several phases of construction, each of which added new ornamentation to the building, inspired by both Western European and Byzantine ideas, which were merged into a unique architectural composition. The Byzantine influence dominates in the interior, although here again it has been given a unique Venetian feel.

Gentile Bellini:
Procession of the Relic of the Cross in the
Piazza S. Marco, 1496
Tempera on canvas, 376 x 745 cm
Gallerie dell' Academia

On public holidays the full splendor of the
Piazza San Marco was displayed in all its
glory, as this painting by Gentile Bellini

shows. Colored pennants were draped
from the windows, while sumptuous flags
were raised before the glittering gold of
the Basilica. The ceremonial parades and
processions themselves added to the rich
ornamentation with the flags and candles
carried by the participants. On other
occasions, such as visits by important
dignitaries, special stages were erected on

possessed since 1393. This painting shows a procession held on St. Mark's Day, April 25, 1444. As the relic is carried past Jacopo Salis, a merchant from Brescia (kneeling in the right foreground), his son is instantaneously cured in answer to his prayers.

Bellini's painting gives an exact depiction of the square in 1496. To the left it shows the medieval Old Procurators' Offices, before they were rebuilt in 1515. The clocktower also predates the current Torre dell'Orologio, which was built after 1496. To the right we see the facade of the church of San Basso, which was destroyed in 1661, while the Casa dei Canonici, the house of the canons of San Marco, can be seen in the piazzetta to the left of San Marco. To the right, beside the clocktower, is the Ospizio Orseolo, which was demolished to make way for the New Procurators' Offices. Between San Marco and the Doges' Palace appears the colorful Porta della Carta. The square itself is paved in typically Venetian, old-style tiles, which today survive only in a few places, mainly in the inner courtyards of certain palazzi.

The fine detail of Bellini's paintings has often led to him being described as the forerunner of the great Venetian Vedutists of the 18th century. His clients were probably far more interested in their own portraits, which the artist incorporated into the painting in 1496, though it depicted an event that had taken place 50 years earlier.

the square, making it even more magnificent. Bellini's picture is one of a cycle of paintings he carried out together with Vittore Carpaccio, Lazzaro Bastiani, Giovanni Mansueti, Bennedetto Diana, and Perugino for the Scuola Grande di San Giovanni Evangelista. The paintings depicted miracles attributed to a precious relic of the Cross which the Scuola had

Facade columns

As Venice grew to become the ruling power in the eastern Mediterranean, treasures, marble, columns, capitals, reliefs, valuable vessels and paintings were collected and sent from the various conquered lands and used to decorate the Basilica di San Marco. The multicolored columns on the building's exterior are an obvious example of this. They originate from different places and periods, and were reassembled here to enhance the facade. Some of the columns were fitted with new, finely worked capitals, which emphasize their value. With their differing colors, they were more than enough in themselves to enliven the original plain brick facade.

The horses of San Marco

In 1204, during the Fourth Crusade, the Venetians brought from Constantinople a *quadriga* of gilded bronze horses (i.e. four in chariot harness) dating from the 4th century. The erection of this fine set of sculptures in the city of St. Mark was a final symbolic act, confirming the end of Venice's old status as a protectorate. In the mid-13th century the horses were positioned on the loggia over the main portal of San Marco, which was where the doge and his entourage appeared on festive occasions. The horses of San Marco, and the building in its entirety, became a symbol of the might of the Venetian state. Although Venice's enemies always threatened to bridle the horses, Napoleon was the first person to actually succeed in removing them. As he prepared to put an end to the Venetian Republic in 1797, Napoleon sent the horses, together with other trophies, to Paris, and it was not until 1815 that they were returned to their old site.

Today the horses are threatened not by foreign invaders as much as by pollution. For this reason, in 1982, the originals were placed in the Museo Marciano, which can be reached via a narrow stairway from the narthex of the Basilica.

Main portal

The main entrance of the basilica, which was originally decorated in blue and gold, consists of a number of recessed arches projecting beyond the gallery above. Three of the arches are decorated with sculpted ornamentation, which provide an idea of the stylistic development of Venetian sculpture during the 13th and 14th centuries.

The inner arch shows early Romanesque, Venetian-Byzantine forms of the early 13th century. The *intrados* (inner face) of this arch shows animals with vine leaves. This column's pedestals bear symbols that may be interpreted either as Terra (Earth) and Oceanus (Sea), or as Church and Heresy. The front of the arch depicts the wilderness and civilized life.

The middle arch, decorated with its naturalistic forms, illustrates the transition from the Romanesque to the Gothic style. The intrados of this arch shows allegorical images of the months, while the front of the arch depicts Christian virtues.

The outer arch's intrados features the main guilds of Venice. The man on crutches biting his fingers is, according to age-old legend, the lame architect of the Basilica, who realizes that his edifice is not perfect. The front of the arch displays figures of the prophets, vines, and Christ giving his blessing. Over the main portal is a mosaic that was added in 1836, representing the Last Judgement.

The allegorical depictions of the months are presented in the form of typical activities corresponding to the time of year, and the signs of the zodiac. The detail shown below, from the intrados of the middle arch, illustrates grain being harvested in June with the zodiacal signs for Gemini and Cancer.

The Transferal of St. Mark's Relics to San Marco, c. 1265
Mosaic over the Porta di Sant'Alipio

The facade mosaics date mainly from the 17th–19th centuries, and replace earlier 13th century works, whose themes they repeat, though mostly using contemporary stylistic methods. An original 13th century mosaic survives above the northern entrance in the main facade, known as the Porta di Sant'Alipio. It shows the mortal remains of St. Mark being transferred to San Marco.

Two Venetian merchants brought the relics of St. Mark from Alexandria to Venice in 828–29. According to legend, it was decided that the priceless relics should first be brought to the Doges' Palace to ensure that they were kept safe until a site for a church in the Evangelist's honor was determined. Just before the relics reached the palace, they suddenly became so heavy that they could not be moved any further. Everybody took this to be a sign from St. Mark that this was where he wanted to be honored in the future.

The mosaic shows the 13th century, rather than the original, Basilica. It is an important record of what San Marco looked like before the renovation work of the 14th and 15th centuries. It shows clearly the flatter domes and the original design of the facade, which does not yet have its Gothic arch finials and sculptures.

South facade

The facade facing the Doges' Palace is the visitor's first sight upon arriving at the Piazetta by boat. It was therefore designed with the magnificence such a position required, while the north facade was relatively neglected. Originally there were two entrances here.

The domes of San Marco

Goethe's description of San Marco as "crab-like" is understandable from an aerial view. The broad main building with its domes really does look like a crab. The domes have two shells: they are flat on the inside, while on the outside they have a taller shell made of lead.

South facade columns

The two rare Syrian columns standing in front of the facade were said to have originally stood before the Genoan fort in Acre. The Venetians reputedly stole them from here, after their victory of 1256 which once again gave Venice's merchants free access to oriental trade. A more recent study, in 1977, has established that the columns are in fact from a church in Constantinople that by 1204 had fallen into ruin. If this is correct, it means that these columns, like so many other elements that decorate the Basilica, did not reach Venice until the time of the Fourth Crusade.

The Tetrarchs

Another remarkable item from Venice's looting campaigns around the eastern Mediterranean is a group sculpture of red porphyry, which stands on the corner of the Treasury. This square, windowless building holds the treasures of San Marco as well as relics and liturgical objects.

The sculpture, which dates from the 4th century, most likely depicts the so-called "Tetrarchs," four joint rulers of the Roman Empire. The stylized portraits are of Emperor Diocletian (284–305) and his sons-in-law and co-regents Maximilian, Constantius, and Valerius. Each one of them ruled over a quarter of the empire. There is one Venetian legend, however, claiming that the figures are four Moors who wanted to steal the treasure of San Marco, but were turned to stone by a miracle of St. Mark, and embedded in the wall at this spot to frighten off future thieves.

San Marco

Modeled on the Church of the Holy Apostles in Constantinople, the third version of San Marco, starting in 1063, was built as an east-facing main building in the shape of a Greek cross with five pendentive domes: one central dome and a dome on each arm of the cross. With an apse to the east and absidal chapels beside the presbytery, the building is focused on the sanctuary, raised over the crypt. This is enhanced by the fact that the domes along the east-west axis are larger than the side domes over the north and south arms of the cross. The plan thus suggests a rectangular building with narrower transverse arms. The narthex, which formerly enclosed the west dome on three sides, lengthens the building westwards, further underlining the effect. The north and west wings have been preserved, while the south arm was given over to the baptistery and the Cappella Zen.

Major mosaics in San Marco

The 12th-century mosaics of the three main domes depict central themes of Christian theology: the prediction of Christianity by the prophets, the Ascension of Christ and related depictions of blessing and judgment, as well as Pentecost and the spreading of the Word. In the apse appears Christ Pantocrator (as Ruler of the World), above Saints Nicholas, Peter, Mark, and Hermagoras, patron saints of Venice.

Major mosaics in San Marco

1 Apse: Christ Pantocrator Giving the Blessing. Below him: Saints Nicholas, Peter, Mark, and Hermagoras. Early 13th and 16th centuries (with remnants of the original late 11th-century decoration)
2 Choir: Scenes from the Life of Mark the Evangelist, some 13th century, but heavily restored
3 Dome of the choir: The Church and Predictions of the Prophets, 12th and 13th centuries
4 Cappella di San Isidoro, 14th century
5 Cappella dei Mascoli, 15th century
6 Cappella di San Giovanni: Scenes from the Life of John the Evangelist, early 13th century
7 Dome of the Ascension, 13th century
8 Dome of St. Leonard: Saints Nicholas, Blaise, Clement, and Leonard, 13th century
9 Entry to Jerusalem, Temptation of Christ, Last Supper, Ablution, late 12th–early 13th century
10 Scenes from the Lives of Christ and the Apostles, 13th century
11 Dome of Pentecost
12 Mary and Prophets, c. 1250
13 Baptistery. Dome over the altar: Christ and the Nine Heavenly Choirs. Dome over the font: Apostles Baptizing Converts, Herod's Feast, and Dance of Salome, 14th century
14 Cappella Zen, 13–15th century
15 Dome of the Creation, c. 1230
16 The Flood, mid-13th century
17 Death of Noah and Tower of Babel, mid-13th century
18 Dome of Abraham, 1240-50
19 Domes of Joseph, c. 1270, heavily restored
20 Dome of Moses, 13th century, heavily restored during the 19th century

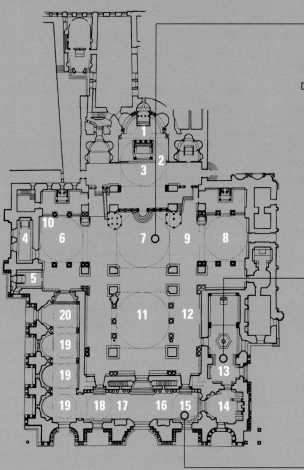

Dome of the Ascension, 13th century, p. 109

Baptistery, 14th century, p. 113

Dome of the Creation, 13th century, p. 104

Dome of the Creation in the narthex, early 13th century

The mosaics in the main body of San Marco are technically and iconographically the most significant works of their kind in Western Europe. *The Creation*, on the southern dome, on the right when viewed from the square, was based on illuminated books from the 6th century. Scenes of the Creation are depicted on the dome in three bands.

The story develops outwards from the middle of the dome in a contraclockwise direction: in the central band, the creation of heaven and earth, the spirit floating over the water, the separation of light and darkness, the creation of the firmament, the moon and the stars, the creation of the fishes, birds and animals, right up to the creation of man. This is followed in the middle band by God giving Adam a soul – depicted as a light pair of wings – and leading him to Eden, where the animals are named. In the outer band we see the creation of Eve and the first human couple, the temptation, their recognition of their nakedness, God's judgment on the sinners, and finally the banishment from Eden. The lunettes over the doors below the dome show scenes from the story of Cain and Abel.

The Building of the Ark, 13th century, southern arch in the narthex

The Flood is depicted with unusually gentle colors, which shape the light and shadow. The construction of the Ark – boatbuilding was a subject the Venetians must have been very familiar with – is presented in various stages. The artists keenly reproduced the smallest details, which greatly help convey the atmosphere. This can be seen in the lowest band, where the Ark is being boarded, while in the foreground small bunches of flowers in bloom are sinking slowly beneath the waters.

The Flood, 13th century, southern arch in the narthex

The opposite side of the arch illustrates the end of the Flood with the same loving detail as the construction of the Ark. The picture at the top left is particularly interesting, showing the effects of the Flood: the artists did not, as was later customary, depict a dramatic struggle with the floodwaters, but instead show people and animals floating dead in the water with eyes closed. A ghostly silence seems to spread under the impenetrable sheets of rain falling from the skies. This makes the image of a dead mother holding her child in her arms all the more poignant. Heaven, rain, and water, all in the same colors of grey, white, blue, black, and gold, are only distinguished by the differing structure of the streaks.

Interior

At first, the interior and exterior of the Basilica consisted simply of bare brick. It was only over the centuries that it became decorated with the mysteriously glowing gold leaf of the mosaics and the marble slabs with their fine texture, which often makes them look like semiprecious stone. The floor, too, is a work of art fashioned from marble. The clear cruciform floor plan is lost under the sheer scale of the structural elements, in particular of the mosaics. They glitter and sparkle in a way which makes it difficult for the eye to distinguish the architectural forms. The initial inlay work was carried out by Byzantine mosaicists. However, a Venetian school soon appeared, which, especially during the 13th century, produced magnificent examples of independent Venetian mosaic work. Famous painters designed mosaics from the 15th century onwards, but these later constructions, based on paintings, did not achieve the same special aesthetic effects reached by the earlier mosaics.

Dome of the Pentecost, 1st half of the 12th century

The mosaics in the western dome were created in the first half of the 12th century, so they are some of the oldest decorations in the present San Marco. The Dome of the Pentecost shows the Apostles spreading the Gospel. In the center is the dove, symbolizing the Holy Spirit. From a throne draped in valuable cloths, the fiery tongues of the Holy Spirit reach out to the Apostles. At window level, below the dome, figures have been painted in pairs, representing the nations to which the Apostles above them have spread the Word. The four Evangelists, Mathew, Mark, Luke, and John, depicted above the pendentive, are included among the Apostles. They are distinguished from the others not just by their cushions, which have more gold embroidery, and the uniform color of their clothes (light blue on purple robes), but also by the fact that they are depicted full face.

The large number of restorations and repaintings to which the dome was subjected (e.g. the pointed shoes worn by the Cretans, which were actually in fashion during the 15th century), have not obscured its clear divisions. These are based on the silver rays which divide the dome into equal sections, and on the symmetry of the colors of the apostles' robes. However, the repairs over the centuries have created an almost entirely new mosaic.

Dome of the Ascension, 1st half of the 13th century

The central dome shows the Ascension of Christ, who gives his blessing, while rising to a blue heaven with gold stars, supported by angels. At the second level Christ is with the Madonna, accompanied by two archangels and the Apostles. Between the small windows at the drum of the dome are female figures embodying the virtues and blessings.

Washing the Feet of the Apostles, southern side aisle

The scenes from the life of Christ on the vaults beside the central dome are in a completely different style from the other mosaics of the late 12th and early 13th centuries. Characteristic of these mosaics are their filigree figures, which look as if they have been drawn in pencil, and the way these seem to hover freely against the golden background, as the representation is very economical with any element indicating space. This is what gives these mosaics their fine ornamental charm. The scene with Christ washing the Apostles' feet (also known as *The Ablution*) depicts all 12 of the Apostles. Six of them are sitting on a high-backed bench; the heads and shoulders of the others appear as busts behind them. While Christ begins to wash the feet of St. Peter, the other seated Apostles are undoing their sandals. Later, a theological controversy arose about whether Judas was in fact present. In the mosaic he is depicted in profile in the right background, distinguished by an exaggerated and distorted hooked nose.

Appearance of the Relics of St. Mark, southern side aisle

In addition to the portraits of the saints on the southern dome and the scenes from the life of the Virgin Mary (reworked during the 17th century), the discovery of St. Mark's relics is also depicted in the south transept, in the right side aisle beneath the vault. This mosaic is in the same style as the *Translation of St. Mark's Relics to San Marco* at the northern entrance of the main facade, known as the Porta di Sant'Alipio, and can also be dated back to the second half of the 13th century. The mosaic shows the pillar containing the remains, which were believed lost, opening before the eyes of the priests, the doge and numerous well-dressed Venetians. The women and girls wear particularly fine jewelry. The anniversary of the reappearance of the relics of Venice's patron saint, June 25, 1094, is still celebrated in the city today.

Place of the reappearance of the relics of St. Mark, southern side aisle

While San Marco was being built during the 11th century, the saint's body was hidden in a secret place known only to the doge and the senior priest. In the confusion at the end of Domenico Selvo's rule in 1084, the details of the secret hideaway were not passed on. It was not until a long period of fasting and prayer under Doge Vitale Falier, in which the entire

population of Venice took part, that the pillar in the south transept, in which the relics had been concealed, miraculously opened. The place where the relics were found is marked by a marble plaque today.

Baptistery

The present baptistery was built under Doge Andrea Dandolo in the first half of the 14th century. He devoted huge sums of money to the mosaics, which show scenes from the life of John the Baptist and the childhood of Christ. The dance of Salome before Herod, in return for which she demanded the head of John the Baptist, is a fine example of the vivid color and effective movement the mosaicists used in their narratives. Not only did Dandolo have his body buried in the baptistery (his tomb is opposite the entrance), but he had himself depicted, together with his chancellor Caresini, on the *Crucifixion* mosaic on the wall behind the altar, where both kneel at the sides of the Cross. The hexagonal font was produced in 1545 to a design by Jacopo Sansovino, whose tombstone was placed behind the altar in 1929. The bronze figure of John the Baptist was executed by Francesco Segala in 1575. The granite block on the altar is thought to have come from Tyre (and, according to legend, to be from the rock on which Christ preached the Sermon on the Mount).

Baldachin over the high altar

A remarkable feature of the high altar, which was given its present form in 1834, are the four alabaster columns of the baldachin (canopy-like structure). They are decorated with reliefs depicting scenes from the lives of Christ and Mary. The columns have been dated by some experts to the 5th or 6th century, and by others to the 13th century.

Iconostasis

As in Byzantine churches, an iconostasis (rood screen) separates the area for the laity from the high altar. This marble partition, open between its columns, supports on its architrave a large cross and the figures of the Virgin Mary and the Apostles by Jacobello and Pietro Paolo dalle Masegne (1393–95), which are key works of the Late Venetian Gothic.

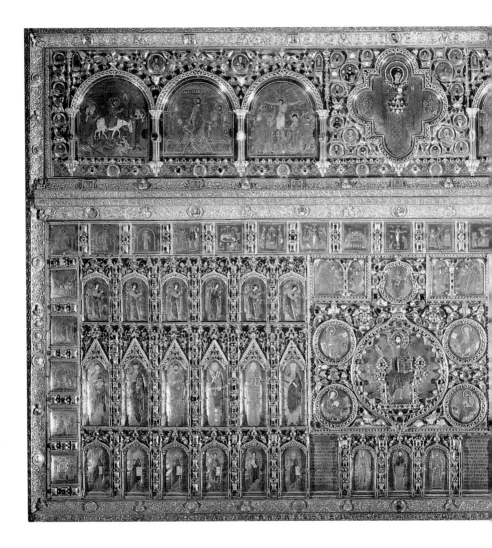

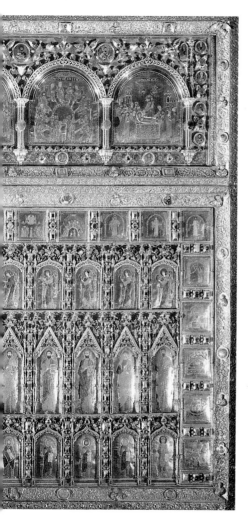

Pala d'Oro, high altar

Numerous Byzantine enamel paintings of the 10th–13th centuries, and valuable jewels, were combined in several phases to make this "golden retable" (Pala d'Oro). The first gold altarpiece was commissioned by Doge Pietro Orseolo I in 976. It was reworked under the Doges Ordelaffo Falier (1105) and Pietro Ziani (1209) and, even more richly decorated, reached its final, present form under Andrea Dandolo in 1342. Measuring 3.45 × 1.45 m, the retable is divided into two zones. In the top third, in the center, is an enamel depiction of the Archangel Michael, flanked by six scenes from the life of Christ set in arches. All seven enamel plaques are 13th century Byzantine work. The lower part of the retable is dominated by a large central rectangle with Christ Enthroned, lavishly bejeweled. The lower part of the middle section bears three plaques depicting the Empress Irene, the Virgin Mary, and the Emperor John Comnenus (1118–45). The last one was later changed into a portrait of Doge Ordelaffo Falier. To the sides of the central area, in three horizontal zones, are the prophets, Apostles and angels. The entire lower section is framed by square plaques showing scenes from the life of Christ and Mark the Evangelist.

Jacopo Sansovino: sacristy door, 1546-69

On entering the sanctuary, it is worth paying attention to the bronze doors of the tabernacle and of the sacristy, which were executed by Jacopo Sansovino in the mid-16th century. The bronze door of the sacristy shows the Entombment and Resurrection of Christ.

In this work, Sansovino referred to Lorenzo Ghiberti's doors to the baptistery in Florence. As did Ghiberti, Sansovino inserted small portraits into the door frame. One of these is Sansovino himself: his long beard is one of his distinguishing features, and he appears with it on other contemporary portraits. The other heads are said to be those of the artists Pietro Aretino, Titian, Paolo Veronese, and Andrea Palladio.

Madonna Nicopeia, 11th century

In the north transept of their city church, the Venetians have housed a particularly valuable icon. This is the Madonna Nicopeia, the Bringer of Victory, which was carried before the Byzantine emperor into battle. The Byzantines believed that this icon, like all those of the Madonna, was based on an actual portrait of the Virgin Mary that Luke the Evangelist was supposed to have painted.

The picture in San Marco, that for many centuries was considered one of the most valuable possessions of the Basilica, is a major example of 11th-century Byzantine painting. As with so many Byzantine works of art, it was brought to Venice in 1204 as booty from the Fourth Crusade. It was immediately incorporated in the city's cult of the Virgin Mary. The fact that such a valuable and auspicious painting had fallen into the hands of the Venetians could only mean, according to the medieval interpretation, that the Madonna herself was placing the Venetian Republic under her special protection.

Capella dei Mascoli (Capella della Madonna dei Mascoli)

This chapel is named after a brotherhood that met here from 1618 onwards. The mosaics, showing scenes from the life of the Virgin Mary, are an unusual example of 15th-century mosaic work. The images adhere closely to contemporary painting. The mosaics were started in 1430 by the Venetian painter Michele Giambono, but were still unfinished 20 years later. The altar, by an unknown Florentine sculptor, is also from around 1430.

Death of the Virgin, 15th century

While the designs for these scenes from the life of the Virgin Mary, which recall an earlier stylistic period, are ascribed to the Venetian Michele Giambono, the *Death of the Virgin* was associated with Andrea del Castagno of Florence, who was responsible for the frescoes of San Zaccharia in Venice. The highly sculpted, almost stone-like effect of the figures and the cool central perspective are reminiscent of the latter

artist's work. It is possible that painters from the circle of Andrea Mantegna, or even Mantegna himself, provided the original design.

The very hard effect of the mosaic, which also linked it with Castagno in the minds of earlier scholars, and the large-eyed, simplified faces, could then be regarded as having been transferred from one medium to the other. Regardless of whether the originator of the mosaic was Castagno, or a local artist such as Mantegna or Jacopo Bellini (who has also been considered as a possible designer), the *Death of the Virgin* maintains a central importance in Venetian painting: it was the starting point from which, in the mid-15th century, local artists began using the new, highly sculpted forms.

A saint is stolen for the Republic

Apart from St. Peter, who is instantly associated with the Vatican, and a long way after that, St. James, who is the patron saint both of Santiago de Compostela in Spain and Santiago de Chile, there is hardly any other saint that can claim as huge a political success as St. Mark, who was proclaimed protector of the Venetian Republic in 829. The Venetians won their victories under his banner. His

symbol, that of a winged lion, became a symbol of Venice and was set up wherever Venetian territory was established. The winged lion also appeared on the Venetian coinage that was used throughout the world. And, beside their ruler's palace, the Venetians built the most magnificent church in Christendom in honor of their patron saint. But how did St. Mark actually get to Venice?

According to legend, St. Mark, who was one of the twelve Apostles and the four Evangelists, was asked by St. Peter to be a missionary in northeast Italy, where he founded the archbishopric of Aquilea. Its territory included Venice, or rather the area that was later to become Venice. On his travels, it is said that St. Mark lost his way in the lagoon and lay down to rest on one of the islands as darkness fell. In his dreams an angel appeared before him, and welcomed him with the words "Pax tibi, Marce" (Peace be with you, Mark). The angel then went on to prophesy that this would be his final place of interment and where he would be most revered.

St. Mark's travels then took him to the Egyptian city of Alexandria, which he also converted to Christianity, and where he established a bishopric. This was where the

St. Mark, mosaic over the main entrance to San Marco, to a 16th-century design by Titian.

ATALEXADRIA PERGIT IN VGIO ALEXADRIA RADIT CALIAM TRAP BS
RAVIT MANS S· SMARC

St. Mark Travels to Alexandria, mosaic, 12th–13th century, San Marco, Venice

saint became a martyr. The pagans, when they regained control, took him prisoner and dragged him to his death. The Christians of Alexandria buried him in his cathedral.

During the 9th century, the city was in the possession of the Muslim Saracens. Their caliph ordered a magnificent palace to be built. As the building materials could not be delivered quickly enough, stones were taken from the local Christian churches. St. Mark's tomb was in danger. Luckily two merchants from Venice, Rusticus and Bonus, happened to be in

Alexandria at the time, their ships with their valuable cargoes having been driven into Alexandria harbor shortly before. One day, as they were paying their respects in St. Mark's cathedral, the Greek monks who were serving there told them of their concern about the caliph's plans. The Venetians immediately made a plan to save the saint's relics. First they had to convince the reluctant monks that it would be better for the relics to be handed over than allowed to fall into the hands of the Saracens. Then they had to sort out the

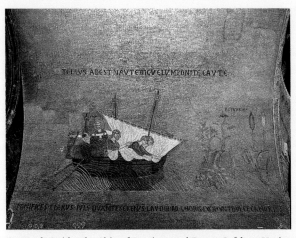

TELLVS ADEST NAVTE DICVELVM PONITE CAVTE

PONTIFICES CLERVS PLS DVX MATER CENS LAVDIBVS HONOR EX ORNAT DVLCE CANORIS

St. Mark Guides the Ship of Rusticus and Bonus Safely to Venice, mosaic, 12th-13th century, San Marco, Venice

through. The saint ensured them a miraculously quick passage across the Mediterranean, and they arrived in Venice on January 31, where the relics were received rapturously by the bishop, the doge, and the population at large. The plan was to take the valuable remains to the Doges' Palace, but, on the way there, the relics became so heavy that they were too much even for several men. This was the very place where the future Basilica would stand. It was only when the doge vowed that a church would be built in the saint's honor on precisely this spot that it was possible to lift the body again and take it to its temporary resting place.

problems that could be expected both from the Christians and the Saracens if the remains of the saint were removed from Alexandria. It was hardly likely that the local Christians would welcome the prospect of having their protector removed. Rusticus and Bonus ardently begged St. Mark to help them. So, when the time came, and they were removing the body from the church, a fierce storm broke out over the city, driving everybody indoors, and enabling them to smuggle the sacred remains out of the church. But the next problem was getting the body past the customs officers. However, here again the Venetians had a trick. They were carrying the body in a box. But, as it emitted such a wonderful odor, they covered it with pork. This was so repulsive to the Muslim customs officers that they waved the Venetians

Thus runs the story of the transfer of the relics of St. Mark to Venice. The fact that this happened just at the time that Venice was involved in a bitter dispute with the archbishopric of Aquilea about an independent diocese for Venice made the Apostle's arrival there a stroke of fortune, because now not even the Pope, let alone the obstinate archbishop of Aquilea, could deny Venice its own bishopric. For this reason, several historians have claimed that Rusticus and Bonus had not travelled to Alexandria as traders at all, but had simply been sent there with the mission of settling the question of Venice's bishopric once and for all by stealing the saint's relics. After all, how certain was it that the right body had been brought to the lagoon, considering that the Apostle had died 700 years earlier? But these are modern-day doubts, and they would hardly have occurred to a medieval Christian. The miracle of the Translation of the Relics makes it all the clearer why this saint honored Venice above all cities. In addition there was a further miracle, whereby the saint indicated that his final resting place would be next to the seat of the temporal ruler, and not in the cathedral: this showed that in Venice secular power was superior to that of the Church. The veneration of St. Mark and belief in the significance of his relics' presence in Venice never died, even though in the course of time the body disappeared on several occasions, only to miraculously reappear unharmed.

And anybody who has visited San Marco and seen the saint's tomb, which is beneath the high altar, will, for the moment at least, find it hard to doubt that he or she really is standing in the church where St. Mark lies buried.

Jacopo Tintoretto: Saving the Body of St. Mark, 1562, Gallerie dell'Accademia, Venice

Doges' Palace

South facade from the Riva degli Schiavoni

When you view the Doges' Palace from the Riva degli Schiavoni, it is evident that it is not in fact a single building, as it appears when viewed from the Piazzetta. The differing colors clearly show that the Gothic brick building is quite distinct from the Renaissance building behind it, with its white stone blocks. This reflects both the history of the palace's construction, and its different functions: city hall, courthouse, and residence of the doge. The oldest part of the palace today is that facing the water, which was built, starting in 1340, as the assembly hall for the Great Council. On July 30, 1419, the Doge Michele Steno held the first meeting in the completed hall. In 1424 Doge Francesco Foscari had part of the palace overlooking the Piazzetta rebuilt. The architects had to copy exactly the Great Council building, which already had seven arcades leading to the Piazzetta. This gave the Doges' Palace its present integrated appearance, which makes it look as if it had all been built contemporaneously.

West and south facades

The form of the building, with its open portico and the balcony on the second floor, was typical of Venetian houses of the period. In the Doges' Palace it is combined with pointed arches and open-work tracery in Gothic designs that were soon to be copied throughout Venice in all the aristocratic palazzi. The white of the

arcades and the richly carved capitals, the play of light and shadow on the tracery, and the light-colored upper story give the Venetian seat of power an upbeat, festive appearance. The two open-arcade stories give the impression that the closed section of the building is floating lightly above the open lower floors. In reality, the huge building, measuring 71 x 75 m, rests on huge timbers of larch wood. Unlike other 14th century rulers' palaces in Europe, the

Doges' Palace is completely unfortified. In the past this was taken by visitors as certain proof that all classes lived peacefully together in the city on the lagoon.

Filippo Calendario:
Noah's Drunkenness,
c. 1344, south facade

Filippo Calendario, who was executed in 1355 as one of the conspirators with Doge Falier, was originally not only the chief architect of the Doges' Palace, but also created a series of excellent sculptures for the arcades. Situated on the right-hand corner of the waterfront is *Noah's Drunkenness*. To the left is Noah, pictured with the vessel of wine slipping from his hands. His two sons, seeing that he is drunk and naked, are shown standing on the other side. One son is covering his father up with a cloth, while the other shows no sympathy. The fine observation in both the figures and the precisely sculpted foliage bear witness to Calendario's remarkable skill and aptitude.

throne are two sins she is suppressing: on the left, anger tearing up its shirt, and on the right, pride, with donkey's ears growing from its helmet.

Porta della Carta, 1438

Doge Francesco Foscari not only had the northwest wing facing the Piazzetta extended, but additionally incorporated into it a new entrance to the inner courtyard, known as the Porta della Carta. Over the entrance he had a kneeling lion depicted.

The origins of the name Porta della Carta (literally, "Paper Gate") is a matter of dispute. Some believe that it derives from the city archives that were once housed here, while others think it refers to the sentences and decrees that were read out here. Yet another explanation is that requests to the government had to be submitted in writing.

In 1438 Foscari, at the height of his power, commissioned the Buon family of sculptors to carve the portal. The prolific Gothic shapes make the portal look as if it were made by a goldsmith. This impression was, in earlier times, reinforced even more by the fact that it was painted in blue and gold.

Western facade

The seven older arcades of the palace on the Piazzetta include Filippo Calendario's open-work tondo depicting Venetia, whose sword simultaneously identifies her as Justice. This is one of the first allegories of the city of Venice. Venetia embodying Justice became one of the Republic's most highly favored symbols. The Venetians regarded justice as one of the main virtues of their city-state. Beneath Venetia's lion

"Futuri Flegrei"
I Campi Flegrei
da Omero a Virgilio
Mostra itinerante sui Campi Flegrei

Palazzo Ducale - Salone del Piovego
1 aprile - 15 giugno 1996

Fortitude, Porta della Carta, 1438

Bartolomeo Buon, who ran a family stone carving workshop together with his father, was considered the best sculptor of his time in Venice. He was not, however, responsible for all the sculptures found on the Porta della Carta. The large-scale workshop which he ran allowed him to produce sculptures at high speed, and meant that he could pass on many of the figures to skilled collaborators. The fine figures of the virtues in the niches – Wisdom, Mercy, Prudence, and Fortitude – were probably not executed by Buon himself. Antonio Bregno, who later carved similar figures for Foscari's tombstone (see p. 235), was the creator of the impressive figure of Fortitude in the first niche from the bottom on the right side.

Scala dei Giganti, 1484–1501

Once you have passed through the Porta della Carta and the dark Arco Foscari, you see before you the last of what were once four stairways leading to the offices on the loggia floor, impressively known as the Giant's Staircase. This was started by Antonio Rizzo in 1484. Its name is derived from the two colossal, far greater than life-size, statues by Jacopo Sansovino that were set up on either side of the staircase in 1567. They depict Mercury, the Roman god of trade, and Neptune, the god of the sea, thereby overtly symbolizing the origins of the wealth of Venice. Equally unmistakable is the Lion of St. Mark over the entrance arch to the loggia, representing the patron saint of Venice and the Venetian state. The Scala dei Giganti was the setting for the magnificent inauguration ceremonies of the doge.

Gabriel Bella:
Inauguration of the Doge on the Scala dei
Giganti, before 1792
Oil on canvas, 95 x 147 cm

The St. Mark's Lion relief over the Scala dei Giganti rises above the statues representing the sea and trade. In this way it was brought home to every visitor who arrived through the Porta della Carta and the magnificent open stairway to enter the Doges' Palace, how Venetian trade and seafaring enjoyed the special protection of the saint. The strength and the symbolism of the relief was revealed when in 1797 it was destroyed by Napoleon's army which marched into the city. The present relief is a copy of the old one. Magnificent, and subtly designed, the stairway played an important role during the reception of official visitors and the inauguration of the doge. Most of this grand ceremony was carried out on the open stairway.

Gabriel Bella recorded, as he did many other aspects of daily Venetian life, the inauguration of the doge on the Scala dei Giganti. Surrounded by senators and all the councils, the new doge would take his oath to the Venetian state and its laws on the highest step. Then the youngest councilor would put on his head the *camauro*, a cap of the finest white cloth, upon which the oldest councilor would set the doges' cap.

Il Doge Viene Incoronato
Sopra La Scala De Siganti

Courtyard

The east wing of the Doges' Palace was rebuilt in 1483 after being badly damaged in a fire. It is likely that undamaged parts of the old building were incorporated into the new one. For a long time the richly decorated facade was believed to be the work of Antonio Rizzo, who was the builder responsible for the palace, and his successor Pietro Lombardo. It is now known, however, that it was designed by Mauro Codussi, Venice's leading Renaissance architect. On no other building did he apply such lavish ornamentation as on the east wing of the palace, where the doge's apartments were. It was not until around 1600 that the arcades in the east and west wings of the palace were opened, thus giving the entire courtyard a more uniform appearance. Previously this had been the vegetable garden of the nuns of San Zaccaria, which is why the name Broglio (garden) was still used for the courtyard. It was a place where officials, councilors, and members of the government could talk in a relaxed atmosphere. These meetings were also used for illegal deals or for trade in offices, as council members' votes could be bought. According to some rumors this was an important source of income for impoverished members of the nobility. Be this as it may, to this day a dishonest deal is described in Italian as a *broglio* in honor of this courtyard.

The Doge and the Councils

Although the title "The doge of Venice" was associated with authority and splendor, it also contained a certain element of mystery. What the city's highest representative actually did, what influence he had, and by what means he ruled were usually concealed behind the mask of pomp and ceremony.

In the beginning, as the city of Venice was gradually emerging, the doges had almost unlimited power. The name of the office originates from the Latin *dux*, which was the title of the Byzantine ruler, who from the 8th century onwards ruled the lagoon. The authority of the early doges, who soon acted largely independently, was so great that from the 8th to the 12th century they frequently managed to appoint their sons or other close relatives as their successors.

During the 12th century, however, the community gained increasing influence. The doge was no longer approved by general acclamation at the public meeting of all citizens of Venice, known as the *Arengo*. The assembly now only elected the doge with the assistance of electors. At the same time, towards the end of the 12th century, the doge came to be assisted by an elected council. The council consisted of one representative of each of the six *sestiere* (districts), who acted as direct advisers to the doge, along with a Great Council (Maggior Consiglio). The members of both councils, known as *Sapientes* (Wise Men),

were dignitaries selected on the basis of their wealth or knowledge, and had previously advised the doge in special situations. Now they became a permanent institution. The six advisers from the districts and the other *Sapientes* were initially chosen through election by the *Arengo*. Theoretically, any Venetian could at any point be elected doge. In reality, only wealthy families which had occupied positions of power for a long time were considered. The fact that other families that had attained wealth and respect in the course of time wanted to take part in governing the city and no longer accepted the supremacy of the old traditional families led to constant quarreling from the 12th to the 14th century. This power struggle culminated in the *Serrata* (Closure) of the Great Council, which was carried out between 1297 and 1323: only those whose forebears had been council members could now be admitted and in 1323 membership became hereditary. The Venetian nobility thus did not stem from imperial or royal families, but was rather a patriciate. The names of the families entitled to sit on the councils, their marriages, and the births of their sons were

Titian: Portrait of Doge Andrea Gritti, c. 1545, Kress Collection, National Gallery, Washington. Painted long after Gritti's death in 1538, this portrait fully captures the image of the doge's power.

recorded in the Libro d'Oro, or Golden Book. In later centuries only very few families, because of special services or wealth, were admitted to the register.

The hereditary nature of the Great Council's membership meant that the number of members grew constantly from the 14th century onwards, making it far too cumbersome as a means of government. This gave rise to numerous committees and subcommittees which dealt with individual problems. The offices of these institutions were filled by the Great Council and occupied by its members.

While the nobility thus grew into a self-governing class and remained so until the end

Doge's cap, Museo Correr, Venice

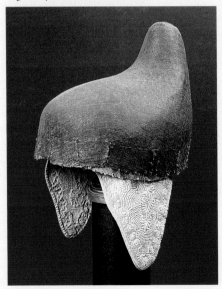

of the Republic, the doge's power gradually waned. From the 13th to the 15th century he became increasingly a prisoner of his own dignity. In 1229, the post of the five "correctores" was established. The nobility checked how the doge had carried out his duties during his rule, and then established the *promissiones*, promises, that the new doge had to make before he took office.

As with all Venetian institutions, it was a punishable offense to refuse the office of doge. The incumbent was chosen by a complicated selection procedure involving the drawing of lots and election. The doge received a kind of salary which in itself was barely enough to cover his expenses. He was forbidden to have his own business, which meant that one of the first preconditions for becoming a doge was wealth. Despite this, he had to pay taxes like all other citizens. Although he presided over all the councils, he was otherwise just an ordinary council member. Only in the Great Council was he able to prevent a member speaking. He was under constant obligation to leave the Doges' Palace only in ceremonial fashion and, except in case of war, forbidden to travel abroad without permission or unaccompanied by a member of the Small Council (known as the Collegio from 1412). He could only receive foreign emissaries in the presence of the Collegio. The councils were allowed to open letters from abroad addressed to the doge, who had to read all other letters in their presence. No letter or ordinance of the doge could leave the palace without signatures from at least four councillors. His sons and grandsons could only accept Venetian posts or marry the daughter of foreign princes with permission of the council. If, despite all these constraints, a doge did manage to exercise great influence, this would be due mainly to his personality.

Real governmental power was in the hands of the Collegio. This consisted of six members, which from the 13th century onwards were elected by the Great Council. To these were added the three presidents of the Quarantia (the judicial institution) and, during the 14th and 15th centuries, ten *Savi*, who were representatives selected from a senate committee. Members of the Collegio were also not allowed to refuse election and, like the doge, were forbidden to conduct their own businesses. They were not allowed to leave Venice without permission of the Great Council, and they had to be unrelated to the doge.

Venetian election urn, Museo Correr, Venice

A unanimous vote by the Collegio was enough to dismiss the doge. If there were differences of opinion between the Collegio and the doge, the council's opinion was final. The Collegio, which also came to be known as the Signoria, presided over all meetings together with the doge. Laws were first discussed in the Collegio, and then were submitted to the senate for advice and finalization.

During the 15th century the senate had some 300 members, including all the doge's sons, nephews, and brothers. Senatorial posts were much aspired to by the Venetian nobility, because they brought with them great prestige but few limitations. Senators could conduct their businesses and did not have to leave the country, as was the case if one was given honorary command of the fleet or appointed governor of a city ruled by Venice. In addition, the time for debates was unlimited in the senate, which meant senators could excel as brilliant orators. Members of the senate also wore a rich purple toga, which was subordinate only to the scarlet toga of the Collegio.

The representatives of the two highest legislative institutions, the Quarantia and the Consiglio dei Deici (the Council of Ten), by contrast, wore black. Feared throughout Europe, the Council of Ten was something like a

Gabriel Bella: A Night Session of the Council of Ten, before 1792, Pinacoteca Querini Stampalia, Venice

secret service with judicial powers, which had been set up to combat the numerous conspiracies afoot during the 14th century. The aim of the body was above all to protect the state from internal enemies. The Council of Ten carried out most of its activities secretly and under cover of night. Witness statements were ignored and torture used to extract

confessions. The time limit for their investigations was two months, however. Outside advisers were taken on for particularly complex cases. Verdicts had to be approved by vote five times: if the votes did not achieve unanimity, the prisoner was released.

The leading institutions had innumerable smaller subordinate ones. The most surprising thing about the Venetian administration was that an office was hardly ever terminated, while new administrative and decision-making committees were continually set up, often with no clear lines of demarcation between them. The distribution of power among the offices was thus finely balanced, with numerous checks made on any decision.

Not only did the Venetians constantly set up new committees, but they also constantly amended their legislation, thus making the motto of "mutate rege mutata lex" (change of government means change of law), coined by Domenico Moresini, a late medieval ship's captain and historian, applicable throughout Venice's history. The extent of this situation can only be judged if we take into account that the majority of government members, apart from the doge, had to leave their posts within a year, or even half a year.

It was not until the end of the Republic that various institutions obstructed one another completely and stalled any kind of policy-making. This may be due to the fact that, as a city-state, Venice was relatively easy to run. The established families, nobles, and citizens knew each other and were bound together in a variety of ways – they might be from the same district, they may have been trading partners, fought in the same wars, or been members of the same *scuola*. This meant that the groundwork for political decisions could be prepared by personal contacts. Indeed, this network may be the secret of the Venetian system of government's survival for 1000 years.

Giudizio De Rei
Nella Quarantia Criminal

Gabriel Bella:
The Quarantia Criminale
(Criminal Court), before 1792
Oil on canvas, 95 x 147 cm
Biblioteca Querini Stampalia, Venice

The courtyard and first two floors of the Doges' Palace were accessible to all of Venice's citizens. These floors also contained scribes' chambers and minor offices. The first floor contained cells for prisoners. The offices of the Avogardi (lawyers) on the ground floor are comparable to a modern government function. Having their offices arranged on this floor meant that the lawyers had access to the prisons and the torture chambers at all times during proceedings. The new prison built in 1560 was linked to the Avogardi on the same level via the famous Bridge of Sighs. The law courts, the rooms of the Quarantia, each of which consisted of 40 lawyers, were on the floor above. Both civil and criminal cases were heard here.

Bella's painting demonstrates how small the group of defendants or witnesses (in their colorful clothes on the left) look in contrast to the large phalanx of lawyers of the criminal court.

denounced as particularly gruesome. But when we compare them with the dark, filthy jails that prisoners were thrown into in the rest of Europe, where they had to share their fate not just with other unfortunate souls but with teeming vermin, perhaps Venice's prisons were not that bad. The Venetians themselves considered them to be particularly humane.

Bocca del Leone

The "lion's mouth" letter box was intended for people to post anonymous letters denouncing fellow citizens for tax avoidance, bribery, or embezzlement.

First Floor, I Pozzi

I Pozzi (wells) was the name given to the prisons on the ground floor of the Doges' Palace because of their dampness. They were built of Istrian stone and faced with thick wooden planking. Beds consisted of a wooden platform. Much of the horror literature of the 19th century depicted Venetian prisons as even more terrible than they were in reality. Because they were associated with the reputation of the Council of Ten, which can be compared to a powerful secret service, the prisons were

Doges' Palace, ground floor and loggia

The Doges' Palace contained government offices, courts, prisons, reception rooms, ceremonial halls, and ballrooms, in addition to the doge's apartments. Depending on their reason for being there, a visitor would be led to their final destination via a series of stairways, passages, corridors, and waiting rooms. On the way, the visitor would pass a collection of paintings depicting the wealth of Venice and the attributes of the office being visited. Innumerable portraits of officials were another typically Venetian decorative feature; these also served to emphasize the Republic's tradition and continuity, and to inspire respect for its virtues, history and wealth.

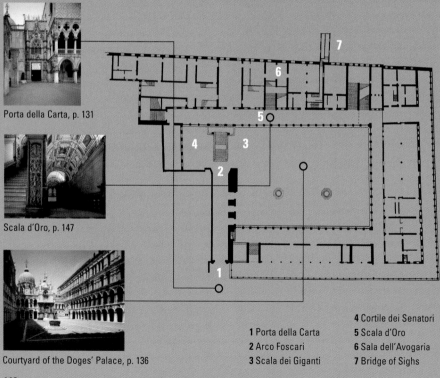

Porta della Carta, p. 131

Scala d'Oro, p. 147

Courtyard of the Doges' Palace, p. 136

1 Porta della Carta
2 Arco Foscari
3 Scala dei Giganti
4 Cortile dei Senatori
5 Scala d'Oro
6 Sala dell'Avogaria
7 Bridge of Sighs

Scala d'Oro

The state rooms were situated in the upper floors of the palace. After 1559, high-ranking visitors were led there from the loggia floor via a magnificent single stairway with a gilded stucco ceiling. The stairway was designed by the renowned architect Jacopo Sansovino. He started its construction in 1530, and it was completed by Antonio Abbondio in 1559. The fine stucco work and the paintings are by Alessandro Vittoria and Giovanni Battista Franco.

Doges' Palace, second floor

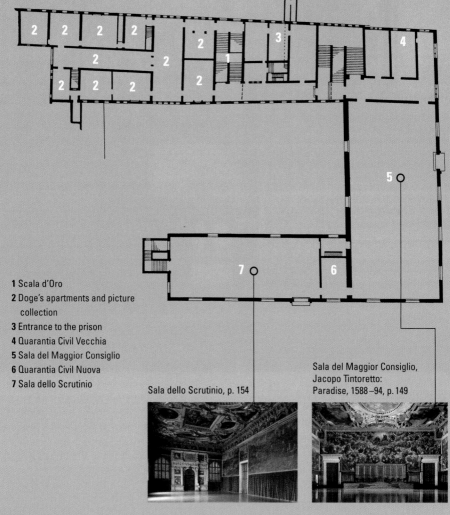

1 Scala d'Oro
2 Doge's apartments and picture collection
3 Entrance to the prison
4 Quarantia Civil Vecchia
5 Sala del Maggior Consiglio
6 Quarantia Civil Nuova
7 Sala dello Scrutinio

Sala dello Scrutinio, p. 154

Sala del Maggior Consiglio,
Jacopo Tintoretto:
Paradise, 1588–94, p. 149

Sala del Maggior Consiglio

The Hall of the Great Council, situated on the south side of the first floor, was the assembly hall for the Maggior Consiglio. All Venetians over 25 and of noble birth were admitted to the hall. It was a kind of parliamentary chamber, even though the members were not elected but had voting rights by birth and so were not representative of the people as a whole. The hall was destroyed in 1577 by a great fire, which consumed all the works of art and fine furnishings that had accumulated there since the 14th century. After a brief consultation on whether to design a building to reflect new styles and tastes, the decision was made to restore the room. Between 1578 and 1594, the Sala was returned to its previous state and fitted with contemporary furnishings. Beneath the finely carved ceiling, three walls of the room are embellished with paintings of the first 76 doges who ruled Venice up to 1556. The rest are in the neighboring Sala dello Scrutinio. The doges' coats of arms are carved into the ceiling above the portraits. One portrait had a black veil painted over it: that of Marino Falier, who tried to overthrow the Republic in 1355.

Gabriel Bella: The Doge Thanks the Great Council for his Election, before 1792
Oil on canvas, 94.5 x 146.5 cm

Jacopo Tintoretto: The Voluntary Subjugation of the Provinces, 1578–85
Oil on canvas

Bella's painting shows the Sala del Maggior Consiglio in full session. The Great Council, whose membership at times exceeded 2000, was far too big to function effectively. For this reason noble officials and council members were selected for various functions. This was rarely done by direct vote; in order to avoid manipulation, election commissions were selected by means of a complicated system of lot-drawing and ballots.

The magnificently carved ceiling of the Sala del Maggior Consiglio was designed by Cristoforo Sorte, an engineer and cartographer by trade, who also worked as a painter and designer. The ceiling contains 35 panels glorifying the Venetian state. The official plan for the paintings and descriptions of them are still in existence. This written record of what was to be represented in the Republic's parliamentary chamber gives us a good idea of the Venetian self-image at the time the ceiling was decorated. But what the document shows above all is that the artist ignored the instructions given to him. Pictures at the side were to show the deeds of Venetians; the central pictures, to show their results. Tintoretto's central painting depicts the subjugation of the Venetian provinces (which are not designated more precisely). They are bringing military insignia and treasure to express their subservience. At the top of the staircase is Doge Nicolò da Ponte (in office 1585–95). In the background, the gables of San Marco are just visible and below the doge on the left are the members of the government. Above it all, Venetia appears in the clouds, St. Mark's Lion beside her with the wreath of victory in its mouth. Although it is supposed to be giving the laurel wreath to Venetia, it looks as if it wants to give it to the doge himself.

Paolo Veronese:
Apotheosis of Venice, 1578–85
Oil on canvas, 904 x 580 cm

While Tintoretto's central painting was regarded negatively by his contemporaries because they felt he had assigned too much work to his workshop, they all agreed on the fine quality of Veronese's painting. It depicts an allegory of Peace, brought by the Venetian government to all its subjects.

Jacopo Tintoretto:
Paradise, 1588–94
Oil on canvas, 700 x 2200 cm

Before the fire, this spot was occupied by a famous painting of the *Coronation of the Virgin* by the 14th-century artist Guariento of Padua, which was also called *Paradise*. Tintoretto's painting similarly culminates in the crowning of Mary. She is surrounded by angels, saints, and holy men. The gigantic painting really does give the viewer the impression of looking straight into heaven where the Madonna's coronation is taking place. Tintoretto successfully manages to show all the gathered saints. Whereas earlier scenes of this kind merely showed a few representative saints, Tintoretto makes the coronation the high point of the assembly.

The fact that the viewer gets lost in the crowd is reinforced by the strong motion of many figures, which interrupt the concentric arrangement. By skillfully arranging light and shade, Tintoretto gives an impression of depth. We would hardly be able to make out the main figures of the painting if he had not left a gap in the throng around them.

Sala dello Scrutinio

The second largest hall on the second floor was built later than the Sala del Maggior Consiglio, when Francesco Foscari extended the palace during the 15th century. This was where the votes of the Maggior Consiglio were counted. It was also the hall where the various electoral commissions, which were formed and re-formed by the drawing of lots, held their sessions, until the doge or another high-ranking officer was finally chosen. This hall was also so badly damaged in the fire of 1577 that it had to be completely redecorated over several years from 1578.

Today, visitors usually enter the Sala dello Scrutinio after the Sala del Maggior Consiglio; however, in the old days, most visitors and members of the councils entered this hall before the Sala del Maggior Consiglio. This is important in order to understand the sequence of the decoration. While the Sala del Maggior Consiglio glorifies the Venetian system of government, the paintings on the walls in the Sala dello Scrutinio show military episodes which led to Venetian supremacy in the eastern Mediterranean sea. The ceiling depicts battles with the other Italian maritime city-states of Pisa and Genoa, which were finally conquered by Venice. The frieze with images of the doges depicts actual portraits.

Doges' Palace, third floor

Sala del Collegio, p. 162

Sala del Senato, p. 163

Sala del Consiglio dei Dieci, p. 164

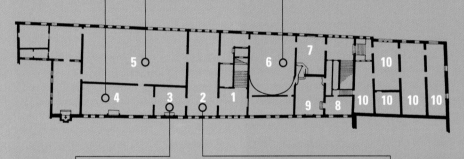

Anticollegio, p. 161

Sala delle Quattro Porte, p. 158

1 Scala d'Oro
2 Sala delle Quattro Porte
3 Anticollegio
4 Sala del Collegio
5 Sala del Senato
6 Sala del Consiglio dei Dieci
7 Sala della Bussola
8 Sala degli Inquisitori
9 Sala dei Tre Capi
10 Armory

**Titian: Doge Antonio Grimani before the
Allegory of Faith, c.1555–after 1576**
Oil on canvas, 365 x 500 cm

Titian's painting of the Doge Antonio Grimani kneeling before the allegory of Faith was twice started by the artist in around 1555, but was not completed until well after his death. It is one of many votive paintings with a kneeling doge which can be found all over the Doges' Palace. Every ruler was obliged to commission one of these pictures during his rule. There are many such portraits depicting the same doge; others, by contrast, only had such portraits painted with reluctance. The authorities, however, were unrelenting. Grimani's painting is unique in that it was ordered by the council ten years after his death. It is possible that the doge's term in office from 1521 to 1523 was too short a period for him to get round to commissioning the painting. After all this, the final completion of the picture was delayed for at least 20 more years.

Sala delle Quattro Porte

The decoration of the original Sala delle Quattro Porte was destroyed in the great fire of 1577. Palladio has been repeatedly mentioned as the architect responsible for the renovation, although the historical sources are not definite enough for us to ascribe the hall's interior decoration to him. It is possible that he only played an advisory role.

The name of the Hall of the Four Doors is almost self-explanatory. The four doors led to the offices of the highest government officials; to the Consiglio dei Dieci; to the assembly hall of the Senate; and, to the Anticollegio. The paintings on the vaults of the ceiling emphasize Venice's rule of the sea, its might, its independence, and its wealth. They also depict cities and regions that were within Venice's domain – Istria with its crown and Verona with its arena. In 1589 sculptures by Alessandro Vittoria and Girolamo Campagna were added above the doors, symbolizing the functions of the rooms beyond them. The door to the Sala del Collegio is surmounted by allegories of Vigilance, Eloquence, and Attention, while the door to the Consiglio dei Dieci depicts the figures Authority, Religion, and Justice.

Anticollegio

From the Sala delle Quattro Porte the visitor is led into another, even more sumptuously decorated, if smaller, waiting room, the Anticollegio. It is the anteroom to the hall where the highest council of state met. The magnificent stucco ceiling was designed by Andrea Palladio and executed in 1576–77. The ceiling frescoes, originally by Paolo Veronese and his workshop, were largely repainted during the 17th century. They illustrate the power and wealth of the Venetians.

When the Republic obtained Paolo Veronese's famous *Rape of Europa* in 1713, a painting which was still famous throughout Europe 150 years after its completion, the whole room was redecorated. The four Tintorettos, which were executed in 1577–78 and originally adorned the main wall, were placed beside the doors. These paintings too, with their scenes of classical mythology, could be interpreted in the light of Venetian virtues and strengths, but the associations were so complex that an explanation was almost always necessary. In a location such as this, where high-ranking visitors, while waiting for admittance, could view them at their leisure, these paintings must have encouraged learned conversations and enabled members of the Collegio to flaunt their erudition.

Jacopo Tintoretto: Marriage of Bacchus and Ariadne, 1577–78
Oil on canvas, 146 x 167 cm

Ariadne, abandoned beside the sea by Theseus, is given a wedding ring by Bacchus. Venus, goddess of love, holds a bridal tiara made of twinkling stars over Ariadne's head. This mythological scene was also taken to be symbolic of Venice as Bride of the Sea.

Sala del Collegio

This assembly hall is probably the most sumptuous room in the whole of the Doges' Palace. This was where the Republic's supreme governing body, the Collegio, also known as the Signoria, met. It consisted of the doge and his six closest advisers, the *Savi*, plus 17 highly placed state officials from the various departments, the chairman of the Council of Ten, and the Grand Chancellor. This was the place where foreign ambassadors

were received, Venetian ambassadors returning from foreign lands gave their reports, and the sessions of other committees were prepared. The walls are covered with large paintings showing various doges kneeling before saints. The entire room was redecorated after 1574.

It is therefore not surprising that, behind the rostrum of the Collegio, along with the other doge paintings, there is a picture depicting the naval Battle of Lepanto against the Turks in 1571. This was the Republic's greatest military victory in that period, and – perhaps for the last time – it reiterated its unique position of power in the eastern Mediterranean. The paintings on the ceilings are allegories of Venice's might, which was a result of Faith. Although in the anteroom classical gods celebrate the Republic in abstruse symbols, here, in the real center of power, it is Christianity that predominates.

Sala del Senato

The Sala del Senato, where the senators met, is near the Sala del Collegio, and can be entered either from here or from the Sala delle Quattro Porte. The Senate was the second highest ruling body, as it approved the bills that were drawn up by the Collegio. According to protocol, the Senate assembled only at the invitation of the Collegio, and so senators were also known as *pregadi* (invitees). Some senators were elected by the Maggior Consiglio, while others were senators by virtue of their high official positions.

In the same way as members of the Consiglio, Venetian senators were allowed to wear purple robes. But the great honor that gave them their rank also entailed a great deal of hard work. During the sessions, which were held at least twice a week, the doors of the hall were locked and not opened until the Senate had discussed all the items on the agenda.

Each senator had the right to speak for as long as necessary, which was perhaps the reason for the two large clocks, showing the signs of the zodiac and the hours, that served to remind senators of the passing of time. Even so, debates often went on late into the night or even until the next morning. Jacopo Tintoretto's huge painting on the ceiling shows Venice's glory as a maritime power.

Sala del Consiglio dei Dieci

To reach the Sala del Consiglio dei Dieci, or Council of Ten, from the actual seat of government, i.e. the Senate or the Collegio, you have to cross the Sala delle Quattro Porte. The Council of Ten was set up in 1310 after a plot against the government had been uncovered. Its function was to keep watch over the Senate, the Collegio, and the doge himself. This was why its office was housed separately from the others. The Council of Ten had to read all mail received and sent by the government. It also had the right to depose the government, and even the doge himself, should he be convicted of a misdemeanor. The Council of Ten had a well-organized system of spies able to keep it informed of all goings-on in the city at all times. In this way it kept watch over the entire life of Venice. The power of this institution to dismiss people, put them on trial, or even to have them secretly assassinated, without warning or accountability, was the sinister side of the all-powerful Venetian administration.

Paolo Veronese:
Juno Showering Grace upon Venice, 1553
Oil on canvas, 365 x 147 cm

It is not clear to this day what the overall plan was for the paintings in the hall. Its theme is evidently the expulsion of the vices. Paolo Veronese, an almost unknown 25-year-old artist, was commissioned to paint the ceiling in 1553. The works he created were true masterpieces. The central painting is a copy of the picture that the French removed to the Louvre in 1797. The side painting, which is in fact the personification of Venice receiving rich gifts from Juno, suggests that Grace also represents Mercy. For the Council of Ten, leniency towards the condemned was a particularly important virtue.

Giovanni Battista Tiepolo:
Neptune Bestowing Gifts upon Venice,
1748–50
Oil on canvas, 135 x 275 cm

Tiepolo's painting was not hung in the Sala del Consiglio dei Dieci until the 20th century. It was originally designed for the Sala delle Quattro Porte, where it was to

replace a damaged 16th century painting. When directly compared with Veronese's ceiling paintings in this hall, it is easy to see how much Tiepolo owes to the color and forms of Veronese, who worked 150 years earlier. However, Tiepolo's turquoise blue, red, and orange are new elements not to be found in the work of his predecessor.

Why was the portrait of one doge painted over?

A visitor to the Doges' Palace is very unlikely to spend a long time examining every single painting on the walls of the Sala del Maggior Consiglio due to their sheer number and, particularly, since only the later portraits are authentic. However, this would mean missing out on one important curiosity in the portrait gallery, namely that the portrait of one 14th century doge has been painted over in black. What terrible crime had this doge committed to have his face obscured forever? A Latin inscription from 1570 simply tells us that his portrait was covered over because of his crime. This inscription replaces an earlier one which had mentioned treachery as the reason. Why did Doge Falier, the most respected person in Venice, commit this crime?

Long before the 70-year-old Falier was elected doge on September 11, 1354, his name frequently came up in conversations as a potential doge. From an old aristocratic family, he was a successful admiral, general, and diplomat. As a member of the Council of Ten, in 1310 he had even been assigned with tracing and eliminating the conspirator Bajamonte Tiepolo (the latter was done between the columns on the Piazzetta). To this day, superstitious Venetians still walk around, not between, the columns. The legend relates that Falier, on hearing of his election to doge while he was ambassador to the Avignon Pope, sailed back to Venice on the state barge in thick fog and landed between the two columns. This made people fear the worst and, what was

Tintoretto: The painted over portrait of Marino Falier, Sala del Maggior Consiglio, Doges' Palace, Venice

Wall paintings (above) in the Sala del Maggior Consiglio

more, as the poet Petrarch wrote in a letter, he set the wrong foot on land first.

The fact is that Falier managed to win over two important non-aristocratic Venetians for his subversive plan: ship's captain and merchant Bertuccio Isarello, and master builder of the Doges' Palace, Filippo Calendario. Their job was to attempt to win over more conspirators. On the pretext that the Genoese, with whom the Venetians were constantly at war, and who had inflicted a crippling defeat on the Venetians in the Battle of Portolongo under the previous doge, had just invaded the lagoon, Falier wanted to call a meeting of the government on the night of April 15, 1355. The plan was that the plotters would then capture the entire government and pronounce Falier as absolute ruler.

Why Falier developed such a plot is a matter of conjecture. What seems certain is that the population of Venice felt highly demoralized after the defeat of Portolongo, believing that the nobility's cowardice had caused the fiasco.

Chronicles also recount that members of the ordinary population were humiliated by the nobility (the conspirator Isarello was such a victim), and were then not adequately compensated. In addition, the population, and possibly also the doge, desperately wanted peace with Genoa, which the government rejected. Falier may also have been inspired by the northern Italian states, where government by the aristocracy had gradually been replaced by one-man rule.

This system seems to have been much more successful for these states as far as trade and warfare were concerned – Genoa was a prime example – than was Venice's. As the doge was already 70 years old and had no male successors, it is clear that his motive was the interests of his native city rather than power for either himself or his family, since he personally stood to gain very little if the plot were a success.

The Venetians, however, had another explanation. They claimed that Michele Steno (a later doge) had written a satirical verse on the Doge's chair in the Sala del Maggior Consiglio, in which he claimed that Falier had been cuckolded by his wife. Although Steno was indicted for defaming Falier, the other nobles gave him a very light sentence of one month's imprisonment. This was what had made Falier's mind up to finally get rid of the partisan rule of the aristocracy. From contemporary documents we know that Steno was indeed sentenced for libel against Falier, though whether the doge's wife was involved is not known. Whatever the reason for the conspiracy, the plot was betrayed and uncovered. The reason for this it seems was that many of the common people whom the plotters had approached had not joined in, and had indeed warned the nobility. The latter then reported to Falier that there was trouble brewing. Falier did not, however, manage to stop a thorough investigation from taking place. First his co-conspirators, and finally he himself, were uncovered, and sentenced to death in secret. Eleven of Falier's more humble conspirators were hanged the following day beneath the windows of the Doges' Palace. They were gagged lest they call out or use passwords to set the coup in motion. On April 17, Falier himself, after being stripped of all his insignia, was beheaded on the steps of the palace, in the very same place where he had been inaugurated just a few months earlier. The bell which tolled for his death was hung in the tower of San Marco without clapper and rope so that it could never be tolled again. Eleven years later his portrait was painted over.

The columns on the Piazzetta between which Bajamonte Tiepolo was executed.

Biblioteca Marciana

In the 16th century a building was erected opposite the Doges' Palace which the procurators of San Marco had planned as their new seat of office. Jacopo Sansovino, who had moved from Rome to Venice in 1527 when imperial troops sacked the Holy City, was commissioned to design it in 1537. He introduced the new Romanesque style, hitherto unknown in Venice. Andrea Palladio, the greatest architect of the late 16th century, described the Libreria as the richest and most ornate building since Antiquity. Work began on the corner of the Campanile and was well advanced when on December 15, 1545, large parts of the incomplete building collapsed. Sansovino was imprisoned and only released through the intervention of influential friends.

In 1547 he was again appointed chief architect, having provided the funds for the reconstruction from his own pocket. In 1554 the building was completed as far as the 16th arcade from the Campanile. It stayed like this until 1582, when Vincenzo Scamozzi extended the structure all the way to the waterfront. Today the building houses the Biblioteca Marciana, one of Italy's foremost libraries. Also under the arcades is the entrance to the Museo Archeologico, which is situated next to the library.

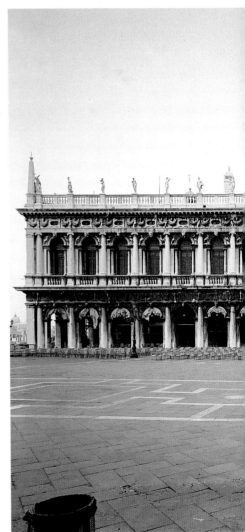

Library hall

The valuable collection of Greek and Latin manuscripts, that the Greek Cardinal Bessarion bequeathed to the Republic in 1468, was housed in the newly completed building. This idea emerged after the procurators had established themselves here in their new headquarters. The cardinal's collection formed the basis for one of the most valuable libraries in Italy. The building was for the Republic above all a status symbol. In accordance with the high value placed on education during the Renaissance, and also as an expression of appreciation for Bessarion's priceless manuscripts, the upper levels of the library hall were richly decorated.

representing the classical deities as embodiments of the Virtues and the Arts. The prize, a valuable gold chain, was won by Paolo Veronese for his picture of Music, Song, and Honor.

Titian's *Wisdom*, in the anteroom, came into being some seven years later. It is like a commentary on the paintings by the younger artists in the hall. Titian takes the bright colors of the younger generation and shows that he is still capable of creating a picture that can compete with the paintings of the younger artists in color, harmony, and the complex depiction of the human body.

The vestibule with Titian's *Wisdom* had originally been planned as a lecture hall, in which scholars would deliver lectures to Venetian aristocrats.

Titian:
Wisdom, c. 1564
Oil on canvas, 179 x 189 cm

In 1556–57 a competition was announced to commission the 21 paintings to cover the gilded ceiling of the library. The chairmen of the jury were Sansovino himself and his close friend Titian, the city's most prominent artist.

The ambitious young painters participating were given the assignment of

View of the Piazzetta from the Bacino di San Marco

The square between the Libreria and the Doges' Palace is known as the Piazzetta, or "small square," in contrast to the large Piazza San Marco. During the 16th century it was covered by numerous little shops, in particular the premises of bakers and butchers. It was not until the advent of

Jacopo Sansovino that measures were taken to rid the square of its many kiosks and sheds. Sansovino created a splendid area that was a fitting reflection of the city. The two massive granite columns at the waterfront had been erected back in the 12th century. They are surmounted by the Lion of St. Mark as a symbol of the city's patron saint, and a statue of St. Theodore, the Greek saint who, although the first patron saint of Venice, has been largely forgotten.

Zecca

The Zecca, or Mint, is attached to the southwestern side of the Libreria. Venice's mint was originally situated near the Rialto, but was moved to its new site in 1277. Its waterfront situation was important, as the sparks that were produced while the metal was being melted could easily start major fires. As part of his general renovation of the entire Piazzetta, in 1536 Sansovino also began to rebuild the Mint. He designed only a two-story building, and the third story, which was added during his lifetime in 1558–66, is not considered part of his work.

The imposing rustication of the stones, which extends over the columns, gives the entire building a severe, fortress-like character. In this way, Sansovino's exterior hints at the hard industrial labor of melting metal, conducted within. The heavy rustication, combined with the simple capitals of the columns the architect employed here, was more suited to a lowly activity, or to a military structure. The fortress-like character of the building also denoted that within it were kept valuable metals and finished coins, which had to be protected. Today, the former mint is part of the Biblioteca Marciana.

Prison (Prigioni Nuove)

Bridge of Sighs

The prison is to the east of the Doges' Palace. The building was erected in two stages. The front section with the facade was started in 1589, and the architect, Antonio da Ponte, like Sansovino with the Mint, used a very expressive style. The rough rustication shows that, as with the Mint, this is a fortified building that one cannot enter or, more importantly, leave.

The Ponte dei Sospiri, or Bridge of Sighs, is probably Venice's most famous bridge after the Rialto Bridge. It links the rooms of the examining judges and the prisons in the Doges' Palace with the new prison. The romantic name derives from the sighs of unhappy condemned prisoners, who would get their last view of daylight, the sea, and freedom from the bridge.

Loggetta

The gathering place of the nobility under the Campanile, which at that time was still surrounded by small shops and stalls, was probably moved in the 15th century, and certainly no later than the 16th century.

In 1537 Jacopo Sansovino designed the present small building, the Loggetta, completed by 1547, at the foot of the Campanile. Its function as a meeting-place for the nobility was short-lived, however. In 1569 the guard of honor of the arsenal workers, which kept watch during the sessions of the Maggior Consiglio in case they needed help, moved in here. It was only in 1663 that the terrace was added, and that the doors were placed beneath the archways.

Jacopo Sansovino:
Mercury
Bronze

The four niches of the Loggetta contain bronze statues of Minerva, the Roman goddess of war and wisdom; Apollo, the god of oracles and prophecy; Mercury, the god of merchants, thieves, and oratory; and, an allegory of Peace. The thin, finely folded robes of Mercury show a certain tenderness, which can also be seen in his youthful face. The muscular arms and legs, by contrast, show power and strength.

Sansovino managed to combine youthfulness and power skilfully. Mercury seems to be looking back towards Apollo on the other side of the door. This impulsive move makes the figure appear to be not completely contained in its niche, but to be in a living dialog with the other statues.

Sansovino was not only a good architect, but also an excellent sculptor. Sometimes, as is the case with the Loggetta, his two talents merge perfectly. The entire building, with its many reliefs, columns, and niches with statues, and particularly with its use of different materials in different colors, is at once a work of sculpture and of architecture.

Piazza San Marco

Campanile

The belltower of San Marco dominates the two squares in front of and beside the Basilica, and is an anchoring point between the large piazza and the smaller Piazzetta. The tower, which was added to by many generations, gained its present-day form in the early 16th century. In 1489 lightning struck the Campanile yet again, so in 1511–14 it was rebuilt. Since then, the summit has been crowned with the Archangel Gabriel.

On the morning of July 14, 1902, the Campanile collapsed. The government of the time promptly decided to restore it to its old dimensions, with a height of 310 feet (95 meters). The tower offers a magnificent view of Venice and the lagoon. On especially clear days, one can even see the Alps.

Torre dell'Orologio (Clocktower)

In 1496, Mauro Codussi had the great honor of being commissioned to build a clocktower at the entrance of the Merceria, the main road leading into the Rialto. The wings were added in 1499. The tower is an architectural masterpiece of colored stone, in blue and gold, which

is just as magical as the mechanical marvel of the clock itself. The first floor is reminiscent of a Roman triumphal arch. The clock above it, in addition to the time of day, displays the phases of the moon and the movement of the sun through the signs of the zodiac. The story above the clock features a bronze statue of the Madonna. The windows beside the statue show the time in five-minute increments. On January 6 and during Rogation week, the Three Kings appear from the side doors. Above these, the Lion of St. Mark stands before a blue, star-studded sky constructed in 1755 by Giorgio Massari. Until 1797 Doge Agostino Barbarigo knelt before the saint. The tower is surmounted by a bronze bell which is struck every hour by two bronze Moors (1497). These had been there as part of Codussi's design.

and also through clever investment, the procurators had very large sums of money at their disposal. From the 12th century onwards they lived in the building which stood on the site of the Old Procurators' Offices. The 16th century architects used the motif of narrow round-arched arcades in the old Veneto-Byzantine style. This once again shows how conservative the architects of Venice were.

On the other side of the piazza, the New Procurators' Offices were started in 1582–84. The work was directed by Vincenzo Scamozzi. These buildings included the residences of the nine procurators of San Marco, who by law were obliged to live in the vicinity of the Basilica.

Old and New Procurators' Offices

The construction of the Clocktower in 1496 marked the beginning of rebuilding on the north side of the Piazza San Marco. The next step was the building of the Procuratie, or Procurators' Offices, adjacent to the Clocktower. The Procuratie were the offices of the procurators of San Marco, who were responsible for the administration of all government building works on the Piazza with the exception of the Doges' Palace. Thanks to the large sums of money that San Marco received from state subsidies and private donations

Scamozzi borrowed the design of the adjacent Libreria for this project, but added a third story to conform with the Old Procurators' Offices opposite. The uniform ground-level arcades that surround the Piazza San Marco on all sides give it an enclosed feeling. At first glance it is quite difficult to tell that the two Procurators' Offices and the connecting building, on the south, north, and west sides of the Piazza, were built at completely different times.

Gabriel Bella: The Old Market on the Piazza on Ascension Day, before 1792
Oil on canvas, 95.6 x 145.5 cm

Bella's painting shows the Piazza San Marco on Ascension Day ("Sensa" in Venetian). Since the Middle Ages, the square was a large market for all the goods produced in Venice. Ascension Day attracted many pilgrims to the city, to whom, according to a special dispensation in 1177 by Pope Alexander III, San Marco was set aside for the day. The Venetians regarded the square as a place of business, but for the pilgrims it was also a chance to pick up some Venetian goods. Bella's painting depicts the Old Market, a jumble of stalls and stands, which was closed down in this form in 1777.

In the background, between the buildings of the two Procurators' Offices, we see the church of San Giminiano. Its facade was rebuilt by Jacopo Sansovino during the 16th century, and the church contains his tomb. In the early 19th century it had to make way for the third wing, which today connects the two Procurators' Offices.

New Procurators' Offices, Napoleonic Wing

Although they occupied Venice for only a few years at the beginning of the 19th century, the French under Napoleon left their mark on the city. Because Napoleon and his entourage needed a suitable residence and a large ballroom, the church of San Giminiano was demolished and the extension, known as the Napoleonic Wing was built between the Old and New Procurators' Offices. In this way, the new ruler took over the heart of the Venetian power base. The architect Giuseppe Soli based his design on the New Procurators' Offices, but, instead of a fourth floor, he built a strict attic story which emphasizes the orderly character of this wing.

New Procurators' Offices, Museo Civico Correr

A magnificent staircase with murals leads to the ceremonial halls that were built on the first floor of the Napoleonic Wing. The nine procurators' apartments were all converted into one single apartment for the emperor. However, Napoleon himself never trod the stairway nor set foot in the rooms. When they were completed in 1820, he had already left the stage of world history. Today the stairway leads to the Museo Civico Correr, which is dedicated to the history of Venice. Together with the Museo Archeologico (entrance through the Libreria arcades), it is housed in the New Procurators' Offices. The core of the museum is the collection of the Venetian nobleman Teodoro Correr, who bequeathed his treasures to the city in 1830. Over the years the city collections have had to be split up over several sites. The Museo Correr today contains mainly items of historical interest. The major collection of Venetian art and culture of the 18th century is in the Ca' Rezzonico.

Antonello da Messina:
The Dead Christ, 1475-76
Oil on wood, 117 x 85 cm

Antonello da Messina (c. 1430–79), who was educated in southern Italy, had an immense influence on 15th and 16th century Venetian art. It is very likely that he brought to Venice the technique of oil painting that was perfected by the painters of the Netherlands and northern France. Messina, like the rest of southern Italy, was under French rule, which was why there was a particularly vigorous interchange of artistic ideas with the north. This gave Antonello the opportunity to learn the secrets of oil painting at a very early age. During Antonello's stay in Venice in 1475–76, Giovanni Bellini learned a great deal from him. Despite the damage that Antonello's *Dead Christ* in the Museo Correr has suffered, it still gives us an idea of his skilled handling of light and landscape.

Giovanni Bellini:
Transfiguration
Tempera on wood, 134 x 68 cm

With the *Transfiguration,* Bellini (c. 1430–1516) was still continuing to work with the traditional technique that involved using tempera and oil. This, however, was adequate enough for him to skillfully depict light and shade, to blend colors, and to give his figures solidity. His figures are still wholly under the influence of his brother-in-law Andrea Mantegna. However, the complex convolutions and the foreshortened bodies of the Disciples at the foot of the mountain bear witness to his skill: the crossed feet of the lying figure are particularly noteworthy. In this work, three of the Evangelists are describing the Transfiguration of Christ, which was witnessed by the Apostles Peter, John, and James the Great.

The End:
Venice's final struggle for independence

When, on May 12, 1797, the Maggior Consiglio, at Napoleon's instigation, proclaimed the end of the Republic of Venice, and shortly afterwards French troops occupied the city, it was the final act in the gradual decline of Venice from its position as the greatest power in the eastern Mediterranean. Many authors have described life in Venice following the Treaty of Passarowitz of 1718, the last treaty which Venice signed as an independent political entity, as a dream from which only a rude awakening could be expected.

In the 18th century, Venice was crippled by lack of money and an inefficient system of

Giuseppe Borsato: The Venetian Provinces Swear loyalty to Emperor Franz I in S. Marco, May 15, 1815, Museo Correr, Venice

government. Centuries of warfare against the Turks had sapped the strength of the state. Despite this, people from all over Europe continued to stream into Venice. They no longer came to trade in goods, but to enjoy the city's unique atmosphere. One festival followed another, and gaming halls and brothels abounded. Fortunes were lost quickly, without new ones taking their place. Napoleon put an end to all this. Many Venetians still longed for their Republic, and the bourgeoisie and nobility started slowly to push through long overdue reforms.

But the freedoms of the French Revolution promised by Napoleon proved hollow. Even before his takeover of Venice, Napoleon had decided to exchange it with Austria for another region. In October 1797, he turned Venice over to the very power against which the Venetians had fought for 200 years. After a brief second episode of French rule, the final handover of Venice to Austria in 1814 shattered all hopes of resurgence in a new spirit. Venice became a provincial capital within Austria, the residence of one

Friedrich von Amerling: Franz I, 1832, oil on canvas, Weltliche Schatzkammer, Hofburg, Vienna

Anonymous: Daniele Manin (1804–57), Museo del Risorgimento, Venice

economic activity. This situation only started to improve in the 1820s, when duties were reduced.

During the 1840s the Austrians started to modernize the dilapidated lagoon city. The street system was improved and gas lighting was installed. In 1846 a railway embankment was built over the lagoon, thus connecting Venice with Milan for the first time, and ending centuries of isolation. All these feats of engineering, however, did little to alleviate the deep-rooted dissatisfaction of the Venetians, and of all northern Italians, at being subjected to Austrian rule and paying high taxes without proper political representation. When they looked at France, where the bourgeoisie was gaining more influence, the Venetians became increasingly dissatisfied with the strict rule of the Habsburgs.

The election of Pope Pius IX in 1846 was like a signal. The reforming Pope revolutionized the feudal Papal States to some extent from the top by giving his subjects more political rights, and recommending that other rulers do the same. Throughout Italy the new Pope was received with enthusiasm, which, for many, also had nationalistic undercurrents.

of the Austrian emperor's representatives. Venice had to share this meager political status with Milan.

Under the Austrians, the whole of northern Italy initially suffered severe hardship. The region was subjected to high taxes and customs duties, which soon crippled all

Italy started to complain against foreign rule. A congress of Italian scientists in Venice in 1847 more or less openly protested against the Austrians. The Venice opera house, the Teatro La Fenice, became a center of nightly protest whenever, in the fourth act of Verdi's *Macbeth,* the chorus sang of having to save the betrayed homeland. The secret police tried in vain to trace those responsible for throwing garlands of flowers in the Italian colors of white, red, and green onto the stage. They were also unable to arrest those opera-goers who wore clothes in which the three colours predominated.

There were no open demonstrations in Venice, however, not even when the news came of deaths in Milan and of students in Padua rising against occupying troops. But the Venetians did attempt to protect themselves against foreign rule by legal means. A lawyer named Daniele Manin (1804–57) was famous

Vincenzo Giacomelli: Daniele Manin and the Insurgents Capture the Arsenal (Daniele Manin Forces the Surrender), 1890, Museo del Risorgimento, Venice

Luigi Querena (1768–1853): The People of Venice Raise the Italian Flag in the Market Place, Museo del Risorgimento, Venice

for his many petitions against the Habsburg rule. Frightened by the disturbances in other cities, the Austrian authorities finally had Manin arrested, together with another ardent opponent of the Austrian occupation, Niccolò Tommaseo, on January 18, 1848. Now Venice finally had its own figurehead in the struggle for liberty.

Dissatisfaction was widespread throughout the Habsburg empire, with revolutionary fervor even reaching the capital, Vienna, where protestors forced the emperor to guarantee a constitutional monarchy. Encouraged by all these events, on March 17, 1848, a furious mob

stormed the residence of the Austrian representative in the New Procurators' Offices, and forced him to release Tommaseo and Manin. The following day there was a skirmish in the Piazza San Marco, resulting in the first Venetian victims, who were solemnly carried to the Café Florian, the stronghold of national resistance.

Daniele Manin and his followers were now resolved to use force if necessary to get rid of the Austrians. When the Venetian and Italian units of the army refused to obey orders, and the weapons from the arsenal fell into the hands of the protesters, the Habsburg army and the government had to withdraw. Daniele Manin was quickly made the leader of the Venetians. With his Venetian dialect, he was able to rouse the common people in the streets as no one else.

In the summer, the Austrians returned to the Veneto with reinforcements. They quickly recaptured some towns in the Friuli, but Venice resisted with the same tenacity as large parts of northern Italy. It was some time before the Habsburgs succeeded in regaining their lost territories. They were helped by the disunity among the Italians concerning their future political system. Even Manin's opinion on the Italian situation was hesitant and undecided. His whole way of thinking and his outlook were focused on his native city. So, time and time again, he missed opportunities to improve Venice's situation by providing military assistance to the mainland. While one region after another fell there, the Venetians managed to hold out. This was mainly due to their natural defense, the lagoon. The more hopeless the situation looked, the more closely the people stood by each other. In autumn, 1848, the city, now a refuge for numerous soldiers who had fled from fallen regions over the summer, was besieged. The state was soon

Luigi Querena: Soldiers on Parade in the Piazza San Marco, Museo del Risorgimento, Venice

Dalla Gribera: Venice Resists at All Costs, Museo del Risorgimento, Venice

unable to afford to feed the population, pay the soldiers, or maintain the military apparatus.

Nevertheless, the Venetians resisted stubbornly. They drew war loans, and wealthy families guaranteed to cover the new paper currency that was issued due to the lack of coinage, and donated their jewellery and silver for the war effort. This last funding campaign alone raised 1.3 million lire. The beleaguered city became a shining example for all Italians who still hoped for freedom. Nobody, however, was prepared or in a position to support the Venetians. A campaign to raise war loans for the city throughout Italy only collected 200,000 lire. Hunger and disease were on the rise in the winter of 1848/9. Food

prices soared: meat, butter, and wine rapidly became unobtainable. But still the Venetians held out.

When, in the spring of 1849, the situation looked completely hopeless after the Battle of Novara, in which troops from the Piemont were defeated by Austria, the Venetians had to reconsider the issue of capitulation. The government under Daniele Manin decided on April 2, 1849, in a poignant meeting in the Doges' Palace, to hold out despite what the Future might bring. This decisim cost the lives of many Venetians, particularly when, in early summer 1849, cholera broke out in a starving city ravaged by bombing.

When Manin received the news on August 13, 1849, that food supplies for the city's inhabitants would completely run out on the 24th, he decided – albeit against the will of part of the population and of the soldiers – to capitulate. On August 27, 1849, Austrian troops once again occupied the Piazza San Marco. It was to be another 17 years before Venice was united with the kingdom of Italy. The days of the old Republic, which Daniele Manin and others had promised would become a new Republic governed by its citizens, was finally past.

Announcement of the abdication of the Manin government, 1849, Museo del Risorgimento, Venice

N. 12752

IL GOVERNO PROVV.
DI VENEZIA

Considerato che una necessità imperiosa costringe ad atti, a' quali non possono prender parte nè l'Assemblea dei rappresentanti, nè un potere emanato da essa,

Dichiara:

1. Il Governo provvisorio cessa dalle sue funzioni.
2. Le attribuzioni governative passano nel Municipio della città di Venezia per tutto il territorio sin qui soggetto ad esso Governo.
3. L'ordine pubblico, la quiete e la sicurezza delle persone e delle proprietà, sono raccomandati alla concordia della popolazione, al patriottismo della Guardia civica ed all'onore dei corpi militari.

Venezia, 24 agosto 1849, ore 2 pom.

IL PRESIDENTE
MANIN.

Per Francesco Andreola, tipograf.

The Moorish Room

During the 19th century, the Café Florian was the meeting place for Venetians who were forging plans to rid themselves of their hated Austrian rulers. The Austrian officers would meet on the opposite side of the square in the equally traditional Café Quadri. The interior decoration of the Café Florian takes the visitor back to the 19th century. Ludovico Cadorin arranged it into four rooms in 1858, each like a drawing room, and named according to its decor. The Moorish Room is decorated with paintings of oriental beauties. It is easy to imagine Lord Byron, Giuseppe Verdi, and other famous visitors to Venice spending their days here among Venetians reading the newspaper or debating in hushed tones. To this day there are many Venetians from old families who insist on having their coffee served at the same seat. The café war that raged silently between the Austrians and Venetians was not confined to politics: Richard Wagner ostentatiously preferred to visit a different café from his rival Verdi.

Café Florian

The Piazza San Marco is famous for more than just its artistic treasures. Under the arcades of the New Procurators' Offices is Italy's first café, the Café Florian. This was opened in 1720 by Floriano Francesconi. At the time, ladies and gentlemen from all parts of the world sipped hot chocolate here. Drinking chocolate was the fashion in the 18th century, and a symbol of wealth and luxury. Pietro Longhi recorded the social significance of chocolate in his wonderful paintings, and the café is also mentioned in world literature. With the demise of luxury-loving rococo society, the bitter drink known as coffee took over. The aroma of coffee and cigars proved highly conducive to discussion and politicking.

San Moisè

Founded in the 8th century, San Moisè has been rebuilt repeatedly. In 1668 it gained its present facade, which was funded by the Fini family. Designed by Alessandro Tremignon, with sculptures by Heinrich Meyring, the facade is a monument to the Finis. Public statues were forbidden in Venice, but funding a building meant that families could dedicate what was probably an even greater monument to themselves. The Fini were one of the new aristocratic families. Vincenzo, whose bust can be seen on an obelisk over the door, had only just purchased this title for a large sum of money. The whole facade seems to reveal a slight excess of aristocratic pride and newly acquired wealth.

Santa Maria Zobenigo (Santa Maria del Giglio)

The name Zobenigo is that of an old Venetian family whose palazzo was near the church. Similarly to San Moisè, the facade of Santa Maria del Giglio was built as a memorial to the rich Barbaro family. The pronounced three-quarter columns and the deep niches for statues provide a more balanced combination of sculpture and architecture than San Moisè, however. It is interesting to note in both these cases that on the facades, in the places usually reserved for the church's patron saint, there are sculptures of mortal men. On the other hand, this practice can be regarded as sound business sense: the churches would gain a rich facade, while wealthy Venetians had the opportunity for public recognition.

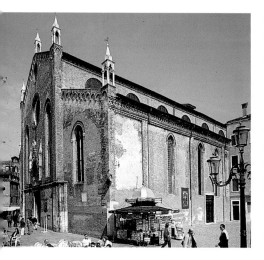

church when it was rebuilt. In order to build a church on such a scale nonetheless, the monks even had to build over a *rio* (stream) at the back of the structure.

Portal

The chief reason why the monks had the main entrance to their church so lavishly decorated was most likely its somewhat concealed and gloomy situation. The majority of researchers have attributed the work to the Buon family of sculptors.

The luxuriant and sumptuous acanthus leaves of the pointed Gothic arch and the

Santo Stefano

Like many of Venice's Gothic ecclesiastical buildings, this church belonged to an order of mendicant monks, the Augustinian hermits. Although it was founded in 1294, the present building dates primarily from the 14th century. The simple, almost unornamented brick architecture is typical of the mendicants' churches in Venice at this time. It is, however, unusual that it is not the facade of the building but its side that faces the large square which it overlooks. Complexities of land ownership and years of quarrels with neighboring landowners meant that the Augustinian hermits were unable to change the orientation of their

fine rope spiral which surround the portal, are considered unusually fine examples of stonecarving.

Interior

The 14th and 15th century interior of the church gives us an excellent impression of a richly decorated Late Gothic Venetian church, combined with the original simple mendicant style. Some of the altars in the side aisles are from a later period. The original interior was somewhat darker than the present one, as large insulated windows have since been installed which make the wooden roof vault with its magnificent ceiling and wallpaintings clearly visible.

The unusual ceiling is shaped like an inverted ship's hull. Also notable are the frescoes on the walls, which, like the ceiling, date from the first half of the 15th century. The brick wall of the upper section was covered with a diamond-shaped pattern, but painted in almost the same color as the brickwork it covered. The pointed arches separating the side aisles from the main aisle, and the curved three-part gable of the ceiling at the choir end were painted grey to look like stone. Even the columns have been included in the red and white color scheme. They alternate between red broccatello from Verona and white Greek marble. As if the natural color of the stone were not decorative enough, the fine capitals are also gilded and painted.

Teatro La Fenice

The opera house's name, which means Phoenix Theater, seems to have proved itself. Like the mythological bird which constantly re-emerges from its ashes, La Fenice has resurrected itself twice in its 200-year history. On January 29, 1996, a fire destroyed the theater which had opened in 1792. After it burned down for the first time in 1836, the Venetians had decided to rebuild it "come era e dove era" (as it was and where it was). This motto, which had been used again with reference to the Campanile di San Marco when it was rebuilt early this century, was revived after heated discussions, as a call to arms for the reconstruction of Venice's famous opera house. Thanks to huge donations from all over the world, but particularly to

the efforts of the Venetians themselves, the theater was reopened in December 2003.

Ateneo Veneto (Scuola di San Girolamo, or Scuola di San Fantin)

This building was originally constructed in 1592–1604 for the Scuola di San Girolamo and the Scuola di Santa Maria della Giustizia, which was also called the Scuola di San Fantin. The community, known as the Brotherhood of the Good Death, accompanied prisoners condemned to death on their final journey. For this not only were the brothers given donations by the general population, but also a certain sum from the Venetian state.

When the Scuola was dissolved in 1806, the Società Veneziana di Medicina, founded under the Napoleonic regime, occupied the building. This medical society soon merged with other scholarly associations into a single organization called the Ateneo Veneto. It still meets regularly today, and invites the public to visit the rooms of the former Scuola. The paintings on the interior are by Jacopo Palma il Giovane and late 17th century artists.

Museo Fortuny
(Palazzo Pesaro degli Orfei)

The aristocratic Pesaro family built this palazzo on the Campo San Beneto in the 15th century, demonstrating that magnificent palazzi are not only found on the Grand Canal. The fine window arcades with their ogee arches are an impressive example of the Venetian Gothic, which many builders still adhered to in the 15th century. In 1786 the Società Filarmonica L'Apollinea had its headquarters here. In front of the palazzo is a raised area, under which the well is situated. The original well rim is still preserved to this day.

Interior

Mariano Fortuny y Madrazo (1871–1949), the son of a famous salon painter from Madrid, specialized in painting for the stage and on fabrics. At the beginning of the 20th century he acquired the Palazzo Pesaro in Venice, which since 1956 has housed a museum for his unusual fabrics, stage backdrops, and paintings. The Late Gothic palazzo provided exactly the right ambience in which to receive his illustrious clientele. These included actresses and dancers, as well as American heiresses who were able to feel like Renaissance princesses in Fortuny's expensive silk dresses. At any rate, they did not have to suffer the discomfort of most dresses from that age. Fortuny's creations were part of the Jugendstil and Art Deco movements. They consisted of incredibly soft, flowing garments that, as original Fortunys, still fetch enormous sums at international fashion auctions.

Palazzo Contarini del Bovolo   Staircase

If you look over the rooftops of Venice from a vantage point such as the Campanile di San Marco, you will easily distinguish a tower-like building whose white arches can be seen at a great distance. This is the staircase tower of the Palazzo Contarini del Bovolo, which has been painstakingly restored in the last few years. External staircases were common in Venetian houses of the 14th and 15th centuries but, even at the time it was built, the staircase of the Palazzo Contarini was unusual due to its size and form. To distinguish it from the other 24 Contarini palazzi in the city, the building was called "del Bovolo" ("snail" in Venetian) due to the spiral staircase. After the 16th century, staircases were usually placed inside houses, and frequently made into sumptuous, richly ornamented reception areas. The staircase tower of the Palazzo Contarini is connected to the main structure via a side addition, which adds four loggias to the building. Loggias were favorite places for Venetians during the summer, particularly if they led out onto a small garden. It is common to find many inner courtyards with loggias leading to an external staircase, but none as magnificent as this.

The spiral staircase was built in 1499 by Giovanni Candi. Arches of white Istrian stone provide the four stories of the staircase with illumination. Combined with the balustrades, which are similarly supported on graceful columns, they are prominent structural elements.

San Salvatore

This church (built 1507–34) is an impressive example of Venetian High Renaissance architecture, which relies mainly on traditional Venetian forms. The architects, Giorgio Spavento and Tullio Lombardo, used a cruciform dome design similar to that of San Marco. The three main domes are arranged in a row above the nave, with each supported by four columns. Each column of the main domes has a pendant, which appears to half vanish into the outside wall as a pilaster. The small square spaces resulting from this have again been vaulted by smaller domes, producing an alternating spatial structure which looks like an infinitely extendible modular system. The old cruciform dome church layout was successfully revived by Mauro Codussi in the 15th century. The fact that the structural elements have been painted gray for emphasis indicates that his work was studied by 16th century builders. Through a glass plate in front of the high altar, the old burial chambers beneath the church can be seen. On the high altar itself is Titian's *Transfiguration of Christ*, which covers a precious gilded silver reredos from the 14th century. This is only revealed between the 3rd to 15th of August and on feast days.

senting Hope in the right-hand niche is believed to have been carved by Sansovino himself, as is Charity on the right. Some, however, believe the latter to be the work of one of his colleagues.

Jacopo Sansovino: Tomb of Doge Francesco Venier, 1555-61
Marble

Caterina Cornaro, the queen of Cyprus, who died in 1510 and whose remains were moved to San Salvatore in the late 16th century, is probably the most renowned person buried there. A more magnificent tomb was built for Doge Francesco Venier, designed by Jacopo Sansovino, the architect of the Libreria.

Architecture and sculpture seem to play equal parts in this monument, whose colored marble and gold leaf produce a spectacular effect. The sculptural aspect of the tomb is quite restrained, although Sansovino ran a renowned sculpture workshop. Scholars disagree as to which figures he executed himself and which he assigned to colleagues and students. The lying figure of the doge, and the relief above it depicting Piety with the doge kneeling before her, are ascribed to Alessandro Vittoria, who was Sansovino's most skillful student. The figure repre-

Copy after Giovanni Bellini: Supper at Emmaus
Oil on wood, 260 × 375 cm

Titian: Annunciation, 1560–65
Oil on canvas, 405 x 235 cm

This horizontal painting was previously believed to be the work of Giovanni Bellini. It was never disputed because of its large format. Stylistically, however, it belongs to a stage later in the 16th century after Bellini's death in 1516. Today it is considered to be an old copy of a painting by Giovanni Bellini from around 1490.

The *Annunciation* in San Salvatore is a fascinating late work by Titian, painted some ten years before his death. The artist depicts the Annunciation as a vision or mystic miracle, and transposes the original textual source into his visual language. The open space in which Mary is sitting is denoted by architectural elements, such as the columns on the left, and furnishings, such as the desk and the vase, on the right. The miracle of the Annunciation fills the entire room as a material apparition. The angel is not just stepping into a fine living room, as was the case in many paintings of the previous century. Here the Archangel Gabriel, who has come to announce to Mary that she is to bear the Son of God, seems to be part of a large, multicolored cloud, from which, on closer inspection, countless figures of angels gradually emerge.

The highly realistic glass vase before the Virgin contains flowers which seem to glow like fire. This is a reference to the story in the Old Testament of the burning bush, which Moses saw in the desert. The flaming bunch of flowers that does not incinerate is a prediction of the birth of Christ to the Virgin Mary.

Sestieri San Polo and Santa Croce

Santa Croce and San Polo

The small districts of Santa Croce and San Polo contain popular residential areas. San Polo is the most densely populated of Venice's districts. Walking through its narrow, crooked streets and small squares, one is constantly surprised by picturesque views. On the other hand, Santa Croce includes districts built as recently as the 19th and 20th centuries on newly created islands. Accordingly, apartments here are often more comfortable than in the older houses. San Polo also contains the Rialto, and thus the present-day market area and former busy mercantile center of the city. It was in this focus of financial power that the Venetian economic authorities, who supervised trade and levied taxes, had their offices. From medieval to modern times, the Rialto has also functioned as a banking center, where the financiers and money changers conducted their business. The Rialto was, naturally, the place where most foreigners were to be found, and so the prostitutes also settled nearby, as evidenced by frank street names such as Ponte delle Tette (Bridge of Breasts).

Scuola Grande di
San Giovanni Evangelista, p. 26

The Frari, Titian: Assumption
the Virgin Mary, 1516–18, p. 2

San Giacomo dell'Orio
(interior), p. 263

Scuola Grande di San Rocco,
Jacopo Tintoretto: Miracle of the Brazen
Serpent, 1575–77, p. 256

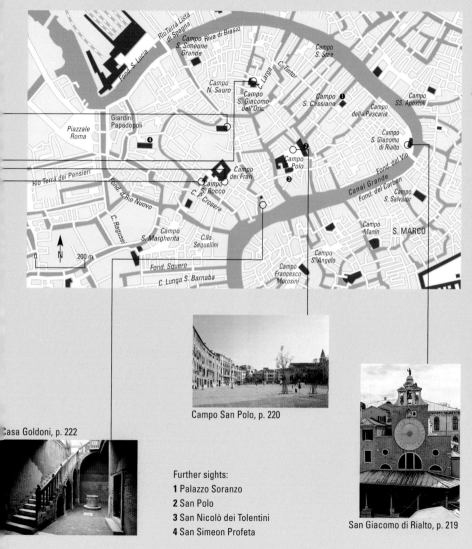

Campo San Polo, p. 220

Casa Goldoni, p. 222

San Giacomo di Rialto, p. 219

Further sights:
1 Palazzo Soranzo
2 San Polo
3 San Nicolò dei Tolentini
4 San Simeon Profeta

Rialto

Rialto (from the Latin *rivo alto* or "high bank") was one of the first areas of Venice to be settled. As the name suggests, it rose high above the waters of the lagoon. This, combined with the Grand Canal, a deep waterway through which even relatively large ships were able to navigate, made it an ideal location for the transshipment of goods.

In the Middle Ages it was the center of Venetian trade. Many ships of the time would travel up the Grand Canal and moor directly alongside the Rialto in order to unload their choice cargo: shimmering silks, rare spices, and other such treasures from the Orient. The place bustled with merchants, brokers, credit negotiators, tax collectors, as well as curious onlookers. Something of the lively activity of the time can still be experienced when Venetians go to buy their daily provisions at the vegetable and fish market. Against the unique backdrop of the Grand Canal, and with all the colors and smells, it is an experience not to be missed.

San Giacomo di Rialto

This small domed basilica in a cruciform shape is one of the oldest places of worship in the city: the foundation stone was laid by 429. Its facade still displays the characteristic porch which, in the past, many Venetian churches possessed. Today it is the only remaining of its kind. In former times, the money changers and bankers would have sat beneath this portico and all around the small square, waiting for their international clientele. Banking transactions were carried out in the open air, monitored by the authorities. The Venetian bankers were famous for their successful credit businesses. It was here that the idea of bills of exchange emerged: clients would go from one banker to another with slips of paper upon which various sums of money were recorded. The impressive clock has been telling merchants the time since 1410.

Campo San Polo

Unlike the Piazza San Marco, all other squares in Venice are referred to by the word *campo*, meaning 'field' or 'meadow.' In fact, most squares were unpaved until well into the modern era, and if not covered with trees, they took the form of a maintained meadow. The Campo San Polo, which takes its name from the neighboring church of St. Paul (*Polo* in the Venetian dialect), was no exception. The main road from the Rialto to the train station runs by here. There has been a church on the site since the 9th century. The present building, dating from the 15th century, was extensively renovated in the early 19th century. It contains paintings and altarpieces by Tintoretto, Giovanni Battista, and Domenico Tiepolo. Although the Campo San Polo is the second largest open space in Venice after the Piazza San Marco, brick paving was not laid here until 1494. This typically Venetian style of paving, with its warm red coloring, gave the paved squares a very different, warmer character than the gray flagstones you see today.

Joseph Heintz the Younger:
Bull Run on the Campo San Polo, c. 1625
Oil on canvas
Museo Correr, Venice

As with other large squares, the Campo San Polo was the scene of public festivals and entertainments of all types. These included the bull run, which enjoyed great popularity in Venice. The German painter Joseph Heintz the Younger (c. 1600 – after 1678), who probably resided in Venice as of 1625, portrayed such an event in one of his paintings. The crowd would hunt the bulls to complete exhaustion with dogs, finally killing them by chopping off their heads. This cruel spectacle, which was also dangerous for the bystanders, continued until 1802, when it was banned following a catastrophic accident in which a wooden grandstand collapsed causing many viewers to die.

Joseph Heintz depicted everyday Venetian life in numerous paintings. He also provided an exact representation of the city's architecture, including the Campo San Polo. On the right of his painting, the double Palazzo Soranzo, Gothic in style can be seen (left: a photograph showing the square from the other side). The appearance of the palazzo remains unchanged to the present day, except for small details. Up to the 17th century a waterway or *rio* ran along one side of the square in front of the palazzo and neighboring houses, as can be clearly seen.

Casa Goldoni

Also to be found in the Sestiere San Polo is the birthplace of the famous Venetian dramatist and comic playwright Carlo Goldoni (1707–93). In his plays, which had their origins in the commedia dell'arte, he gave an unrivaled depiction of life in 18th century Venice.

The Late Gothic Palazzo Centani-Rizzi today serves as a memorial to this great playwright, who was born in Venice on February 26, 1707. Commemorative plays are performed here. The palazzo also houses the theatrical department of the Museo Civico and an institute for theater studies. It is well worth a visit, even for those who are not experts in the theater, principally because of Goldoni, but also because of the palazzo itself. Virtually nowhere else can the well-preserved inner courtyard of a Venetian residence be seen. It is not certain whether the paving is actually the 15th century original, but the herringbone pattern of the bricks is typical of the period. The same is true of the staircase running around two sides of the courtyard, resting on ascending pointed arches. Also preserved in the small inner courtyard is a particularly fine wellhead or *vera da pozzo*, such as was common in Venetian residences of this type. Here, water would be drawn from the cisterns below the courtyard.

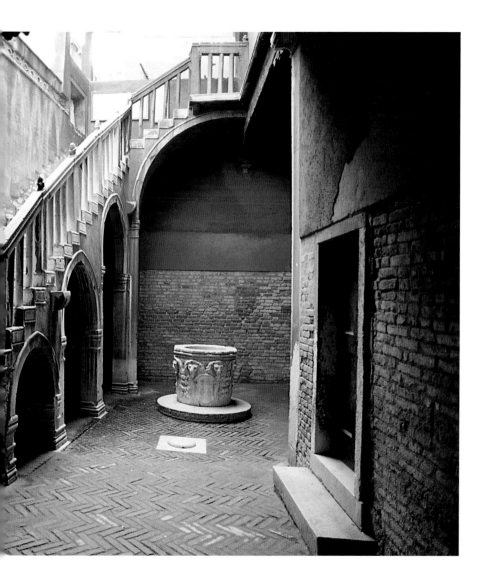

Water in a city surrounded by the sea

Few visitors to Venice today consider how difficult it must have been in centuries past to
obtain the water people needed to survive.
Many a castaway has died of thirst by drinking
seawater, and the same problem presented
itself in Venice. Like a ship at sea, it was surrounded by water but had great difficulty in
obtaining drinking water.

Even in its early days, the needs of the city
could scarcely be met using wells, which could
only be sunk in a very few places on the highest
islands. From the time of the first settlement,
therefore, people began to collect rainwater in
cisterns. Drinking water was also brought by
ship from the mainland, since both the cisterns
and the few wells were in constant danger of

*Wellhead, vera da pozzo, in the inner courtyard
of the Ca' d'Oro, 14th century*

Diagram of a Venetian well

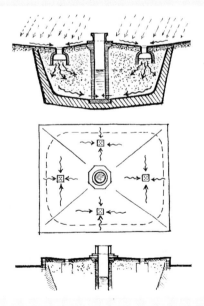

Courtyard of the Ca' Lion-Morosini, with well, 13th century

being flooded and thus rendered unusable. The well installations were perfected over the course of time.

The design of these water-collecting basins had to ensure that they caught as much rain-water as possible, that no seawater got into them, even during a flood, and that the drinking water was not polluted by any other means. Venetian wells, as they have evolved since medieval times, are perfectly suited to these tasks, and they are complicated and costly installations. Every suitable open space was used for obtaining water. Most water was collected by paving the area around the cisterns to the water inlets and sloping it towards several drains. In addition, gutters of flat stone were sometimes used to channel water into the openings, which were positioned around the well. These open gutters and drain inlets can still be seen in most squares, but you

may not realize what lies beneath. The water does not run directly into the cisterns, but passes first through an ingenious filtration system. First of all, a deep pit was dug, often encompassing the whole area of the public square, and almost always the entire extent of a palazzo courtyard. This excavation was lined with clay or loam, and then filled with sand. Into the sand was set a brick well shaft, which opened out just before the layer of clay. Beneath the rainwater drain inlets were shallow, walled chambers, sealed at the bottom with unpointed natural stone. These allowed both large amounts of water to be stored when it rained and water to seep into the sand. Only when there was sufficient water pressure, i.e. when enough water was stored in the sand contained in the impermeable loam tank, did the water rise up into the well. Having passed through the entire layer of sand, the water had thus been purified.

The city wells played a crucial role in construction planning, since it was extremely difficult to relocate an existing well without demolishing and rebuilding the entire house. Once installed, therefore, the wells determined the ground plan of all future construction work. In order to collect as much water as possible, the entire courtyard of private houses had to be paved. No flower beds, not even a plant pot, could be allowed to compete with the cisterns for water. This explains why Venetian courtyards were generally neither covered nor

Well in the Campo Sant'Angelo. The campo has clearly been raised in order to prevent water entering the openings of the well.

227

planted. Cistern wells, their shaft heads crowned with stone (the *vera da pozzo*), were formerly to be found in almost every square, and also in the palazzi of the nobles and large housing developments. Sometimes the area of the square around the well would be elevated to prevent the entry of seawater during flooding. This can still be seen in many locations today, e.g. in the Campo San Trovaso or the Campo Sant'Angelo.

The heads of public wells were covered and locked. A town official, responsible for monitoring water use, would open them up for the public only at certain times. This was done not only to regulate water use, but also to prevent pollution of the water. In previous centuries, contamination of the wells was a constant threat. In times of war it was (and is still today in other regions of the world) a dangerous means of terrorizing the civilian population. People's fear was so great that accusations of having contaminated a well were a popular way of stirring up feeling against a particular person or group of people, be it witches, Jews, or heretics. That could never happen in Venice, however, because the water supply, like so many other matters, was regulated and controlled by the State to the satisfaction and for the safety of the people. Nevertheless, the State was not the sole provider of wells. Wealthy private individuals would have wells built in the squares where they lived, for the general good. These would usually be decorated with the noble benefactor's coat of arms. Even with the regulation of the water supply, one problem still faced the Venetians for centuries, and it was only solved

under Napoleon. The cemeteries were often adjacent to public squares used for water collection. During floods the water would force the corpses upwards and, when the waters receded, the decomposing bodies got into the wells, contaminating them. It was not until 1807 and the filling of the canal between San Michele and San Cristoforo della Pace that a separate cemetery island was created.

The *vere da pozzo*, the stone heads of well shafts, were a familiar sight on the *campi* of Venice until the beginning of the 20th century. They were frequently decorated with ornamental stonework. A particularly fine example dating from the 16th century can still be seen in the little square facing the side aisle of Santi Giovanni e Paolo. Seeming superfluous after the introduction of a central water supply, the most beautiful wellheads have now disappeared from the majority of squares, their value as small works of art not acknowledged. Along with wellheads from private houses, many of these testaments to Venetian life now lead a meager existence, perhaps as goldfish ponds in the villas of the rich. A few have ended up in museums, where their original function as an object of everyday use takes far greater precedence over their character as a piece of sculpture. It is only in recent years that there has been a move toward preserving the remaining few specimens in their original locations, as living monuments to the past. Only there can they convey to locals and tourists not only something of the everyday culture of the city of Venice, but also the fact that ingenious technology and artistic sensibility are not necessarily mutually exclusive.

16th century wellhead outside the side aisle of the church of Santi Giovanni e Paolo

The Frari (Santa Maria Gloriosa dei Frari or Santa Maria Assunta)

The Franciscan friars arrived in Venice in 1222, shortly after their order was founded by St. Francis. They soon became known to the Venetians as "I frari" (the Venetian form of *frati*, "brothers"). Around 1250, they began the construction of a church, the forerunner of the present-day Frari. Like the Dominicans, the Franciscans did not withdraw to isolated monasteries: their calling was above all to care for and support the population. The two orders sometimes became competitors in these activities, and so it was sensible to allocate them plots of land in districts which were a good distance from one another. (The Dominican church is Santi Giovanni e Paolo).

So many people flocked to hear the Franciscans preach that the church was soon too small. In 1340, work began to enlarge the building and make it one of largest churches in the city. It was completed in 1445, a century later.

The Frari is a brick construction, like all medieval Venetian churches, with elements of white *Pietra d'Istria* enlivening the effect of the bricks. The exterior appears very plain, therefore, but a second look reveals many architectural refinements, such as the rich, graduated, curved pediments, the surrounding arch friezes, filigree tracery windows, and the finely profiled window frames.

and altarpieces donated by religious orders or rich families, also bears witness to the popularity of the Franciscans.

The term "preaching barn," which was coined for the huge, unadorned churches of the men-dicant orders, is certainly not applicable to the Frari. The friars' choir is preserved in the nave, and is unique in present-day Venice. It was in this area, enclosed by marble choir screens and separated from the lay worshippers, that the brothers would sit during services. Only their singing and their prayers could be heard by the faithful.

Interior

The three-aisled Frari church is T-shaped. Seven apses form chapels adjoining the southwest transept. Six smooth, circular pillars of cut stone allow the eyes to wander into each of the slightly lower side aisles, giving the church the spatial characteristics of a hall. In addition, the painted wooden beams stabilize the wide cross vaulting in the nave. In this way, the church afforded sufficient room and an unobstructed view to the crowds who gathered for services. The magnificent interior decoration of the church, with its numerous works of art

The Frari

Titian: Assumption, 1516–18, p. 242

Titian: Madonna di Ca'Pesaro, 1519–26, p. 244

Other items of interest:
1 Tomb of Titian
2 Tomb of Doge Nicolò Tron
3 Tomb of Claudio Monteverdi, altar by Alvise Vivarini and Marco Basaiti (1503)
4 Tomb of Antonio Canova

0   5

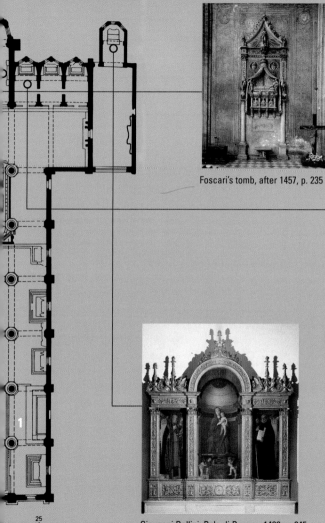

Foscari's tomb, after 1457, p. 235

Giovanni Bellini: Pala di Pesaro, 1488, p. 245

25

Donatello: John the Baptist, 1438, p. 243

Chancel

The chancel is decorated with rows of delicate tracery windows set one above the other over two stories. The Frari church was built with its high altar in the southwest. It was not built in the usual east-facing position as a result of construction difficulties presented by the site. In the early evening in particular, when the sunlight slants through the windows, the fine lace-like patterns in the windows create an especially beautiful effect. Built into the side walls of the chancel are two magnificent tombs.

Antonio and Paolo Bregno:
Tomb of Doge Francesco Foscari,
after 1457
Marble

Along the right-hand wall of the sanctuary lies the tomb of Francesco Foscari, one of the most powerful and important doges in the history of Venice. The proud Foscari was in office from 1423 to 1457, when he was forced out of office because people feared he might set himself up as a dictator. Only after his death did the Republic celebrate him as one of their greatest. His memorial, combining Gothic style with that of the Early Renaissance, was commissioned by his nephew from Antonio and Paolo Bregno and completed after 1457, the year in which Foscari died. It shows the deceased surrounded by female figures personifying the virtues of a ruler: wisdom, justice, moderation, and power. On the opposite wall is the huge tomb of Doge Nicolò Tron (1471–73), a masterpiece of the Venetian Early Renaissance by Antonio Rizzo. The Gothic touches still displayed by Foscari's tomb have been set aside here in favor of classically oriented forms.

A simple grave for a great musician: Claudio Monteverdi (1567–1643)

In the Frari, before the altar in the chapel of St. Ambrose, a memorial stone is set into the floor. There are often flowers on the grave, and a simple inscription informs the visitor that this is the last resting place of Claudio Monteverdi, one of the greatest Italian composers. His works were the first in Europe to blend vocal and instrumental elements with equal weight, without simply substituting an instrument for the human voice. He was also the first to emphasize the solo voice, paving the way for opera in its modern form.

Like all composers of his time, he primarily devoted his efforts to the madrigal, an elaborate song form which pervades his work from his first book of madrigals as a 20-year-old to his eighth and final book, which he published himself five years before his death. The madrigal, a song based on lyric texts, was the most important form of chamber music in the 16th century. The main goal of early examples was to interweave in an intricate manner usually five voices in different registers, thus giving the text a harmonious sound. Monteverdi took the existing polyphonic form, which was based on the motet, and developed it into cantata-like pieces or even concertos for voices, in which solo voices were married with instruments. His harmonies became increasingly chromatic, i.e. they made use of notes a semitone away from those of the diatonic scale. He was also not afraid to employ dissonance.

In addition to the madrigals, he also wrote ten operas, only three of which have been preserved in their entirety.

Monteverdi liked to combine different musical forms. Madrigals and instrumental passages can be found alongside recitatives

Domenico Fetti: Claudio Monteverdi, c.1623, oil on canvas, Gallerie dell'Accademia, Venice

and arias. This lent his operas diversity and vivacity and made every one of them a sweeping success.

Solely his sacred works, to which he only really turned during the second half of his life in Venice, remained rooted in existing principles of composition. Many of them display an "old-fashioned" polyphonic harmony. One reason for this may be that his sacred works were written for San Marco, and that a significant proportion of existing church music had been written by great composers such as Adrian Willaert and Andrea Gabrieli specifically for the acoustics of the Basilica, with its domes and galleries. Any music lover who has the chance to hear a polyphonic composition by Monteverdi or one of his predecessors performed in San Marco should on no account miss the opportunity. In his other works, however, Monteverdi consistently followed the "seconda maniera," the new style which also characterized his madrigals. It is distinguished by virtuoso passages for solo voices, a rich instrumental accompaniment, and musical interpretation according to the emotions of the text.

Although Monteverdi enjoyed his greatest success in Venice, he was not a Venetian by birth. Born in Cremona in 1567, he came into contact with Venetian music at an early age through his teacher Marcantonio Ingegneri. Originally from Verona, Ingegneri was *maestro di capella* at Cremona Cathedral and a solid supporter of Venetian polyphony. Following his musical studies and first successes, Monteverdi entered the service of Duke Vincenzo I of Mantua in 1590, where he started as a lute player in the court ensemble.

Start of the "Possente Spirito" in the third act of Monteverdi's first opera, Orfeo (1607), published in 1609

When, in 1595, Vincenzo obeyed a summons from Emperor Rudolph II to aid Habsburg troops against the Turks, Monteverdi was appointed leader of the ensemble that accompanied the duke. Despite a continual lack of funds, a military expedition befitting the duke's status encompassed not only three companies of horse-archers, but also a retinue of pages, scribes, doctors, cooks, butlers, and musicians. The expedition appeared more like a pleasure trip, taking in Innsbruck, Vienna, and Prague, where grand banquets afforded people the

Interior view of San Marco

opportunity of hearing the artistry of the duke's ensemble. When they finally arrived in Vysehrad, however, where the emperor's troops were laying siege to the citadel held by the Turks, the duke and a large number of his troops fell ill, and the military expedition ended with an immediate return to Mantua. As for Monteverdi, it became clear during this undertaking that there was one detail of life at the Mantuan court which was bound to continually hamper his future musical creativity. As members of the court, artists such as Monteverdi occupied a social standing somewhere between the ordinary employees and the noble courtiers. A rigid code of behavior made life in the presence of the ruler an eternal scholarly game, and artists were seen less as employees than as a members of court society. However, there was a world of difference between appearances and reality. Above all, this meant that it was made very difficult for artists to ask for their salaries to be paid when money was tight, which it always was in Mantua at the time of Monteverdi. Nevertheless, the necessary elegant clothes and other equipment that members of court were expected to have for trips abroad had to be financed from their own pockets. Added to this were the numerous intrigues to which everyone at court was constantly subjected. In any case, Monteverdi had to wait a long time before obtaining the post he desired as leader of the court ensemble. He was so successful that he attracted the most virulent hostility. One priest from Bologna wrote a polemical treatise vehemently condemning the new style of music developed by Monteverdi, with its dissonance and strongly accentuated solo voices. At first, Monteverdi was extremely hurt by this, but was vindicated by his successes. At the Mantuan court, he continued to wait for his promotion. In 1599 he was consoled with a position similar to the one he had occupied in 1595, when he accompanied the duke on a trip of several months taking the waters in Spa. This at least gave him the opportunity to acquaint himself with the new declamatory style of singing used by the French composers, which he was probably the first to introduce to Italy. When, in 1601, he was finally given the long-awaited post as leader of the court ensemble, his situation did not really improve. He was continually having to wait to receive payment for his music, and to beg for money in the most degrading of circumstances. The duke's never-fulfilled promise of future payments often had to suffice to secure him credit to obtain items for his day-to-day needs. The constant disputes over money and reputation at court, together with the damp climate in Mantua, took a heavy toll on his health.

When his wife died in 1607, his situation seemed to become intolerable. Monteverdi fell seriously ill and returned to his father in Cremona, who strongly advised him not to go back to Mantua.

Nevertheless, Monteverdi was once more enticed by the duke's promises, and once again his health suffered badly. When Duke Vincenzo died, he left the State's finances in utter ruins. This economic situation led his son Francesco, the new duke, to dismiss all members of the court that he considered unnecessary, including the now 45-year-old leader of the court ensemble, Monteverdi. One of the most famous

Title page from Orfeo. 1609 edition

L'ORFEO
FAVOLA IN MVSICA
DA CLAVDIO MONTEVERDI
RAPPRESENTATA IN MANTOVA

Anno 1607 & nouamente data in luce

AL SERENISSIMO SIGNOR
D. FRANCESCO GONZAGA
Prencipe di Mantoua, & di Monferato, &c

In Venetia Appresso Ricciardo Amadino

M D C I X.

composers in Italy was literally thrown out on the street. Had it not been for his elderly father in Cremona, Monteverdi would have had nowhere to live. News of his dismissal spread like wildfire throughout Italy, and the music-loving Venetians saw their chance. They made the destitute ex-courtier what was an almost unbelievable offer. As the new conductor of the Capella di San Marco, he was promised the princely salary of 400 ducats, free accommodation, and other privileges. Monteverdi was now able to experience Venetian freedom, so vastly different from the artificial atmosphere of a royal court. Not without good reason had other artists, such as Titian, refused to exchange their lives in Venice for any court in the world. Not only did the Venetians pay on time, they also allowed their "divine Claudio," as they enthusiastically called him, to continue to accept other commissions. As soon as the financial situation had been consolidated, the Mantuan court also made new approaches to the famous composer. It is a joy to read in his letters the cold indifference with which Monteverdi was now able to treat his former masters, thanks to his secure position in Venice, although he did indeed continue to work for them. His financial situation was now settled once and for all, and the Venetians, who were exceedingly knowledgeable and enthusiastic about music, venerated "their" Monteverdi. There was no offer tempting enough to entice the composer away from Venice.

It is probably true to say that the last 39 years of Monteverdi's life, which once again bore the stamp of great creative power, were the happiest and most peaceful for him. When he eventually died in his 84th year, the doge and the government honored him with a solemn service in San Marco. The State had only ever held such a ceremony for one other artist, namely Titian, and it was in the same church in which the famous painter and numerous doges were interred that Monteverdi found his own final resting place. Venetians honor the great musician, just as they do Titian, because through his work, he too made a contribution to the fame and glory of the "Serenissima."

View of Mantua, 1575

Titian: Assumption of the Virgin, 1516–18
Oil on wood, 690 x 380 cm

The vast high altar with Titian's depiction of the *Assumption of the Virgin Mary* immediately catches your attention as you enter the church. The imaginary triangle formed by the bright red colors of the robes of the Apostles, Mary, and God makes Mary's assumption to heaven look physical. Only in the church itself is it possible to sense how precisely the artist had attuned his painting to its surroundings. When the work was finally unveiled in 1518, it immediately caused the greatest astonishment and instant rejection, which quickly turned into fascination. This was something that had not been seen in Venice before. Unheard of were not only the beautiful Virgin Mary, but above all, the Apostles watching the Assumption. Their gestures, expressions, and movements all express wonder, shock, and religious ecstasy at the prodigious scene above their heads. God's golden heaven is separated from the blue sky of earth by a wreath of clouds and angels bearing Mary aloft. Heaven appears to open like a golden dome. Titian's *Assumption* is a masterpiece of the High Renaissance in Venice.

Cappella dei Fiorentini

To the right beside the presbytery is the Florentine Chapel, which has been there since the 19th century. Previously, perhaps as early as 1436, its altar was in the left side aisle. 1436 was the year of an agreement with the Franciscan friars on the establishment of a Florentine chapel. Interestingly, the Florentines seem to have had an altar before, and perhaps even after 1436, in the Dominican church of Santi Giovanni e Paolo. It was not until 1443 that the Council of Ten permitted the chapel's transfer to the Frari. It is unfortunately not known what exactly moved the Florentine brotherhood to take this step.

Donatello: John the Baptist, 1438
Wood, height: 141 cm

The monochrome wooden figure of John the Baptist was created for the Florentine Chapel. Since the 16th century it had been regarded as a work dating from the last year of Donatello's stay in Padua (1443–53). The emaciated figure of John the Baptist, with his large hands and his non-idealized features, are in keeping with the artist's later works. When the figure was being restored during the 1970s, however, the year 1438 was found carved into its base.

commemorates a naval victory over the Turks, at which point Pesaro was commander of the papal fleet. The fact that Titian took the unprecedented step of moving the Virgin Mary from the center of the picture to the right side was determined by the interior layout of the church. When you approach the painting from the main entrance, the Virgin Mary is visible from afar. In this way Titian created a dynamic composition, which also has connotative dimensions. The patron kneels directly in front of the Madonna, who is facing him and St. Peter with the same attention, while the heavenly figures communicate only indirectly with the rest of the Pesaro family.

Giovanni Bellini: Pala di Pesaro, 1488
Oil on wood

Giovanni Bellini executed this altarpiece (*pala*), signed 1488, for the many-branched Pesaro family. It is located in the sacristy, which used to serve as the Pesaro Chapel. The Madonna and the saints are still presented, as was usual in earlier times, on separate panels of the triptych, yet in the same space. The altarpiece thus has a very realistic effect, also achieved by the powerful figures of the saints in their voluminous garments. They made an impression on Albrecht Dürer, who praised Bellini as the best of Venice's painters. Dürer used the figures as models for his *Four Apostles*.

Titian: Madonna di Ca' Pesaro, 1519–26
Oil on canvas, 385 x 270 cm

With his *Madonna di Ca' Pesaro*, Titian created a further masterpiece for the Frari. The donor, Jacopo Pesaro, wearing a black brocade gown, is kneeling before the Virgin Mary. On the other side are other members of his family, with St. Antony of Padua above them. Jacopo is depicted together with a knight bearing a flag with the coat of arms of the Pesaro family and of Pope Alexander VI. The banner

Scuola Grande di San Marco, late 15th century

The Scuole: more than just fine buildings and insurance

An observant visitor to Venice will notice numerous sumptuous buildings which are neither churches nor the seats of wealthy families. These are the assembly halls of the *scuole*, brotherhoods of laymen which played an important role in the public life of the city-state. Such religious organizations of laymen existed in other Italian cities, although nowhere was their influence and importance as great as in Venice.

Although descended from the flagellant movement of the Middle Ages, displays of atonement like public whipping played a very minor role, if any, in the lives of the *scuole*. They were religious associations which met for prayer sessions, collecting money for good causes, and above all for holding masses for their members that were sick, dying, or dead. In a time when people lived in existential fear of punishment in the afterlife for sins committed in this life, the *scuole* played an important role. For only donations and good deeds were capable of alleviating the punishment that awaited you. People who could not afford to make donations to foundations or masses on their own were able, through the combined efforts of the confraternities, to fulfill these important religious duties. Being a member of a *scuola* meant that you were secured a place in the afterlife.

Most *scuole* were based on a trade or a region, i.e. on a particular craftsmen's guild or associations of Florentines, Levantines, Germans, and so on. In addition there were the *scuole grandi*, charitable organizations with more than 500 members, in which membership was a great honor. They had fine assembly halls, in contrast with the smaller and less prosperous *scuole*, which had to make do with a modest building or even just an altar in a church. The smaller *scuole* limited their charitable activities primarily to their own members.

Members of the Scuola Grande di S. Giovanni Evangelista before the saint, 14th century, Scuola Grande di S. Giovanni Evangelista, Venice

In this way they secured their members not only in the afterlife, but also against eventualities in this life. Regional and trade-based *scuole* were the forerunners of modern employment insurance. The payments made by rich and poor members according to their wealth, which the *scuole* invested with profit, were used to support elderly and sick members or their widows and children. A typically Venetian feature of these *scuole* was appointing a substitute for galley duty. Venetian gal-

leys were rowed not by slaves, but by the Venetians themselves. In theory, every parish had the duty to provide a certain number of oarsmen in case of war. But people were able to avoid this duty if they could name a replacement, who was paid a certain sum of money. During the Middle Ages, when the Venetians were mainly fishermen and mariners, this system worked. This changed, however, when, with the country's growing wealth in the 13th century and after the great plague during

Gentile Bellini: Members of the Scuola Grande di San Giovanni Evangelista in a procession in the Piazza San Marco (detail), 1496, Gallerie dell'Accademia, Venice

the 14th century, an increasing number of people from the mainland sought refuge in Venice. These new Venetians had nothing to do with the sea, but were craftsmen who were ill-suited to the hard maritime life. So the guilds took over the task of providing the necessary oarsmen, though it was usually the *scuole* attached to the guilds that actually paid for the substitutes. Another important function of the *scuole* was to provide the daughters of needy members with dowries to enable them to marry. This was the only way in which girls could be kept out of prostitution,

which might explain why exceptionally pretty women were given precedence in receiving such assistance.

The *scuole grandi* were the successors of the old flagellant brotherhoods. Due to their large memberships, which also included very wealthy Venetians, they gradually accumulated huge sums of money. Although aristocrats could be accepted into the *scuole*, they were always run by ordinary citizens, those 5-10% who did not need the support of the *scuole*. They were the only ones who could be appointed to the *banca*, or managing committee,

Assembly hall on the second floor of the Scuola Grande di San Rocco

of the brotherhood. In addition to religious and charitable works, the *scuole grandi* also provided another important service to the populace, namely, formal representation. The *banca* of the *scuole* were allowed to wear garments similar to those worn by senators and procurators. The *guardian grande*, or chairman, even wore clothes of office modeled on those of the doge. The *scuole* also participated in the big processions and public appearances of the city government.

The common efforts of the members of the *scuole* and the skilled management of their funds also allowed them to make their presence felt in another field that carried great status, architecture, and enabled them to decorate their assembly houses with valuable works of art. The *scuole* and, above all, the *scuole grandi* thus played an important role in the city's political system. It enabled people who were not members of the aristocracy to achieve a status which no other activity in the city permitted them. Not even the office of grand chancellor, which was the highest office open to an ordinary citizen of Venice (and this was only one post, requiring a very high level of education), could offer such splendor. Even the lowliest member of a brotherhood was thus able to feel part of a community which owned fine buildings and richly decorated altars. It is therefore not surprising that the *scuole grandi* were in strong competition with one another.

Such rivalry sometimes almost led to the ruin of a confraternity, as was the case with the Scuola Grande della Misericordia. In its striving to build a finer and more magnificent building than all the other *scuole*, it commissioned a new assembly hall in 1532, designed by the city's leading architect, Jacopo Sansovino, who was then engaged in redesigning the Piazzetta. The ambitious building project of the brotherhood turned out to be more than it could afford, however. Although the building was finished and decorated with fine frescoes on the inside, the exterior does not have the magnificent stone facade befitting such an impressive interior. To this day the exterior of the Scuola Grande della Misericordia's splendid building remains unfinished.

The incomplete building of the Scuola Grande della Misericordia

Scuola Grande di San Rocco

The Scuola was founded after an epidemic of the great plague in 1477, and it brought together two St. Roch confraternities. St. Roch, who was stricken by the plague himself while on a journey, was the saint to whom those infected by the plague prayed. In 1485, the Scuola succeeded in bringing the remains of their patron to Venice from the South of France. Possession of this significant relic meant that the brotherhood, which cared for the sick, became very popular and enjoyed a high income. By 1489, the Scuola was able to start building a church. In 1516, work began on the confraternity house, the front of which is lavishly decorated with colored stone. This magnificent facade had to compete with the Scuola Grande della Misericordia, which had designed its new building with free-standing columns. As a result, the Roch confraternity decided to remodel it in 1550 and commissioned the architect Gian Giacomo de Grigi to make the facade even more ornate and splendid.

Sala dell'Albergo

In terms of art history, the treasures to be found in the Scuola are hidden on the inside. Jacopo Tintoretto (1518–94) worked for the Scuola di San Rocco throughout his life, and completed almost all of its decoration. This was despite the fact that many members of the Scuola strongly disapproved of his style, some even sanctioning money for paintings with specific instructions that none of it was to be spent on works by Tintoretto.

Jacopo Tintoretto: St. Roch, 1564
Oil on canvas, 240 x 360 cm

Tintoretto's supporters continually pre-vailed, but it must also be said that he submitted offers which were impossible to resist. In 1564, when work began on the interior of the Scuola Grande di San Rocco, the Scuola invited a number of artists to submit drawings. While the others delivered sketches for the ceiling of the Sala dell'Albergo, the confra-ternity's board meeting room, Tintoretto completed an entire painting overnight and offered it to the Scuola free of charge. As a result, he became a member of the Scuola himself and was even elected to the *banca*, its inner committee. Since Tintoretto's earliest works are located in the Sala dell'Albergo, it is recommended that his works be viewed in the upper hall first.

Jacopo Tintoretto: Christ before Pilate, 1565
Oil on canvas, 515 x 380 cm

Jacopo Tintoretto: Crucifixion, 1565
Oil on canvas, 536 x 1224 cm

After submitting such an offer, it almost goes without saying that Tintoretto was also awarded the commission for the other paintings in the Sala dell'Albergo. The ceiling is devoted to the patron saint of the Scuola; to the Virtues; and finally, to Venice and the other major *scuole*. The walls are covered with scenes from the Passion of Christ. The painting *Christ before Pilate* is a little less dynamic than *Christ Carrying the Cross* or the breathtaking *Crucifixion*. Its effect lies mainly in the contrast between the figure of Christ standing calmly before Pilate with the unruly mob behind him. Wrapped in a bright white robe, all of the light in the picture appears to be concentrated on him, indeed to emanate from his form. The deep calm of Christ already extends beyond the Passion.

The *Crucifixion* is one of the few dated and signed paintings by Tintoretto. Although he continually produced new and unusual interpretations of this theme, this version is one of his most important. The wide format across the wall was quite unusual. Cleverly, the artist did not choose the moment of the Crucifixion itself, but instead the actual raising of the Cross, so that his picture does not require the same height as usual. The free space in the middle of the painting is a wide circular area, at the center of which is Christ's Cross. The crowd appears to be circling round the Cross. Tintoretto strengthens his composition with the heightened halo underneath the crossbeam.

Jacopo Tintoretto:
Miracle of the Brazen Serpent, 1575–77
Oil on canvas, 840 x 520 cm

When it was decided to commission paintings for the upper hall, Tintoretto again applied for this contract. Many of the members spoke out against him, but again he made the Scuola a very tempting offer. Instead of asking for a high fee, which would be payable in one installment by the

confraternity, he undertook to complete the decoration of the entire room for a lifelong stipend of 100 ducats. Again, this offer by Tintoretto, a crafty businessman, could hardly be refused. From 1575 to 1581 he worked on decorating the upper hall. The paintings on the ceiling are of scenes from the Old Testament and those on the walls depict instances from the New Testament. The three main paintings on the ceiling, namely the *Gathering of Manna*, *Moses Striking Water from the Rock* and the *Miracle of the Brazen Serpent*, depict the themes of feeding the hungry, giving drink to the thirsty, and looking after the sick, all charitable activities to which the Scuola was committed. The scenes from the life of Christ on the side walls add particular weight to this theme.

Over the course of time, the magnificent meeting hall continued to be furnished splendidly either by the wealthy Scuola itself or by donations from its well-to-do members. Thus, the Scuola acquired Titian's *Annuciation* of 1525 and two early works by Giovanni Battista Tiepolo, *Abraham with the Angels* and the *Banishment of Hagar*. The wooden paneling with scenes from the life of St. Roch by Giovanni Marchiori (1743) are some of the most important works of 18th century Venetian painting. The twelve caricatured figures are by Francesco Pianto il Giovane (late 1700s). The *Mercury* (up the stairs, on the right) holds a written scroll with explanations.

Jacopo Tintoretto: Mary Magdalene, 1583–87
Oil on canvas, 425 x 209 cm

The devotional room in the lower hall remained undecorated for a long time. The simple architectural design was sufficient for holding prayer services and meetings and for giving out alms. As was also the case in other *scuole*, the upper hall met the requirements for representation. It was only when the decoration of this was complete that thoughts were turned to decorating the lower hall with scenes from the life of the Virgin. The Sala Terrena was therefore the last room which Tintoretto painted, from 1583 to 1587. By then he had spent 20 years of his life in the service of the Scuola, the result being an impressive monument to both himself and his art.

The major role which light played in the later work of the artist is particularly evident in the paintings in the lower hall. In the narrow paintings of the two female hermits, Mary Magdalene and Mary of Egypt, individual parts of the landscape are lit as if with bolts of lightning. The lonely landscapes have a magical air. The deeply religious experience of the saints can thus be understood by the viewer. The grand staircase leading up from the first floor may have been erected 1544–46 by Antonio Abondi (known as Lo Scarpagnino), under the supervision of Jacopo Sansovino. It is an important forerunner of the splendid staircases of the Baroque period.

Jacopo Tintoretto: Flight into Egypt, 1583–87
Oil on canvas, 422 x 580 cm

The quality of Tintoretto's paintings in the lower hall is much disputed. Even his contemporaries accused him of being a hasty, careless painter. But, in addition to this, the composition of the pictures also perplexed viewers by raising questions about how realistic the works are. This applies in particular to the *Annunciation* and to the *Flight into Egypt*. In the *Annunciation*, the scene takes place in a poor tradesman's home with dilapidated walls and worn out stools, though, at the same time, one sees a magnificent Venetian ceiling and a white feather bed with a red silk curtain, worthy of the future Queen of Heaven.

The *Flight into Egypt* is also disconcerting to the viewer. The fleeing family are depicted from the front, right on the edge of a huge landscape. They are separated from other people peacefully carrying out their daily tasks on the opposite side of the river, by an impenetrable bush and by the water. They themselves would appear not to have any more space in the peaceful landscape, as they are so tightly squeezed into the corner of the picture. One has the impression that they will disappear in the next moment. Their homelessness and exile are impressively portrayed.

Scuola Grande di San Giovanni Evangelista

The Confraternity of St. John the Evangelist, founded in 1261, is one of the oldest *scuole* in Venice. In 1369, it received a relic of the Holy Cross as a donation, which brought it great prestige and thus a very large income. At the beginning of the 15th century, work was able to begin on expanding the brotherhood's meeting hall.

When building work on its lavish inner staircase was complete, Pietro Lombardo was commissioned in 1478 to erect a splendid entrance door into the courtyard of the Scuola. In a lunette over the entrance, an eagle appears as a symbol for John the Evangelist, and also as the emblem of the Scuola. In appointing Lombardo, they could be certain that their door would be just the right mix of fashionable Renaissance style and late Gothic opulence, which would fulfill the representational requirements of a wealthy *scuola* and provide firm proof of its culture and prosperity.

Gentile Bellini: Miracle of the Cross on San Lorenzo Bridge, late 1500, (now in the Accademia)
Oil on canvas, 323 x 430 cm

Today the Scuola has been largely robbed of its once rich treasures. The paintings with which it was decorated in the 15th century came from the workshop of the Bellini family, who were then the leading painters in Venice. Despite the fact that the paintings by the father on the ground floor are lost, one can still see today the huge series from the workshop of

the younger generation in the Accademia. The relic of the Cross, which contributed so greatly to the Scuola's standing, was the focus of each painting. Gentile Bellini's paintings depict a miracle which supposedly took place between 1370 and 1382. During a procession, the relic apparently fell into the canal from the San Lorenzo bridge. It continued to slip out of the hands of the brothers. The grand guardian of the Scuola, Andrea Vendramin, was the first to manage to reach it. The picture shows the moment when he takes the relic in his hands and brings it back to the canal bank.

The pictures of episodes involving the Scuola's relic are not just descriptions of events, but are also significant testaments to the life and appearance of Venice in the 15th century. These paintings also contain many portraits. Who the people kneeling on the right are is disputed (they were wrongly taken to be members of the Bellini family). On the left is the Queen of Cyprus, Caterina Cornaro, with her royal household.

San Giacomo dell'Orio

At Campo San Giacomo dell'Orio one sees that, away from the hordes of tourists, Venice is still able to assume the tranquil air of a small Italian town. It is particularly worth visiting at Carnival time, when the inhabitants organize celebrations in their local squares, which are very different from the mass spectacle which takes place in the Piazza San Marco. The church is named after a laurel tree (*lauro* in Italian) which once stood here. Another story relates that the church, which is one of the oldest in the city (9th century), was built on an island inhabited by wolves. In this case, the name would derive from the Italian for wolf (*lupo* or *lupao*). The unusual position of the tall church tower from the 12th or 13th century, which is next to the church rather than in front of it, is explained by the many renovations (in the 13th and 15th–17th centuries) it has undergone. In the Middle Ages, the facade and the main entrance to the church were where the tower is now.

Interior

The church's interior also shows clear traces of the extensive rebuilding. Some of the marble columns are booty from the eastern Mediterranean, as is the case in other very old Venetian churches. The tulip-shaped pulpit leans against a granite column which must have been part of an earlier church building. With its rich ornamentation, the pulpit itself is reminiscent of the works of the Lombardo school of the early 16th century. Like few other churches, San Giacomo dell'Orio has been able to maintain the character of a true parish church. No important family or religious house paid for the decoration here. It was completely fitted out only very gradually.

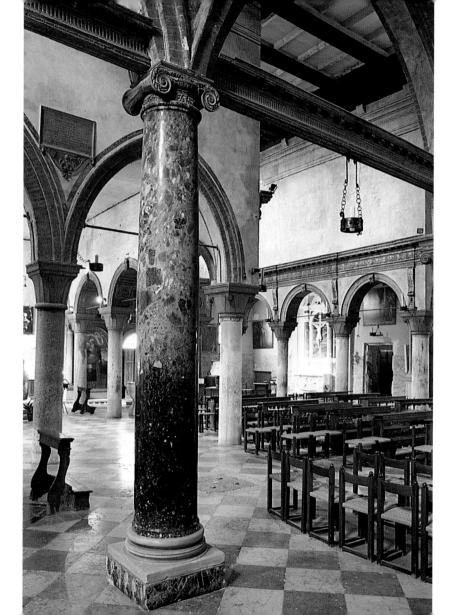

Sestiere Dorsoduro

Dorsoduro

The *dorso duro* (hard back), is the most southwesterly district of Venice, so named because, unlike every other part of Venice, it is solid, and in places rocky ground even predominates. Along the Dorsoduro is the most distinguished part of the Grand Canal, with the church of Santa Maria della Salute, the Accademia and the Guggenheim Collection. It also contains parts of the university, the harbor, the once ordinary area around San Nicolò dei Mendicoli, and the Giudecca.

Scuola Grande dei Carmini (Scuola Grande di Santa Maria del Carmelo), Giovanni Battista Tiepolo: Madonna with Child Presents the Blessed Simon Stock with the Scapular, 1739–49, p. 285

San Nicolò dei Mendicoli, p. 296

San Sebastiano, Paolo Veronese: Coronation of Esther, 1555–56, p. 292

Gesuati Church (Santa Maria del Rosario), Giovanni Battista Tiepolo: Pala delle Tre Sante, c. 1748, p. 305

Carmelite Church (Santa Maria del Carmelo; interior), p. 287

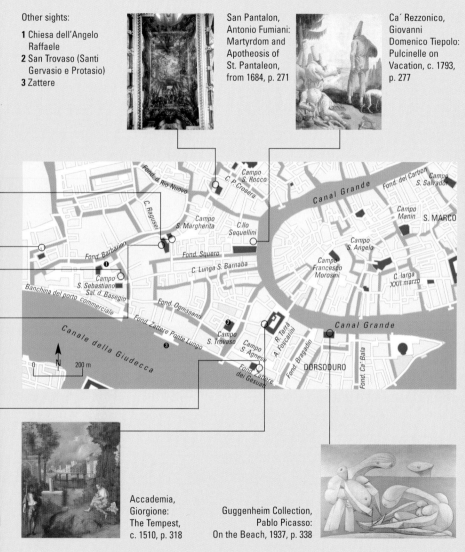

Other sights:

1 Chiesa dell'Angelo Raffaele
2 San Trovaso (Santi Gervasio e Protasio)
3 Zattere

San Pantalon, Antonio Fumiani: Martyrdom and Apotheosis of St. Pantaleon, from 1684, p. 271

Ca' Rezzonico, Giovanni Domenico Tiepolo: Pulcinelle on Vacation, c. 1793, p. 277

Accademia, Giorgione: The Tempest, c. 1510, p. 318

Guggenheim Collection, Pablo Picasso: On the Beach, 1937, p. 338

Zattere

On beautiful spring and summer evenings, many Venetians take to the Zattere. From the Punta della Dogana, one can stroll all along the wide, half mile long strip of canal bank by the *bacino* (basin) almost as far as the westernmost point of Venice. There are a few cafés along the way, whose lovely views across to the Giudecca are inviting to the visitor.

The name of the promenade comes from the Venetian *arzere*, or beach. In earlier times, great rafts carrying wood landed here. The wood was shipped from the mountains to supply the Venetian demand for building materials, and also to provide for the energy requirements of the large city.

Giovanni d'Alemagna and Antonio Vivarini from 1444, in the left choir chapel.

Giovanni Antonio Fumiani: Martyrdom and Apotheosis of St. Pantaleon, from 1684
Oil on canvas

Giovanni Antonio Fumiani (1643–1710) devoted nearly 25 years of his life to the decoration of the church ceiling, from 1684 on. He is also buried here. Fumiani painted on canvas. At first glance, one can only see the tremendous architecture in this painting, which seems to open up the church's space into the vast heavens. After a time, one can make out the different scenes of the martyrdom of St. Pantaleon. On the right of the painting, under a tent roof, is the Roman emperor Diocletian, who ordered the torture and death of the saint. St. Pantaleon himself appears surrendering to his fate, under a high arch, framed by an aura of bright light. Henchmen show him the tools of torture. The sky is open, ready to accept the soul of the saint.

San Pantalon (San Pantaleone)

The appearance of the church, which since its construction in the late 17th century has been missing a proper facade, does not in any way prepare the impartial viewer for the marvelous Baroque visual feast in its interior. Also worth viewing is the beautiful *Coronation of the Virgin* by

Ca' Rezzonico

Museo del Settecento Veneziano

After the Rezzonico family had acquired and completed the construction of this Baroque building, work commenced on its lavish decoration. Giovanni Battista Tiepolo, Andrea Brustolon and other artists worked on it. The interior decor offers a unique and authentic backdrop to the 18th century Venetian art displayed here. In addition to works of art, there is a collection of porcelain, furniture, clothing, and other useful items. The elegant stairwell which leads up to the magnificent rooms on the second floor, and to the exhibition rooms, was executed by Giorgio Massari.

Giovanni Battista Tiepolo:
Triumph of Zephyr and Flora, 1731–32
Oil on canvas, 395 x 225 cm

The painting shows the divine personification of the west wind with the goddess of flowers and spring. While Zephyr has a pair of soft, diaphanous wings, Flora, whom he is gently embracing, is supported by a putto. The pair are floating upwards on a rising, dark cloud formation. Underneath, Cupid points to them. The color palette is typical of Tiepolo, giving the painting luminosity and brightness.

The painting originally belonged not to the Ca' Rezzonico, but to the Ca' Pesaro, and was probably painted for the marriage of Antonio Pesaro and Caterina Sagredo in 1732. However, the couple were denied good fortune and fertility, both promises portrayed in the painting. Antonio died shortly after they were married and Caterina was left a childless widow.

Giovanni Battista Tiepolo:
Allegory of the Marriage of Ludovico Rezzonico
and Faustina Savorgnan, 1758
Fresco, 630 x 1030 cm

On the occasion of the marriage of
Faustina Savorgnan to Ludovico Rezzonico
on January 16, 1758, the family had the
ceilings of two rooms painted by Giovanni
Battista Tiepolo (1696–1770) and his
collaborator Gerolamo Mengozzi Colonna.
The two frescoes refer directly to the
fortunate match. In the so-called Sala
dell'Allegoria Nuziale (Hall of the Nuptial
Allegory), the newly-weds are seated in
Apollo's place in the golden chariot drawn
by magnificent white horses. Apollo, who
was the Greek god of the sun, among
other things, stands behind them. They
are surrounded by the Three Graces and
the figures of Glory, Wisdom, and Noble
Service, which promise them a fortunate
future. The gentle light of the rays of sunshine in the sky also point to future luck
and happiness.

Weddings were often a welcome
occasion for the refurbishment of a single
room or even an entire palazzo. This was
particularly the case if they succeeded in
bringing two important noble families
together. That the couple would get along
well was of little importance in aristocratic
marriages. It was by no means the case,
however, that marriages were made only
for material reasons.

Men's clothing in the 18th century

The museum in the Ca' Rezzonico displays a multitude of *objets* from the 18th century, when the cream of European society gathered in Venice to enjoy life. The visitors mostly purchased luxury Venetian goods, such as glass and lace, examples of which can be admired in this museum. The Ca' Rezzonico also has an important collection of clothing from the Rococo period.

Giovanni Domenico (Giandomenico) Tiepolo: Pulcinelle on Vacation, c. 1793
Fresco (removed), 198 x 150 cm

In 1753, the artist Giovanni Battista Tiepolo, who had in the meantime earned a considerable fortune, bought a country villa, like other wealthy Venetians. This was located in Zianigo not far from Mestre. His son Dominico (1727–1804), who learned his trade in his father's studio and who worked regularly with his father, spent many years decorating the villa with frescoes. Unlike other works of this kind, the paintings in the artist's villa do not extol any significant family tradition. Giovanni Domenico gave free rein to his imagination and decorated the rooms with centaurs and scenes from everyday life or, as in this case, with characters from the commedia dell'arte.

At first glance, the amusing scene of a group of the traditionally white-clad clowns (*pulcinelle*) devoting themselves to the pleasures of life at the villa, predominates. On closer inspection, one sees an ironic, partly satirical, overall undertone of social criticism. With the beloved figures of the commedia dell'arte, who in their characteristic roles already had some negative traits, such as greed, sloth, and gluttony, a theme was to emerge which was quite different from what had hitherto been the norm in villa paintings. The frescoes were removed in 1906 and have been on display in the Ca' Rezzonico since 1936.

under a portrait of Doge Carlo Ruzzini (in office 1723–35); she is probably a member of the Ruzzini family. On the table we see a mirror, a valuable porcelain powder case, combs, and powder puffs, all required for a lady's toilet. The table is covered with a fine white cloth, and there is gold fabric piled up behind the mirror. It is not clear whether this is used to cover the table, or if it is part of an item of clothing which the woman has yet to put on. A wet nurse, with red cheeks and unpowdered hair, carrying a small child, stands to the side while the woman has her hair done. The red coat trimmed with expensive ermine would imply that the noblewoman is preparing for a party or similar occasion. The coat immediately highlights the doge's gown in the portrait which hangs behind her. Even the child's red cap is a reminder of the doge's red-gold cap. All of these are possible playful references to an important family tradition.

Pietro Longhi:
The Hairdresser and the Lady, c. 1760
Oil on wood, 63 x 51 cm

The museum also contains a large collection of work by Pietro Longhi (1702–75), who faithfully portrayed 18th century Venetian life like no other painter. This painting shows an elegant woman of the Rococo period, sitting at her dressing table

Pietro Longhi:
Visit of the Bauta, c. 1760–70
Oil on wood, 62 x 50 cm

A young woman in a red and blue dress, reminiscent in both cut and color of a smart uniform, sits with two men at a sewing table. She is occupied with some delicate embroidery work. A notebook protrudes from the pocket of the man standing up. The other man is seen wearing the traditional mask, known as a *bauta*, which high-ranking Venetians of the late 18th century wore almost all the time. A servant is bringing in a small pot and two cups: this was probably cocoa, which was the fashionable drink in the Rococo period. The sewing table, and the elegant bonnet on the wig-stand on top of the chest of drawers on the right, give the impression that this is the young lady's private chamber. The man standing, for whom there is neither a chair nor a cup, might possibly be the music teacher, whose presence would mitigate the awkward situation of a male visiting the rooms of a young lady. Although the obvious lower status of the music teacher is made clear, within the picture he has more significance than the aristocratic man. The latter is hidden behind his mask, while the lady, her teacher, and even the little servant girl are portrayed.

Not only a talented lover:
Giacomo Casanova (1725–98)

It was a wondrous creature whom Joseph Charles Emmanuel, the Count of Waldstein, employed at Castle Duchcov in Bohemia as his librarian, for an annual salary of 1000 florins plus coachman and servant, as well as free room and board. He was an aging, tall, and once handsome Venetian who, with his old-fashioned French, his plumed hat, his gold-embroidered waistcoats, and his powdered hair must have seemed like an apparition from the previous century to the other residents of the castle. In his last years, which he spent there from 1785 to 1798, Giacomo Casanova, the librarian, was a relic of his time, who had been exiled in the upheavals of the French Revolution. The new age which, after his death, began throughout Europe, which believed in Romantic values such as honesty, fidelity, and patriotism, had no meaning for Casanova, the gallant swindler, subtle cheat, and chameleon cosmopolitan, who felt at home all over the world. He was an elegant lover, who was very attractive to women, although he was quite unable to limit himself to just one. Already forgotten by his

Altera nunc rerum facies, me quero, nec adsum:
Non sum qui fueram non putor esse: fui

Johann Berka:
Giacomo Casanova, aged 63,
colored engraving

contemporaries (with the exception of his many creditors), at Castle Duchcov (formerly Dux Castle) he devoted himself to what he probably felt were his best interests: alchemical research and writing his *Mémoires*.

Although Casanova's description of his life reports so colorfully and frivolously from the ultimately supressed darker side of the Rococo period, it was not published until after the author's death. When the book finally appeared, it was in a form which excluded many of Casanova's erotic adventures. An enthusiastic 19th century editor, who prepared the biography for the public and completely failed to understand the great ease, sympathy, and discretion with which Casanova reported on his various amorous exploits, altered them with dramatic embellishments.

Thus Casanova's name later became synonymous with male potency, and was used equally by enthusiastic seducers and by shady establishments. However, the real Casanova was much more than this. With his love of gambling and masquerade, he was a thoroughly typical figure of the 18th century. This also included undisguised enjoyment of the erotic,

Louis Marin Bonnet: The Broken Fan, c. 1780, color engraving after Jean-Baptiste Huet, Archiv für Kunst und Geschichte, Berlin

which for today's reader of his autobiography is very difficult to imagine after the prudishness of the 19th century.

Casanova was born in 1725 in Venice, in the 18th century a city of pleasure and eternal carnival, the son of a well-known actress and a theater director. His family intended for him to study theology, but he himself was much more interested in medicine, the universal science of his time. During his studies in Padua, he also trained in this subject area. In Venice, he completed his studies in all scientific areas at the monastery of Santa Maria della Salute under Pater Barbarigo, one of the leading specialists in Italy.

That Casanova used his extensive knowledge for cheating, among other things, does not seem to have damaged his popularity in Europe's highest circles. His knowledge not only enabled him to produce ink which became invisible after a time and was ideally suited to writing love letters and signing bills, but he was

Prison door at the Doges' Palace

able to use it to feign the expansion of mercury when working for the French crown to produce a national lottery, and also to manufacture seductive fragrances, to write a utopian novel, or to develop dye for the weavers of his last patron, Count Waldstein. In addition, it also freed him once from an extremely precarious situation which could have brought his career to a premature end.

The Venetian authorities were prepared to turn a blind eye to minor cases of cheating, which continually occurred in popular *ridotti* games. One area, however, in which it did not tolerate sharp practice in the least was espionage and the trade of state secrets. Casanova had the best possible contacts with the French ambassador, available to him through the mistress they shared. This alone was enough for the Venetians to arrest him on the night of July 25, 1755, on a very flimsy pretext and to imprison him without trial in the prison under the Doges' Palace known as the "Piombi" (the "Leads"). It is recorded that he was sentenced to five years. He was not informed of either the reason for his detention or of the judgment, and could only have presumed that he would remain in prison for the rest of his life. He managed to escape, something no one had succeeded in doing before him.

While taking a walk on the roof of the Doges' Palace, which he was permitted to do while his cell was being cleaned, he found a piece of iron and a piece of marble. With the help of a stone, he made a tool. He was also able to make a lamp out of cotton, salad oil, and sponges which he had sewn into his jacket to protect against perspiration stains, and sulfur, which he was able to obtain for his toothache; it was thus that he worked at night to dig a hole in the floor of his cell.

This first attempt at escape was discovered, however, and Casanova was moved to a different cell. Nonetheless, he managed to save the tool which, since he was now frequently checked, he hid in a fellow prisoner's Bible. He instructed the latter, the monk Marino Balbi, to make a hole in the ceiling of the cell. The second attempt was successful. The pair climbed out over the roofs of the Doges' Palace. The doorman was alerted and released the supposedly mistakenly imprisoned pair, who jumped into the next gondola and left Venice before their escape was discovered.

The story of his escape, which was published in 1787 in Prague under the title *Histoires de ma fuite* (Story of My Escape), was Casanova's entry ticket to Europe's high society and it remained valid as long as social circumstances did not change. In the isolation of Castle Duchcov, no one was any longer interested in the adventures of an odd and capricious old man. Only now, 200 years after his death, is Casanova's great general education in all the essential subject areas of his time appreciated once again. Giacomo Casanova can be regarded as more than just a gifted lover or a tenacious seducer.

Heinrich Berka: Casanova's escape from the "Leads" in the Doges' Palace, 1788, engraving, in the first edition of Histoires de ma fuite

Scuola Grande dei Carmini (Scuola Grande di Santa Maria del Carmelo)

The Scuola Grande dei Carmini was, in 1594, the last new *scuola* founded belonging to one of the six main confraternities. It was placed under the patronage of Mary of Carmel and closely modeled after the Carmelite monastery,

near which, beginning in 1427, the brotherhood also built its house. Despite its riches, the facade of the building is not at all pompous, but has slender columns and delicate ornamentation. It is attributed to Baldassare Longhena. The Scuola enjoyed great popularity in the 17th and 18th centuries and was one of the most important institutions of lay devotion and charitable works in Venice. In 1675, it had 75,000 members, i.e. almost half of the population of Venice. The Scuola was dissolved under Napoleon's rule, though its good name (and also the good reputation of its members) outlived the short reign of the self-crowned emperor. In 1840, under Austrian rule, Emperor Ferdinand I authorized the reestablishment of the famous Scuola, which is active to this day. And, as the plaques on the first floor listing the names of its members show, today women may also be members.

Giovanni Battista Tiepolo:
Madonna with Child Appear to the Blessed Simon Stock, 1739–49
Oil on canvas, 533 x 342 cm

The wealthy Scuola commissioned the leading 18th century Venetian painter to complete a work for the ceiling of the Sala Capitolare (chapter hall) on the upper floor. For the lower floor, which was traditionally less richly decorated, Nicolò Bambini completed monochrome paintings depicting scenes from the life of the Virgin.

Tiepolo's ceiling on the upper floor shows Simon Stock, an English general of the Carmelite Order in the 13th century, being presented with the scapular (two pieces of white cloth joined by strings, the wearing of which distinguishes the Carmelites). After their expulsion from the Holy Land, he had reformed the Carmelites from hermits into mendicant friars living in the city. For Carmelites, the scapular is the sign of their devotion to the Virgin: the Mother of God gave it to Simon Stock in a vision as a sign of her protection, it is said. Around the central picture are personifications of the cardinal virtues: Faith, Hope, Charity, Justice, Temperance, Prudence, and Fortitude, as well as angels. In the rich collection of the Scuola, Giovanni Battista Piazzetta's work of *Judith and Holofernes*, in the hall between the Sala dell' Albergo and the Archivio, is of particular interest.

monastery on Campo dei Carmini, was changed in the early 16th century. Over the entrance one can still see part of the bricked up round window from the old church. The facade has a typically simple Venetian brick front, which, on closer inspection, is extraordinarily effective. The usual access to the church is through its original side entrance from Campo Santa Margherita.

Carmelite Church
(Santa Maria del Carmelo)

Interior

The church of the former Carmelite monastery of Santa Maria del Carmelo, abbreviated by Venetians to the Carmini, is tucked away off Campo Santa Margherita. Construction of the church began in 1286, which means that the Carmelites were already established in Venice shortly after the reform of their Order in the middle of the 13th century. Under the new rules of the Order, they forsook their hermit status, their vow of silence, and their ban on eating meat, and established themselves as a mendicant order devoted to the spiritual welfare of the city's population. The main facade of the church, next to the

The basic structure of the Gothic building is still clearly recognizable. Slender columns separate the transepts. The choir was changed after 1514 to its present form. It is interesting to see how the architect, Sebastiano Mariano from Lugano, succeeded in smoothly blending the Gothic choir, incorporating ribbed vaulting, with the Renaissance style. He split the high, narrow, uppermost arches into three window areas and put round-arched windows in the upper row. The powerful, partly gilded, and painted carvings in the nave originate from the late 16th and early 17th centuries.

Lorenzo Lotto: Apotheosis of St. Nicholas with John the Baptist and St. Lucia, 1527–29
Oil on canvas, 335 x 188 cm

In addition to a remarkable altarpiece of the *Birth of Christ* by Cima da Conegliano (c. 1510), in the right aisle, the Carmini also has a particularly fine altarpiece by Lorenzo Lotto (c. 1480–1556/57) next to the side entrance. The colors are most unusual for Lotto: deep blue, green, and purple tones. Hardly any viewers today, however, would endorse the negative verdict of Lodovico Dolce, a 16th-century art theoretician, that the picture is an example of "terrible colors."

St. Nicholas appears with halo; at his feet, John the Baptist and St. Lucia. Beside her, two eyes lie in a small dish as a sign of her martyrdom. According to legend, Lucia tore her eyes out, whereupon the Holy Virgin gave her even more beautiful eyes.

The most unusual feature of this altarpiece, however, is the magnificent, broad landscape in the lowest quarter of the painting. Hardly any other early 16th century artist painted landscapes of such romantic beauty.

Francesco di Giorgio Martini: Descent from the Cross, c. 1475
Oil on canvas, 86 x 52 cm

The most astonishing work of art in this church is Francesco di Giorgio's bronze relief depicting the Descent from the Cross. The small bronze plaque, which dates from about 1475, was made by the Sienese artist, who also acted as the architect, architectural theorist, and painter for the Oratorio of Santa Croce in Siena. It was stolen from Siena by Napoleon and brought to Milan. The picture then belonged to the Baron Margrani, who gave it to the Carmelite Church in Venice.

Francesco di Giorgio's painting combines great expressiveness and infinite tenderness. One can see the Magdalene gesticulating wildly; the dramatic movement of her upper body and flowing hair depict her sadness and pain. The mourning angels around the Cross are also very moving and are in extraordinarily fine relief. It is only on close inspection that one sees a kind of cloud transforming into gentle angels. The artist uses his medium fully and aims for plasticity and a painterly effect.

San Sebastiano

The church of St. Sebastian was renovated in the 16th century by the Hieronymites, who had established their monastery on this site in the 15th century. An unusual event, which research has not yet uncovered, must have led the brothers to renovate the building only a few years after the previous work was completed. The original church was first completed in 1468. The plan for the new building was almost certainly by Antonio Abondio (known as Lo Scarpagnino), one of the architects who, in the first half of the 16th century, built mostly simple standard architecture rather than buildings remarkable for their astonishing architectural quality.

Interior

The first impression of the interior of the church is that is it very simply built. The only surprise is the gallery: it is not only, as is common in other Venetian churches, over the entrance, but spans the entire nave. As a result, there is room for six smaller chapels on the sides. The sacristy, which is accessed via a door under the organ, was decorated with paintings from 1551 onwards by artists from Verona. That no Venetians were comissioned was probably because the prior of the monastery, Bernardo Torlioni, was himself from

Verona. In 1555, he summoned another young artist from his home town to paint the areas on the relatively low, richly gilded ceilings. The name of the artist was Paolo Veronese. In the following ten years, he was called on again and again to work on the decoration of the church.

Paolo Veronese:
Coronation of Esther, 1555–56
Oil on canvas, 500 x 370 cm

The second task which Veronese completed for San Sebastiano was the oil paintings on canvas which were to be mounted on sections of the ceiling. In 1555–56, he painted these with scenes from the life of the Old Testament heroine Esther. The young Jewish woman lived with her uncle, Mordecai. When the powerful king Ahasuerus dismissed his wife Vashti (shown in the first oval picture), he chose the beautiful Esther as his new consort and queen. When the viceroy, Haman, planned to massacre all of the Jews, Esther saved the people of Israel by interceding with the king. To the Church Fathers, Queen Esther soon became the personification of the Church, and the portrayal of her story must be seen in the context of beliefs at the time. Esther is here the symbol of the Catholic Church who, beautifully adorned and crowned, saves believers and destroys enemies. For Veronese, this story gave him the opportunity to show off his talent for portraying magnificent fabrics, jewelry and other such things. These paintings gave him further opportunities to win important Venetian commissions for his work.

Veronese did not, however, just use the decoration of the church as a springboard for his career. No other building gives such a complete impression of his religious paintings. It is only logical that the great artist would also be buried in this church: his grave (and that of his brother, Benedetto) can be found in front of the chapel on the left, beside the presbytery.

Paolo Veronese:
Martyrdom of St. Sebastian, 1558
Fresco, 350 x 480 cm

In the upper story, visible only from the gallery, Veronese painted frescoes with scenes from the legend of the saint to whom the church is dedicated. Here, the saint's body is tied to a bench and he is being beaten with heavy clubs by his torturers. With their intricate movements, the torturers demonstrate Veronese's mastery in dealing with difficult body positions and foreshortening. Veronese painted only stories from Sebastian's legend in these upper-level frescoes. The painted architectural structures framing them give the illusion of a building opening up at the sides. The reality of real and painted space is blurred: soldiers who are aiming arrows at St. Sebastian are placed on one side of the gallery, while their victim is on the opposite side.

Sant'Angelo Raffaele

There are two churches, San Sebastiano and Sant'Angelo Raffaele, on the many-cornered Campo San Sebastiano.

Sant'Angelo Raffaele adopted a new orientation, onto Rio dell'Angelo Raffaele, when it was rebuilt (1618–39). Originally it was planned that all sides of the church would have decorated facades but, as in so many cases, the front had to suffice.

Giovanni Antonio or Francesco Guardi:
Tobit, Tobias, and the Angel, 1558
Oil on canvas, 80 x 91 cm

The interior of the church is decorated with paintings from the 16th and 17th centuries. The most significant painting, however, was placed in the organ loft over the main entrance in the middle of the 18th century. In five scenes, it shows the story of Tobias, whom the Archangel Raphael accompanied on a journey.

San Nicolò dei Mendicoli

The western end of Venice was, like Castello in the east, always a quarter for ordinary people, sailors and fishermen. They are called *Nicolotti* to this day, after their parish church. Beggars, however, as the words *dei Mendicoli* (beggars) would imply, they were not. On the contrary, a column in front of the church bearing the Lion of St. Mark shows the precise social position of the inhabitants of this district. They chose a single leader, a fisherman from their ranks, who was known as the "doge of the Nicolotti." Like the doge of the Republic, he appeared in a red robe when on official duties. Following his election, the doge of Nicoletti, accompanied by numerous residents from his district, proceeded to the Doges' Palace, where he was received by the doge of Venice with a fraternal kiss in a festive ceremony. Thus the government demonstrated symbolically how important ordinary people and fishermen were for the city.

The front facade of the church still displays a small porch, like many medieval churches in Venice.

Unfortunately all of these have disappeared today. They once served as protection for the beggars in the church's district. In other porches of this nature, poor nuns lived, almost like beggars. They were called *pinzochere*.

trodden inhabitants of the quarter. This included the fishermen threatened by the dangers of the sea as well as their families, who often lived on the borderline of poverty. The gilding of the sculpture is an expression of how fervently St. Nicholas was worshipped.

St. Nicholas

On the high altar there is no painting, as is often the case, but instead a large wooden sculpture of St. Nicholas dating back to the mid-15th century. The saint is clad in a heavily gilded bishop's robe. Nicholas, who is also the patron saint of sailors, blesses the community with a raised hand.

On the Saint's lap are the golden balls which remind us that, according to the "Golden Legend," three maidens, of no means and with no dowries, and who were thus facing a possible life of prostitution, were saved from this terrible fate by St. Nicholas, who gave them gifts of golden balls during the night. This sculpture of the good bishop had enormous meaning for the poor and down-

Interior

The richly decorated interior shows how much the inhabitants of the district loved their church. In this poor quarter, where fishermen, seafaring folk and industrial workers lived, there were not enough funds to radically rebuild the church. So, evidently, the 12th century building was modernized bit by bit or the dilapidated parts replaced. The church of San Nicolò dei Mendicoli is, however, a particularly atmospheric Venetian church since, despite many centuries of redecoration, it has completely retained its original function.

In the 14th century, the interior was renovated and the arch to the presbytery and transept raised. This still shows decorative paintwork from that period. The capitals in the nave were renovated as well (two of them are dated 1361 and 1364) and the roof truss was newly constructed. The next major work was done in 1580, when the main nave was decorated with carved and gilded woodwork, and episodes from the life of Christ were included in the paintings. On top of the columns are carved figures of the Twelve Apostles. The sculptured Crucifixion, with Mary, Joseph and two angels, was also completed at this stage.

Gondola docks at San Trovaso

One of the three remaining gondola dockyards in Venice is situated on Rio San Trovaso. Even though today not as many gondolas are needed as in the past, when they provided almost all transport, the demand for the expensive boats (they cost more than €20,000) is still very high.

There is a waiting list several years long for new gondolas, which are made from eight different kinds of wood making them very durable. The boat is about 36 ft (11 m) long and about $4^1/_2$ ft (1.4 m) wide; the right hand side is $9^1/_2$ inches (24 cm) narrower than the left, to allow for steering with just a single oar, which is as long as the gondola itself.

Anyone can buy a gondola, but only Venetians are permitted to work as gondoliers and they are the only ones granted the licenses required. The training period, which is essential in order to be able to steer the boats elegantly and safely, takes ten years. There is no shortage of trainees, although it is mostly the sons of gondolier families who continue the profession of their ancestors.

San Trovaso
(Santi Gervasio e Protasio)

The Venetians have shortened the title of the church from the saints' names to San Trovaso. An earlier church for the two martyrs already existed on this site in the 9th century. The area around San Trovaso was one of the districts which stood high out of the waters of the lagoon and was therefore inhabited early on. In 1028, the Barbarigo family funded a new church, which was destroyed in 1105 by a fire. The 12th century church was so dilapidated by the 16th century that it collapsed and was finally replaced, starting in 1585. The new building was not consecrated until 1657. The church has two identical facades, onto Campo San Trovaso and Rio San Trovaso.

Chiesa dei Gesuati (Santa Maria del Rosario)

Because of its similar name, some people think that the Chiesa dei Gesuati, as the Venetians call it for short, is a Jesuit church. However, the Gesuiti, or Santa Maria Assunta, is situated at the other end of the city. The "poor Jesuates" were a Venetian order founded at the end of the 14th century, long before the Roman Jesuits.

At the beginning of the 16th century, they set up a monastery dedicated to St. Jerome on the Zattere. The facade of its Renaissance church is on the left of the Chiesa dei Gesuati. In 1668 the Order was dissolved and the monastery was taken over by the Dominicans, who built the church, though it continues to bear the name of their predecessors. The facade echoes the churches on the Giudecca opposite.

Giovanni Battista Tiepolo: Donation of the Rosary, 1738–39
Fresco, 1400 x 450 cm

Soon after the church was consecrated, Tiepolo began the frescoes for the ceiling. These contain three narrative scenes from the history of St. Dominic and the Dominican Order. Hanging over the entrance is the *Apotheosis of St. Dominic* and, over the altar, the saint is depicted blessing another Dominican, possibly Fra Paolo, who built the church. The central painting is of the donation of the rosary to St. Dominic, who passes on the valuable gift of the Virgin to the faithful. The doge appears to be the first to reach for the beneficial gift: church and state are thus ideally united. The Dominicans make reference to their city and at the same time show that the believer must stand in the foreground, as the saint must stand nearer to the Virgin than even the highest representative of the State. The wicked, however, plunge into a dark hole at the bottom of the scene. Tiepolo gives particular significance to color and light. From the foot of the painting up to the Virgin, the brightness increases continually, so that he succeeds in giving the horizontal surface the impression of a vertically increasing space.

Giovanni Battista Piazzetta:
Santi Vincent Ferrer, Hyacinth, and Louis
Bertrand, c. 1738–39
Oil on canvas, 345 x 172 cm

In the third side chapel on the right, along with Piazzetta's altarpiece, there is a painting which forms a sort of counterpart to Tiepolo's *Pala delle Tre Sante* in the first chapel. It shows the three Dominican saints, Vincent Ferrer, Hyacinth, and Louis Bertrand. Piazzetta set himself the task of making a composition with several individual figures. Two very similar paintings from two consecutive generations of painters come together here. Piazzetta belonged to the generation known as *tenebristi* (from the Italian, *tenebroso*, meaning "dark" or "dim"). These artists often painted their pictures using few and dark colors. Typical of the style used by many of his generation is the way in which the figures emerge from the colors in the background. The angel at the top of the painting is a breathtaking piece of artwork, whose foreshortening and execution is highly effective in terms of color, considering that just one basic color is involved. Piazzetta's masterpiece combines the old principles of form with a new, brighter palette which still, however, keeps to black, brown, gray, and beige tones.

Giovanni Battista Tiepolo:
Pala delle Tre Sante, c. 1748
Oil on canvas, 340 x 168 cm

About ten years after Piazzetta's altarpiece was created, Tiepolo painted this work showing the Virgin with Saints Catherine of Siena, Rosa of Lima, and Agnes. In contrast to the diffuse light of the sky, under which the saints gather in Piazzetta's work, the Virgin and saints in this painting appear to be in a fixed place. A goldfinch, which could fly away at any time, is resting on the bar across the top of the column. The rest of the space remains strangely abstract and only the sky behind the figures is visible. Tiepolo's composition and the way in which the light shimmers on the garments of the women was clearly influenced by the work of Paolo Veronese, a 16th century artist. The golden cloud on which the Virgin is seated, and the way in which Tiepolo gives the garments of the standing saints different shades of the same color, show that he learned from this painter's methods, which also influenced Piazzetta and his generation. Together they unite in a virtuoso treatment of color, which no other painter in Venice had mastered so brilliantly since Titian.

Comic doctors, farmers stupid and clever, and a rich old man, who always ends up poorly

When the famous Venetian poet, Carlo Goldoni, transferred the characters of the commedia dell'arte – the colorful masked theater populated by rich old men, comic doctors, scholars, and clowns acting as servants – into his plays, the characters both reached perfection and met their ultimate demise. In its heyday, during the transition from the 16th to the 17th centuries, the commedia provoked storms of laughter and enthusiasm in audiences throughout Europe, under the title *Commedia sogetto* or *Commedia all'improviso alla Italiana*. Venice was its main home, as its strong roots lay in that city and in the coarse pieces by Angelo Beolco, known as Il Ruzzante, from Padua. These plays could be performed anywhere, even on the street, without props or elaborate sets, and the humorous sketches took aim at contemporary issues and figures. Goldoni and his contemporaries developed these themes. However, the older figures who, with their very stylized masks, were an essential part of the commedia dell'arte, finally disappeared from the stage in the late 18th century. Their spirit remains in plays such as

The Servant of Two Masters, The Barber of Seville, and *The Maid as Mistress*. Their once well-known characters have little meaning for contemporary theatergoers, even though theater producers such as Dario Fo, the Nobel prize winner, tried to revive the genre in the 20th century.

What was the cast of characters in the commedia dell'arte like? The types can be divided into young (*giovani*) and old (*vecchi*), and into those figures who wore masks and those who did not. The younger members generally came out much better in the plays than the old. But their weaknesses, such as gullibility, blind love,

Gabriel Bella: A Troupe of Actors on the Piazzetta (detail), before 1792, Pinacoteca Querini Stampalia, Venice

corruptibility, naiveté, and pleasure craving were caricatured just as much as the miserliness, lasciviousness, affected youthful behaviour, and conspicuous pseudo-culture of the old. Among the young people, there was always a pair of lovers, the *amorosi*, whose beautiful young faces were not hidden behind masks.

The young woman could also be a courtesan and did not have to be true to her naive young lover under every circumstance, for example if money were involved. The old servant of the young woman almost always displayed avarice and corruptibility, and she frequently acted as a matchmaker.

Like her, Pantalone, one of the major figures, was also one of the older generation. Pantalone was always masked. He wore a much too youthful, close-fitting red suit, a black cap, a wide, black cape, and had a big, long nose and a goatee beard. A bulging bag, filled to the brim, symbolized both wealth and miserliness. He was the embodiment of a rich Venetian businessman, who spoke in his native dialect and tried to woo young, beautiful women. The other figures were always busy trying to get his money. By the end of the play he had always been duped and was made a laughing stock. Playing opposite him often was the Doctor, dressed in black with a large monocle, representing a scholar who had trained at the famous University of Bologna. With pompous behavior and incessant talk replete with empty phrases and foreign words, he was the perfect embodiment of the inflated intellectual, be it a doctor, lawyer, or philosopher, giving opinions the world over. Another of

Der fritff 3ende Arlequin.   Arlequin fouivant.
Jo fritff.ßet Arlequin und fan fall inchts mehr fprechen, Arlequin fouivant, fe prefente à nos yeux,
Er thut, ale wolle thin das Hertz im Leib Zerbrechen. Et ridiculement il fait toujours fes yeux.

Anonymous: Harlequin, colored engraving, Raccolta Teatrale del Burcardo, Rome

the older generation was the Capitano, a resplendent dandy full of his own heroic soldierly deeds, but who would disappear like a coward the moment a situation became in any way precarious. He was often made fun of for his foreign-sounding speech, a pastiche of many soldiers who came to Italy from Spain, Germany, and other places. The most important roles beside Pantalone and the young lovers

Martin Engelbrecht: Pantalone, colored engraving, Augsburg, Biblioteca e Raccolta Teatrale del Burcardo, Rome

At their side, they carried a (wooden) knife as a symbol of their pugnacity and their great gluttony. To modern eyes, this was a rather coarse parody of the extremely poor, often starving farmers who had to seek a living as porters and servants in the cities. The character of the Zanni swung from foolish and outrageous to crafty and cunning; they were always suspicious and inquisitive. Their true or acted stupidity gave the best opportunities for clowning. The servant was often accompanied by Harlequin, a figure who originated in France and was recognizable by his colorful patchwork costume. Harlequin needed to be particularly acrobatic and was extremely wily and foppish. More often than not he was the one who held in his hands the threads of the dénouement, which would finally lead to the young lovers finding each other and Pantalone standing by looking sheepish.

were the Zanni (Venetian for Giovanni). There were often several of these and in the course of time they were given other names too. Mostly servants to the wealthy Pantalone, their costumes of white shirts and trousers were reminiscent of the light dress of farmers from Bergamo, whose dialect they spoke and who came in the thousands to the northern Italian harbor towns such as Venice and Genoa to work as porters. Their mask, which covered half of the face, had very coarse features.

An essential element in the success of the commedia dell'arte was the familiarity of the masks and the subject matter, which were continuously varied in a humorous way. Everyone knew the rich and stingy businessman, Pantalone, and his servants, the Zanni, and their many companions, who varied from one theater company to the next. For the audiences, it was already clear, from the masks on the characters, which of the piece's features and problems would turn out to be funny. Thus, a large part of the story was already known. The individual attraction of a play then lay in the improvisation and in the *lazzi* (jokes), which were as enjoyable as the breakneck acrobatic interludes.

Although we know how much the commedia dell'arte was loved, today we can no longer comprehend its wit, its tempo, and the appeal of the fast and funny dialog, which was often rather lewd and never lost sight of the politics of the day. In times of strict political control and the religious Inquisition, it was wise to commit only the inoffensive to paper. Thus, nowadays, the pieces often seem rather tedious. For the audiences of their day, however, they were a source of endless amusement.

The openness of the dialog was a particularly attractive element of this form of theater, as the audience was able to participate in the play. During the Carnival in Venice, rich and poor alike would don costumes from the commedia dell'arte and participate in the play taking place. Although the commedia dell'arte was made obsolete by new forms of theater in the 18th century, the appearance of its characters survives in the many paintings which remain to this day in the various museums of Venice.

Giovanni Domenico Tiepolo: Pulcinelle on the Tightrope, 1793, Ca' Rezzonico, Venice
Pulcinelle are Neapolitan relatives of the Zanni, who appeared in the commedia dell'arte from the end of the 16th century

Gallerie dell'Accademia

**Paolo Veneziano: Santa Chiara Polyptych
(central panel)**
Wood, 98 x 63 cm

The *Coronation of the Virgin* is the central
panel of the polyptych (an altarpiece made
up of several small panels put together to
form a single work). The polyptych comes
from the Church of Santa Chiara in Venice.
Besides the main panel showing the Virgin,
there are eight scenes from the life of Christ;
in the coping on the left, a Pentecost scene;
on the right, Christ the
Judge; in between, scenes
with St. Francis, St. Clare,
the Four Evangelists; and,
on the side above the Virgin,
David and the prophet
Isaiah. The beautiful Gothic
frame is partly original: it
was restored in the 19th
century. Paolo Veneziano
(died c. 1360) belongs to the
first school of Venetian
artists whom we know by
name. Between 1333 and
1358, he signed several
works. Typical for him and
his Venetian contemporaries
is the close observance of
Byzantine tradition. They
were clearly not interested
in the masterpieces which
the Tuscan Giotto was
already producing in nearby
Padua at the beginning of
the 14th century – paintings
which demonstrated a com-
pletely new concern with
the depiction of dimensional
bodies as well as a portrayal

rich in detail. This is particularly clear in the *Coronation of the Virgin*. The bodies disappear completely under the expensive brocade, which gives the whole image an expensive, festive tone.

Jacobello del Fiore: Madonna with the Cloak (central panel), 1436?
Wood, 86 x 113 cm (in total)

The central panel of the triptych shows the Virgin with St. John the Baptist in the left-hand panel and St. John the Evangelist in the panel on the right. The original, richly decorated, gilded wooden frame has not survived. The Virgin, who is shown sheltering supplicants under her cloak, is a beloved symbol of protection, the Mother of God providing shelter from evil forces and an expression of hope for believers in her intercession at the Last Judgment. This type of picture became more widespread in the West in the 13th century. This *Madonna with the Cloak* by Jacobello del Fiore (1394–1439) followed a theme found in a Byzantine cult of the Virgin's cloak. This was because in 1204 a piece of the cloak from a church in Constantinople came to San Marco.

The figure of the Christ Child, who appears at the Virgin's breast, is reminiscent of an Eastern Church Madonna. Madonna figures with cloaks similar to this were found in works by earlier Venetian painters. The softly falling folds and lining, the soft curls, and colored petals infused with bright strips of light, on which the Virgin and St. John the Evangelist are standing are stylistically different from older Venetian art. St. John the Baptist is out in the wilderness, standing on rocky ground.

The 15th century, during which the foundation for the wondrous Venetian painting of the following century was laid, is represented in the Accademia by many examples of exceptional quality. In

Giovanni Bellini, a number of whose masterpieces can be seen in the Accademia.

Giovanni Bellini:
Madonna of the Trees, 1487
Wood, 74 x 58 cm

The series of Madonna paintings by Giovanni Bellini (1430–1516) were already highly valued during his lifetime. More than 80 works on this theme created by his workshop have been preserved. The *Madonna of the Trees* is his first known painting of the Virgin to be dated. In addition to the religious content, also depicted is the inner and vivid relationship of mother and child, which is still fascinating to a modern viewer of the painting, for whom its religious significance may have little meaning.

addition to masterpieces by the Bellini family and Vivarini, there are also key works by artists such as Cima da Conegliano and Vittore Carpaccio.

Some of the largest cycles of paintings by workshops and by individual artists can also be found in the gallery, providing an impression of 15th century Venetian life. The greatest painter in Venice in the 15th century, however, was undoubtedly

Giovanni Bellini: Pietà, c. 1505
Wood, 65 x 87 cm

People who know this painting from reproductions are always astounded at how small the original actually is, for, in their isolation, the figures seem quite monumental against the breadth of the landscape behind them. Even when one sees that this is Mary who, shortly before Christ's burial, is bidding farewell to her son, this interpretation of a precise moment is in no way forced upon us. On the contrary, the sorrow of the mother grieving over her dead son is timeless. Their position in the foreground is separated from the remaining landscape by the different flowers, which form a sort of arc behind them. The wide surface between them and the town suggests separation from any earthly events. The devout viewer can concentrate his compassion and prayers fully on the figures in the foreground.

Gallerie dell'Accademia

Paolo Veronese: Supper in the House of
Levi, 1573, p. 322–323

Titian:
St. John the Baptist,
c. 1540, p. 319

Marco Ricci: Landscape
with Washerwomen,
c. 1720, p. 326

Rosalba Carriera:
Self-Portrait, before
1744?, p. 329

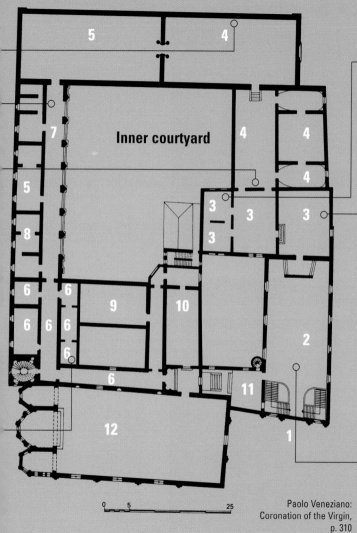

5

4

Giorgione:
The Tempest,
c. 1510, p. 318

7

Inner courtyard

4

4

4

5

8

3

3

3

Giovanni Bellini: Pala di S.
Giobbe, c. 1480, p. 316

3

3

6

6

9

10

6

6

6

6

6

2

6

6

11

12

1

0   5   25

Paolo Veneziano:
Coronation of the Virgin,
p. 310

Giovanni Bellini:
Pala di San Giobbe, c.1480
Oil on Wood, 471 x 258 cm

This work comes from the church of San Giobbe in Venice, which still has the original frame. In painting this altarpiece to St. Job, Bellini included exact replicas of the church's pillars in the frame so that, for a viewer in the church, it must have seemed as if the barrel vaulting in the picture came from the pillars in the frame, continuing on behind their painted counterparts. This gives the impression of the small chapel in the painting actually opening up off the altar, where the various saints are gathered around the Virgin. This painting had an extraordinary effect on Bellini's contemporaries, not only because of its remarkable perspective, but also because of the light, realistic colors, which a chronicler of the late 16th century attributes to the artist's first use of oils.

Giovanni Battista da Conegliano (Cima da Conegliano): Madonna of the Orange Tree, 1497–98
Wood, 212 x 139 cm

Paintings by Cima da Conegliano (c. 1459–1517/1518) are captivating for, among other things, the charming landscapes which often included places from his homeland in the foothills of the Alps. The castle on the left has been identified as that of San Salvatore di Colalto. His figures are a little stiff and have none of the liveliness of Bellini's. When he places his Madonna in a landscape with saints, he gives the usual scenery of such a picture an extra dimension in terms of content. In the distance on the left, St. Joseph is waiting with an ass. And so, at the same time, the Madonna becomes Mary on the flight into Egypt, resting under an orange tree. In the foreground, however, Cima emphasizes the severe sitting position of the Virgin, as if on a throne, and he uses the presence of St. Jerome and St. Louis, who historically were not present at the flight into Egypt, to depict a *sacra conversazione,* a holy conversation.

Giorgione: The Tempest, c. 1510
Oil on canvas, 68 x 59 cm

Titian: St. John the Baptist, c. 1540
Oil on canvas, 201 x 134 cm

Unlike almost any other of the few works by Giorgione (1478–1510) which have survived, this painting has always been accepted as an original. However, there has been no agreement as to its interpretation. A whole book has already been devoted to the various quests by art historians to uncover the meaning of this work, but its subject continues to remain a mystery. This was, of course, both the artist's intention and that of the person who commissioned it, Gabriele Vendramin. Paintings whose meaning was clear only to a small circle of the initiated were particularly admired by the young nobles for whom Giorgione often worked at the beginning of the 16th century. And even for the uninitiated, the warm, humid atmosphere of the storm is clear, seeming to sway between melancholy, menace, and a strong affinity with nature. Giorgione was, next to Giovanni Bellini, the second and much younger artist to be emulated by Venetian painters in the early 16th century. His paintings show something of the yearning for the far-off, close to nature, happy lives portrayed in classical poetry and also found in contemporary works such as Jacopo Sannazaro's *Arcadia* of 1499.

Titian (c. 1488–1576) was one of the painters influenced by Giorgione. In 1540, the date of his painting of St. John the Baptist, he had already long been juxtaposing figures and landscapes. The river in the background here signifies the baptism of Christ by the saint.

Titian: Presentation of the Virgin at the Temple, 1534–38
Oil on canvas, 335 x 775 cm

The Accademia of today includes the building of the former Scuola Grande di Santa Maria della Carità. In 1534, the board of the Scuola commissioned a painting for the confraternity's meeting hall from Titian, at the time the most famous (and probably also the most expensive) painter in the city. The result is that Titian's *Presentation of the Virgin* is now part of the gallery, while remaining in the original site for which it was commissioned. Titian portrays the legend of the Virgin who, as a small child only three years old, climbs the steep steps of the temple very ably, although completely unassisted. On the left, a group of people (including the grand guardian of the Scuola) stand in front of a wide Alpine landscape. On the right, the Blessed Virgin climbs the steps alone and a golden aureole envelopes the holy child. The building behind her closes off the view into the distance. Titian manages to bring together and yet separate the contextual planes of a group portrait and of the sacred event. Portraits and holy scenes rarely occur in the same picture. However, in his choice of background, the artist subtly differentiates between the two. At the same time, he enables the viewer to concentrate separately on the two themes.

huge storm breaks, enabling the Venetians to carry off the precious body, while all around them are fleeing the storm.

Jacopo Tintoretto:
Saving the Body of St. Mark,
1562
Oil on canvas, 398 x 315 cm

Fourteen years after the sensational success of his *Miracle of St. Mark Freeing a Slave*, painted in 1548 for the Scuola di San Marco (also in the Accademia), Tintoretto received a commission for a further painting for the main hall of the Scuola, with scenes from the life of St. Mark. As in the *Miracle of St. Mark Freeing a Slave*, the depiction of space plays a key role in the drama of the painting, which owes less to the breathtaking foreshortening of the body and more to the perspective of the entire painting. The moment shown is when a

Paolo Veronese (Paolo Caliari):
Supper in the House of Levi, 1573
Oil on canvas, 555 x 1310 cm

Originally this painting was situated on
the refectory wall in the Dominican monastery of Santi Giovanni e Paolo. It replaced
a painting of the *Last Supper* by Titian,

which had been destroyed by fire in 1571.
Veronese's commission was also for a
painting of the *Last Supper*. However, on
July 18, 1573, the artist was called before
the Inquisition. In any place other than
Venice, where the inquisitors did not have
such a powerful influence on government,
this would have been an extremely

to give free rein to his imagination. Asked by the inquisitors to change certain things, he altered only the title and the *Last Supper* became the *Supper in the House of Levi* (the wealthy and still unconverted tax collector). There appeared a magnificent, colorful feast, appropriate for a Last Supper.

In this work, Veronese develops his artistic style. Unlike any other 16th century painter, he specialized in depicting expensive materials, precious stones, and pearls. For both Titian and Veronese, color was the most important tool. Unlike the great Titian, however, who in his late works avoided the use of local color and dissolved his paintings in a sort of tonal haze, color was always connected to the subject for Veronese. The expensive silk material which he integrated into his painting is a pretext for showing the maximum number of shades, without freeing the colors from the actual subject.

Despite what the Inquisition might have said about the artist's underlining intentions in the work, we can assume that, among other things, Veronese was exploring the decorative aspects of his painting. It is precisely this well thought out play of color that gives the entire composition its impressive effect.

dangerous situation. The inquisitors complained that the picture was inappropriate and asked the artist why he had included drunks, German farm-hands, and even a man with a nosebleed. Veronese responded with an astonishing awareness of artistic freedom, in which he made it clear that a painter at times should be entitled

Giovanni Battista Tiepolo: Miracle of the Holy House of Loreto, 1744–45
Oil on canvas, 124 x 85 cm

During the night of October 27, 1915, Austrian bombs destroyed the roof of the Venetian church of Santa Maria degli Scalzi (see p. 34). Tiepolo's enormous ceiling painting of the transport of the Santa Casa (house of Mary at Nazareth) to Loreto was destroyed. Fortunately, two sketches for the central piece survived (the other is in London). The draft shows what can be seen on old photographs, but not the complete version, only the central theme. However, even the sketch manages to reveal the main theme in the center of the painting, which gives the whole work its dynamic force. Borne by angels and accompanied by musician angels, the Santa Casa was taken first to Dalmatia and a little later from there to Loreto in Italy. This miracle was said to have taken place in 1295. Loreto is still one of the most important Marian pilgrimage sites.

Giovanni Battista Pittoni:
Annunciation, 1757
Oil on canvas, 153 x 205 cm

The Venetian-born Giovanni Battista Pittoni (1687–1767) was only a little older than Tiepolo, whose work influenced him, along with that of other central Italian painters of his time. In his youth, Pittoni spent much time in Rome and Emilia-Romagna. Unlike his famous contemporary Tiepolo, Pittoni lived only in Venice, although his paintings were coveted throughout Europe. A mark of his work, which is also visible in the *Annunciation*, is the use of pink and green-blue tones in all shades, together with a soft light brown which epitomizes the Rococo style of his paintings. However, the paintings also show Pittoni's typical weakness in the hesitant draftsmanship.

Marco Ricci:
Landscape with Washerwomen, c. 1720
Oil on canvas, 136 x 198 cm

From as early as the 16th century, Venetians were very fond of landscape paintings. These early pictures included, in particular, fresco painting in their villas. From the 17th and 18th centuries on, there are a large number of medium and small-sized paintings which wealthy Venetians used to decorate their palazzi. Marco Ricci (1676–1730) was the founder of 18th century Venetian/northern Italian landscape painting. The next generation of painters was influenced by his broad, varied, and finely colored landscapes. Ricci himself had not only studied Venetian landscapes from previous generations and the paintings by the southern Italian Salvator Rosa, but, on a visit to England lasting several years, he also came across the work of the Dutch landscape painters. The *Landscape with Washerwomen* shows the Piave valley, which he portrayed many times in his landscapes.

Giovanni Battista Tiepolo:
Diana and Actaeon, 1720–22
Oil on canvas, 100 x 135 cm

This work belongs to a series of four paintings depicting scenes from Ovid's *Metamorphoses*. The hunter Actaeon sees Diana, the virgin goddess of hunting, bathing with her nymphs. When she sees him, she turns him into a stag and he is torn to pieces by his own hounds. For a long time the painting was attributed to Sebastiano Ricci. In 1922, it was discovered that it was the work of the young Tiepolo when he was still wholly influenced by the preceding Venetian artists of the 17th century. Tiepolo portrays a grotto far from any civilization except for the farmhouse in the distance. The light bodies of the nymphs and the silvery half moon over Diana form a shimmering contrast to the dark blue of the water.

Francesco Guardi:
St. Mark's Basin with San Giorgio Maggiore
and the Giudecca, 1780–90
Oil on canvas, 72 x 97 cm

During his lifetime, Francesco Guardi (1712–93) painted the monastery island of San Giorgio Maggiore many times. In this late version, it is particularly clear that Guardi, in his numerous paintings of his home town, was not merely documenting the buildings and places or the occupa- tions of the Venetians. Although the essential elements of the architecture, boats, and ships are recognizable, the sole theme of the painting seems to be light and color. The landscape is lit by gentle sunlight. There are gentle ripples on the water which reflect the boats and San Giorgio. But these are only fine rays of light on a mirror-like surface, which the basin would hardly have been like, even on a very calm day. No one will ever have observed San Giorgio reflected in the water as if it were situated on a flat, dark lake. The bright sky with white-gray clouds reiterates in lighter shades the colors of the water, the ships, and the buildings. Guardi chose his colors for reasons of composition, and not to reproduce the actual colors of the island and the sea. At the same time however, he also portrays typical Venetian coloring, which can be found hundreds of times on a slightly overcast day in both the sea and the sky. The harmonious coloring and the still water give the picture a very calm atmosphere, despite the numerous activities of the people we can see. San Giorgio Maggiore and the Giudecca do not appear as small islands, but more as if they were huge ships traveling between the sky and the water.

Rosalba Carriera:
Self-Portrait, before 1744?
Pastel on paper, 31 x 25 cm

When the young Rosalba Carriera (1675–1757) applied for a place at the famous art academy in Rome, the Accademia di San Luca, in 1705, its director, the painter Carlo Maratta, compared her to Guido Reni, who was the most famous artist of the 17th century. From then on, the career of Rosalba was a triumphal march. Already very early on, she found significant patrons and was supported by all the leading royal houses of Europe. Rosalba Carriera was renowned for her sensitive portraits. She did not create momentous oil paintings, but fine, gentle pastels (i.e. chalks) on paper. She fulfilled the demand in the early Rococo period for simplicity and intimacy with the closeness of her pictures, which were not portraits taken from a respectful distance, but just the head and a small part of the upper body. This self-portrait shows her at the age of about 70.

Venice, the way it was

The image we have of the city on the lagoon has been strongly influenced by 18th century landscape paintings of Venice by the artists known as *vedutisti* (painters of views). To this day in Venice, tourists continue to seek out their colors and light. Besides Francesco Guardi, the most important Venetian *vedutista* was undoubtedly Antonio Canal, known as Il Canaletto.

Canaletto: Rio dei Mendicanti, 1723, Collezione M. Crespo, Milan
The Rio dei Mendicanti leads northwards by San Zanipolo. The partial, brightly lit church facade on the left is San Lazzaro dei Mendicanti. Within it were the monastery and the Scuola Grande di San Marco – not much different today from then.

Canaletto: The Molo seen against the Libreria, before 1740. Civiche Raccolte d'Arte Antica Castello Sforzesco, Milan.
The Libreria is on the right of the picture. Behind it, along the length of the Molo, is the Zecca or State Mint, the ground floor of which was sealed off but for a small opening for light, unlike today. Like bars on a window, this was for protection against thieves. A grain store was added, which was demolished in the 19th century to make way for a royal garden.

Canaletto was born on October 18, 1697 in Venice and died there on April 20, 1768. His father, Bernardo Canal, was a famous painter of theatrical scenery. Antonio also trained in this profession before he became a painter of views. The excellent knowledge of perspective and the effect of buildings, which he learned as a theatrical artist, was to stand him in very good stead later, when he finally began to paint the views that surrounded him.

In addition to theater brochures, he soon began to paint the city views which were much loved by foreigners, particular wealthy English tourists keen to improve their education. From 1730 on, he often worked on commission for Joseph Smith, an English merchant who came to Venice c. 1720 and was appointed British consul in 1744. The Englishman, who was the absolute authority on questions of taste, not only for Britons staying in Venice, kept some of

Canaletto: The Molo seen against the Zecca (detail), before 1740. Civiche Raccolte d'Arte Antica Castello Sforzesco, Milan.

Even after Jacopo Sansovino had banished the food stalls and taverns with their booths from the Piazzetta in the 16th century, the Molo and part of the Piazzetta were still the setting for a colorful market which offered more than just luxury items in the 18th century. The traders laid out their wares for sale under makeshift awnings, which could be mounted quickly on poles.

Canaletto's paintings for himself, and sold the majority to his countrymen. He continually found new, sophisticated clients for Canaletto's work, clients who wanted lifelike views of Venice, the much admired "Mistress of the Seas". At first sight, the paintings have the effect of portraying the city as if it were under glass, as the art historian Michael Levey once put it.

This capturing of the moment, the impression that the life of the city portrayed would immediately continue, was determined by the paintings' *staffage*. These figures, in contrast to the precisely portrayed buildings, appear to be just dashes of color and their faces always remain anonymous, but they are actually much

more. Everywhere, the traces of city life are evident: a carpenter's window, the open door of a church, a half-closed well, a curtain flapping. The arrangement of the buildings in the paintings also contributes to this impression, as they are not shown in full. Everywhere, the impression is that the city carries on behind and beside what is shown.

Canaletto's paintings, however, were much more than just an exact portrait of Venice. For him, the city views were an opportunity to contrast light and shade intensively. His paintings are always stamped with a particular light effect. It could be a portrayal of extreme shade and glistening sunlight together, or that he masterfully succeeded in capturing the milky light of the foggy lagoon. Other than this interest in light, lifelike detail was rarely found in the background. Nevertheless, his paintings provide the opportunity to retreat into 18th century Venice.

Canaletto: The Bucintoro in front of the Doges' Palace on Ascension Day, 1729, Aldo Crespi Collection, Milan.
The symbolic marriage of the doge with the sea was the most important official feast day in the Republic. Here, the gilded state barge carrying the doge and members of the government is still anchored in front of the Doges' Palace. Many gondolas are visible in the foreground. These include not only the black gondolas common today, albeit without the awnings, but also some extremely expensive gilded gondolas.

Peggy Guggenheim Collection

Peggy Guggenheim (1898–1979) was a niece of the great American art collector, Solomon R. Guggenheim. Because of the business losses of her father, who died on the Titanic, she belonged to the less wealthy branch of the family. In 1919, however, she inherited a considerable sum, with which she took off to Paris. It was there that she got to know and love modern art. At times she planned to set up a gallery but it was not until 1940, when none of her artist friends were able to sell their work because of the war, that she began to collect in earnest. In 1941, she took her collection to New York, but had returned to Europe by 1946. She bought the Palazzo Venier dei Leoni (see p. 73), where she lived in the company of her many dogs. In 1976, she donated her significant collection of 20th century art to the Solomon R. Guggenheim Foundation, which has been in charge of it since Peggy's death in 1979.

Marino Marini: The Angel of the Citadel, 1949

Peggy Guggenheim placed a sculpture of a rider by Marino Marini (1901–80) on the terrace overlooking the Grand Canal where it could enjoy full sunshine. It is a typical example of such an "angel of the citadel" or "rider," of which Marini made many versions during his career. For most people, the overall effect of his strained posture, as if holding in his breath, and his nakedness, which clearly shows his gender, is humorous. It is almost impossible to imagine how provocative the sculpture would have seemed in the 1950s. As Peggy Guggenheim wrote in her memoirs, his penis was regularly unscrewed so as not to offend churchgoers passing by on the Grand Canal.

Max Ernst: Zoomorphic Couple under Formation, 1933
Oil on canvas, 91.9 x 73.3 cm

In the works of the late 1920s by Max Ernst (1891–1976), again and again we see human and animal figures intertwined. He developed the new techniques of *frottage* and *collage*, which involved rubbing and scraping the structure of natural materials. Paper or canvas was used as the base. Neither process was used for the animal couple here, where the black color is difficult to lift off the underlayer. Nevertheless, Ernst's interest in chance surfaces is still clear. The black muddy mass seems to form a human-animal figure all of its own. The pink, yellow, and blue colored lines which cross through the mass act like chains, from which the form frees itself, but at the same time, resemble entrails and mysterious veins, the inseparable components of growing living things. The picture seems to be an illustration to an article, which Max Ernst had written the previous year, on the subject of artistic inspiration. In this, he described the creative process as a continual change of form. This transformation is set in motion by the artist himself, as he continually recognizes and works out new aspects of things which already exist.

Giorgio de Chirico:
The Red Tower, 1913
Oil on canvas, 73.5 x 100.5 cm

Among other things, the dreamlike empty spaces in paintings by de Chirico (1888–1978) influenced the Surrealists, who tried to uncover what was hidden behind reality. Typical of de Chirico's *pittura metafisca* (metaphysical painting) are cityscapes consisting of huge, simply constructed buildings always accompanied by sculptures. Varied perspective and threatening shadows increase the mysterious atmosphere of his works. The viewer is overwhelmed by the dark perspective of the street in the foreground, linking up with the red tower, which stands menacingly against the backdrop of a blackening sky. Although on the left the silhouette of an equestrian statue can be seen, the tower attracts the greatest attention.

Pablo Picasso: The Bathers, 1937
Oil, chalk, and conté crayon on canvas,
129 x 194 cm

In the foreground, two naked girls are playing with a small boat. In order to depict their swollen, round forms conspicuously, Picasso (1881–1973) places the buttocks of the girl on the left just underneath her neck. On the horizon, another head emerges from the blue tide. One cannot tell if this is another girl or a man watching the two playing. However, drawings do exist for this painting which clearly indicate that the head is a male because of its hair and beard. In the painting, the head of the woman playing with the boat is similar to that of the male, deliberately leaving the painting open to playful interpretation. Since the figure in the background is also looking at the viewer as well as the girls, it seems as if the viewer is mirrored in the painting. Here, Picasso deals again with the theme of beach scenes, which had previously occupied him in the late 1920s and early 1930s.

Jackson Pollock:
Enchanted Forest, 1947
Oil on canvas, 114.6 x 221.3 cm

In 1942, in her New York
gallery, Peggy Guggenheim
was already exhibiting and
sponsoring young American
artists who had been in-
fluenced by the Surrealist
movement in Europe. These
included the then 30-year
old Jackson Pollock (1912–
56). In his early paintings,
Pollock used mainly models
and symbols. These pictures
were already showing the
style of his later paintings,
or the so-called "drip and
splash" method which was
to characterize his work.
He would spontaneously
drip or pour paint onto
canvases laid on the floor.
Extensive accents would
result from the splashing
of the paint. Lines and surfaces were the expression
and image of a continually
developing process. These
drip paintings were the
basis of what
was to become known as
"Action Painting."

Giudecca

Giudecca

The poor Giudecca belongs to the Dorsoduro district, while San Giorgio di Maggiore, with its distinguished Benedictine monastery, is separated by a small channel of water from the Giudecca and is part of the wealthy Sestiere San Marco. Originally, the island was named after its fish bone *spina longa* shape. Where the name Giudecca comes from is not clear: it may relate to the fact that it was originally settled by Jews (*Giudei*). Another interpretation is that the name comes from the Venetian *zudegà* (*giudicati* in Italian), meaning convicted, because previously high-ranking Venetians who were exiled were given land here. Later, wealthy Venetians built their villas in this Venetian hinterland, but before that there were some gardens and summer houses on the island. Later, craft workers and laborers settled there and the Giudecca increasingly became a residential quarter for poorer Venetians.

Mulino Stucky, p. 348

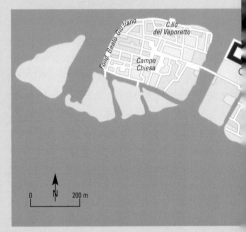

Further sights:
1 Teatro Verde
2 Santa Eufemia di Giudecca
3 Santi Cosma e Damiano

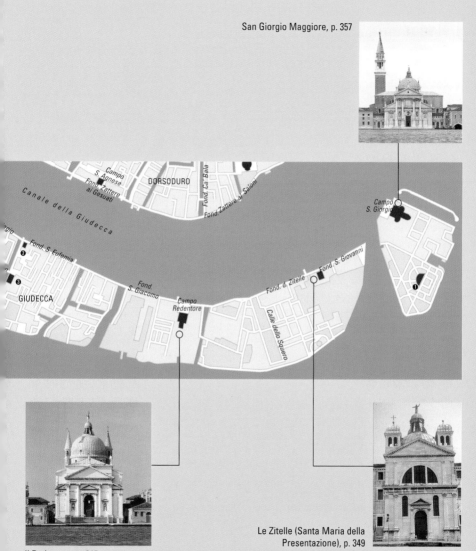

San Giorgio Maggiore, p. 357

DORSODURO

Campo
S. Agnese

Fond. Zattere
ai Gesuati

Fond. Ca' Bala

Fond. Zattere ai Saloni

Canale della Giudecca

Campo
S. Giorgio

Fond. S. Eufemia

GIUDECCA

Fond.
S. Giacomo

Fond. d. Zitelle

Fond. S. Giovanni

Campo
Redentore

Calle dello Squero

Le Zitelle (Santa Maria della
Presentazione), p. 349

Il Redentore, p. 345

Il Redentore

In 1575–76, a terrible plague struck Venice. It raged for over a year and more than half of the population died. In this time of greatest distress, the Senate commissioned the building of a church to honor the Redeemer (*Il Redentore*) for saving them from the disease. The chosen site was the Giudecca, in order to provide a particularly good view of the church from the main island. The surviving Venetians were to be reminded to give praise for the help which Christ had given them in fighting the plague. A committee was set up to oversee closely the appearance and the situation of the church. The most important Venetian architect of the time, Andrea Palladio, was commissioned to produce a draft design. The next decision was whether to build a traditional long building or a modern centralized building. The member of the committee who was interested in architecture, Palladio's friend and patron Marcantonio Barbaro, favored a centralized plan, which many Renaissance architects regarded as the epitome of architectural perfection. The majority of the committee members, however, voted in favor of a longitudinal plan. (It was originally Baldassare Longhena who, again on the occasion of a plague, built a votive church on centralized principles: his Santa Maria della Salute). The Tridentine Council had recently decreed that a long building corresponded best to the requirements for worship. At the Council of Trent (1545–63), which renewed the Catholic faith after the turbulence of the Reformation, the preferred basilica arrangement of the church around a high altar was set out. Palladio resolved this problem, as he had done ten years previously at San Giorgio Maggiore, with captivating results. In brilliant white stone and with noble proportions, the church stands out exotically from the simple low buildings of its surroundings. The theme of overlapping gables, which he had already used at San Giorgio Maggiore, is completed to perfection here. The high dome combines with the facade to give an overall block effect. Everything is concentrated on, and intensifies around, the center. The external facade is unstructured up to the flat pilasters. Sculpture niches with small round gables stand on either side of the great portal built over columns with a single tympanum. The round-arched entrance corresponds visually to the roundness of the dome and thus draws the worshiper straight into the church. From a distance, the dome, with its statue of the Redeemer, has the effect of being the pinnacle of the facade. The Feast of the Redemption is still celebrated on the third Sunday in July. The evening before is particularly atmospheric, Venetians traveling in illuminated boats up and down the canal, their picnics on board.

Interior and Choir

The clear layout of the interior, in which the fundamental and lasting elements of architecture are clearly defined and the proportions of the individual elements are balanced with each other, is typical of Palladio's style. The space is even more strongly standardized than at San Giorgio Maggiore. Among other things, the high columns go from small rectangular bases on the floor almost as far as the roof.

Between the three chapels on either side, there is an arcade with niches. Palladio continued this wall motif on both sides before the crossing, where it is spanned by a large, round arch. Thus he gives the impression that the main space ends here and that, behind, something new begins. At the same time, he brings the high altar, over which there is also a round arch, optically nearer.

This separation and joining of varied spatial compartments is achieved seamlessly. The area of the domed crossing and the curves of the transepts, called conches, at the sides, can also be interpreted as an indentation, as a central space before the monks' choir, to which the main transept connects like a long arm. In this way, Palladio brought together the various plans which he had for Il Redentore. For liturgical reasons, a longitudinal space was developed, but the centralized theme clearly comes to its full force in the choir.

Feast of the Redemption

Because of the church's distance from the main island, one not only gained a viewpoint further away, but the opportunity for a long procession route was created. Once a year, the doge, his retinue, and all the other Venetians would visit the church of Il Redentore in a huge procession of thanks for their salvation from the plague. Boats were used to create a special wooden bridge to ferry participants over the wide Giudecca Canal. To this day, on the eve of the third Sunday in July, the Feast of the Redemption takes place. The Giudecca is then lit by fireworks.

Mulino Stucky

The western end of the Giudecca is dominated by a large industrial complex dating from the late 19th century, the form of which appears more English or northern German. The businessman Giovanni Stucky had his large mill built in 1896 by the German Ernst Wullekopf. The great industrial works have been empty since the 1950s and are slowly becoming more dilapidated. No one seems to agree about how they should be used in the future.

Le Zitelle (Santa Maria della Presentazione)

On the Giudecca, a second church with a civic architecture theme was built with Palladio's participation, namely Santa Maria della Presentazione, known to Venetians as Le Zitelle for short. Palladian forms, such as the large thermal window and the dome with twin belltowers, point to the work of the great architect. However, architectural historians are very much in agreement that Palladio himself was not

involved in the final work: the walls are too flat and the pilasters barely protrude. The construction of the facade with the large window is similar to that at S. Trovaso (see p. 301), the rebuilding of which began at about the same time. It is probable that another architect extensively reworked Palladio's plan, though the sources required to reach a more precise conclusion do not exist. It is known only that in 1566, the Jesuits acquired the land on the Giudecca to build a school for destitute young girls, an institute that was supported by many religious Venetians. Young girls who were orphans, or whose parents did not have the means for a dowry to enable them to get married or enter a convent, often fell into a life of prostitution. In the religious school of Santa Maria della Presentazione they received training in handicrafts which considerably increased their prospects for marriage. The girls from Le Zitelle were renowned for their artistic excellence.

The Venetian Courtesans: Glamor or Suffering?

The very word "courtesan" conjures up images of beautiful women, entertaining in luxurious surroundings, and an eroticism not typically associated with ordinary prostitutes. An exalted view, mainly from the 19th century, contributed to the myths surrounding courtesans.

While Rome and Paris may well claim courtesans who were as famous, if not more famous, the independent and commercially minded Venice was the stronghold of the courtesan from the 16th to the 18th century. In the 16th century, Pietro Aretino (1492–1556), a writer living in Venice, gave a rather malicious account in his famous *Dialogues with Courtesans* not only of the sexual practices of the courtesans, but also of their business methods. The emphasis of 18th century literature was on luxurious eroticism. We know very little about the actual lives of those women who chose to earn a living this way: the majority of literary works wanted nothing more than to provide erotic

Paris Bordone: Two Lovers, c. 1525–30, oil on canvas, 95 x 80 cm, Pinacoteca di Brera, Milan. It is not certain if this is a portrait of a courtesan and her lover. The rather conspicuous presence of gold in the painting would suggest that this is the case.

stimulation and entertainment for their readers. However, once again a Venetian proved the exception here. Veronica Franco (died 1591) was one of the most famous courtesans of her time and also a celebrated literary figure. In her letters and poems she wrote about her own feelings, coming across as an intelligent and warm-hearted woman who portrayed both real suffering and joy at the hands of love. Courtesanship, in its most liberal and chic form, had developed into quite a unique form of venal love at the papal court of the late 15th and early 16th centuries, but it was there that it fell into steady decline with the start of the Counter-Reformation. The Venetian courtesans, on the other hand, maintained their reputation across Europe until the 18th century. The 16th century, notably, was a unique period for women in Venice. At no other time, with the possible exception of antiquity, was it possible for women to achieve such an independent and, to a certain extent, respected lifestyle through selling their bodies, as it was during this century. According to contemporary Venetian sources, both simple prostitutes and courtesans were regarded as important factors in the economy of the city. Only the courtesans, however, could assume the title of *onesta meretrix* (honorable whore). The term *cortegiana,* derived from the masculine *cortegiano* (courtier), gives some indication of their high social standing in comparison to a poor, despised *puttana* (whore). Courtesans remained outside decent society yet they also escaped the massive poverty of their time. Young, beautiful women managing to secure one or more long-term lovers who provided

Veronica Franco: Frontispiece for her poetry collection Terze Rime, which did not appear in the 1576 edition, probably because she was already 30 by then, and not 23 as stated.

accommodation, food, clothing, and a monthly salary could enjoy a good or even luxurious standard of living which they would never have been able to experience under any other circumstances. They earned as much as a senior cleric or a good ship's captain and more than twice the wages of a master tradesman. No other profession of the time offered this

Gabriel Bella: Procession of Courtesans on the Rio della Sensa, before 1792, oil on canvas, Biblioteca Querini Stampalia, Venice

level of financial reward to women. For the courtesans, the end of their career did not always mean the suffering and misery wished upon them by contemporary moral treatises. Many former courtesans managed to save enough money to allow them to marry with a respectable dowry. Since they were often beautiful women who also had a certain standard of education, they could entertain their wealthy clientele with readings, intellectual conversation, singing, music, and dance. Coupled with their extensive sexual experience and financial assets, this meant they were much coveted candidates for marriage. They usually married tradesmen or merchants, although the Venetian chronicle of the early 16th century reported on more than one occasion the marriage of a courtesan and her former noble lover. Such marriages were regarded as minor scandals but came to be accepted after the initial outrage. Nevertheless, the rise in social standing was only one side of the coin. The other consisted of the massive dependence of the women upon their patrons. Brutality was not uncommon, ranging from ruining their reputation (something even a courtesan possessed in this era) to sexual perversions, the infliction of disfiguring facial injuries, and even murder by rejected lovers. The women were defenseless against these acts of violence, which were perpetrated by the upper social classes – mainly because they were the only ones who could afford courtesans – unless they had another lover who would support them.

The social status of the courtesan was also decidedly ambivalent. The much lauded "creatures of luxury" were morally ostracized and sexually exploited women. Indeed, the Venetian state contributed to this in that it regarded courtesans on the one hand as important factors in the Venetian economy, while, on the other, it constantly issued laws, primarily regarding their attire, which would clearly set them apart from equally wealthy female citizens and nobles. If we are to believe sources of the time, this was not only to degrade them, but also because the Venetian courtesans were so famous throughout Europe for their elegance and beauty that ignorant visitors often made rather suggestive advances to the honorable aristocracy. As an indication of just how difficult it was to distinguish between courtesans and ladies of the nobility, a painting by Carpaccio shows two women who were long thought to be courtesans, because of their exotic animals and lavish clothing. Research has now shown, however, that the picture in fact portrays two noble ladies from the house of Torelli.

Vittore Carpaccio: Venetian Ladies, known as "The Courtesans", c. 1490, oil on wood, 94 x 64 cm, Museo Correr, Venice

San Giorgio Maggiore

San Giorgio Maggiore

The island of San Giorgio Maggiore, along with the Giudecca, dominates the Venetian cityscape on the south of the lagoon. The oldest accounts of Venice describe it as a "cypress island." In the early days of Venice, fruit gardens and vineyards were located there, as well as a mill, a salt reclaiming plant, and a small church. In 982, Benedictine monks settled on the island, under the leadership of Giovanni Morosini. Over the centuries, their monastery was to become one of the most important Benedictine monasteries in Italy. In 1109, the relics of St. Stephen came to the island from Constantinople.

As of then, the church played an important part in Venetian Christmas celebrations. On the eve of the second day of Christmas (St. Stephen's Day) and on 26th December itself, the doge and the entire Signoria visited, accompanied by many Venetians, to worship joyfully and pay homage to the martyr. In 1800, when the French were threatening the papacy in Rome, the conclave was moved to the Venetian island. Pope Pius VII was elected at the monastery on San Giorgio. This, however, was the last high point in the history of the monastery. The French plundered here and, of all the precious works of art and valuable books collected over many centuries, nothing remained on the island.

The facade

Just after he had finished work on a new refectory for the Benedictines, Andrea Palladio was commissioned in 1565 to build them a new church. Palladio only supervised the building himself until 1568, but all of his plans were implemented. The monks could not have chosen a better architect than Palladio. The Vicenza architect had long been involved in designing villas and was therefore experienced in the construction of buildings designed to be seen from a distance.

Palladio's inspired design made San Giorgio a perfect counterpart to the buildings of the Piazza San Marco on the other side of the Basin. He placed two dazzling white temple fronts made of Istrian marble behind and above one another. The central, higher front has three-quarter columns on high pedestals and a complete triangular pediment. This facade gives the impression that the lower front, which appears to lie behind, is forced up by pilasters, so that the pediment is only partly

visible. The two forms have a very stylish effect. The space of the basilica is reflected in the tripartite facade with the high central part and the lower side compartments. The dome, with its high towering lanterns, supports the vertical dynamic of the facade structure.

Interior

The interior of the church also has a very clear layout. Palladio chose the basic form of a Latin cross, that is, a basilica with a transept and side aisles. The ceiling consists of a simple barrel vault with a semicircular thermal window, a type of window which gives the space even light. As with the exterior, columns – in this case half-columns – are placed on high pedestals which are also accompanied by a smaller order of pilasters. The functions of all the architectural forms are exact and comprehensible.

The high columns support the ceiling; the pilasters support the arch openings into the aisles. The harmonic proportions of the building give it great serenity, while the sheer size of the structure commands respect.

View from the monks' choir into the nave

According to the requirements of the Counter-Reformation Council of Trent, which had finished just before Palladio began work on the church, the architect placed the monks' choir (or seats for the monastery's large community) behind the high altar. Beyond the high altar with its sculptures, the monks' choir remained visible behind columns, connected to the main space. The separation of the brothers from the lay community, which had been ensured by choir screens before the Council of Trent, remained intact, without denying the community an uninterrupted view of the high altar and the masses celebrated there, as decreed by the Council.

Jacopo Tintoretto:
Gathering of Manna, c. 1590
Oil on canvas, 377 x 576 cm

In 1975, an essay by Nicola Ivanoff, an Italian art historian, drew attention to notable features in this painting. Hitherto, the painting had been interpreted as depicting the shower of manna. Ivanoff, however, observed that the Israelites are not concerned with gathering up the holy food from the heavens, which God had sent them on their journey in the desert. He suggests that this is actually another scene from the Fourth Book of Moses in which the Israelites are refusing to obey because they are weary. The crowd of people in the background on the left and the man speaking angrily to Moses, seated on the right in the foreground, could be evidence of this. The scene is conspicuously lacking in drama, on the contrary, the different activities in a landscape, redolent with water and woodland give the impression of an idyll.

The fact that a man appears behind Moses wearing 16th century armor does not have a negative effect on the scene: a donor would hardly have wanted to be included among the discontented.

Jacopo Tintoretto:
Last Supper, 1592-94
Oil on canvas, 365 x 568 cm

The *Last Supper* hangs opposite the *Gathering of Manna*. That both paintings were planned for these locations is evident from Tintoretto's conspicuous lighting, which is designed for the precise spots where the paintings hang. Both paintings relate to the celebration of mass at the altar. The Last Supper was also a celebratory meal, and the subject of the gathering of manna was seen as pre-figuring this meal in the Old Testament.

Tintoretto does not portray the large dining table from the front, but places it rather at an angle in the picture. At first glance, he thereby emphasizes the naturalness of the evening meal, which, with the many extra figures, is a particularly festive occasion. At the same time, the painting gains an immense spatial dynamic. And, despite the many auxiliary figures, the most important aspect is immediately clear to the viewer from the bright light shining round Christ. The tender presence of many angels, invisible to the participants, emphasizes the mystical nature of the event.

Sestiere Cannaregio

Cannaregio

The name of this *sestiere* derives from the Italian word for reeds, *canna*, which previously grew in abundance in the marshy lagoon between the island and the northwestern tip of Venice. These times are long since gone. In the 16th century, in the northern part of Cannaregio (in the area to the right behind the train station), a light and airy settlement area was laid out to an orderly plan, which was designed for industrial workers, among others. Here the canals were always accompanied, at least on one side, by wide paths (called *fondamenta*). Simple and slightly dilapidated houses mark this western district of Cannaregio. Despite this, it has developed, particularly because of the cheaper rents, into a residential area which is always popular with young people. The further one travels eastwards and the nearer one comes to the Rialto, the narrower and also better cared for are the buildings.

Madonna dell'Orto, p. 380

San Giobbe,
ceiling of the Cappella Martini,
p. 367

Palazzo Labia,
Giovanni Battista Tiepolo:
Cleopatra's Banquet, 1746–47,
p. 370

Ca' d'Oro,
Andrea Mantegna:
St. Sebastian,
1504–06, p. 388

Other sights:
1 Scuola Vecchia dell'Abbazia
2 Scuola Nuova di Misericordia
3 La Maddalena
4 Ghetto Nuovo

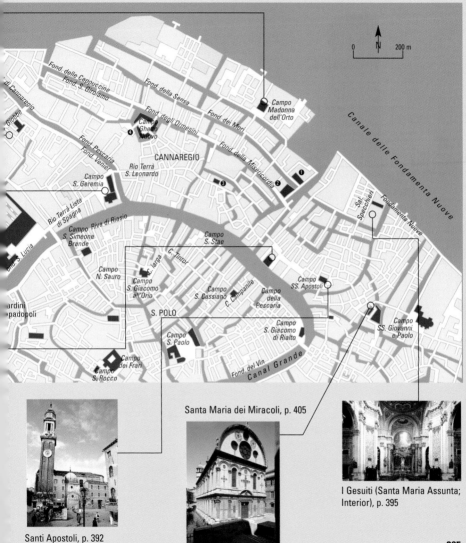

Fond. delle Cappuccine
Fond. S. Girolamo
Fond. della Sensa
Fond. degli Ormesini
Fond. dei Mori
di Cannaregio
Gribbe
Campo
Madonna
dell'Orto
Canale delle Fondamenta Nuove
Campo
Ghetto
Nuovo
④
Fond. Pescaria
Fond. Venier
Fond. della Misericordia
CANNAREGIO
①
②
③
Rio Terrà
S. Leonardo
Campo
S. Geremia
Fondamenta Nuova
Sal.
Spacchieri
Rio Terrà Lista
di Spagna
na S. Lucia
Campo Riva di Biasio
Campo
S. Simeone
Brande
Campo
S. Stae
C. larga
C. Tintor
Campo
N. Sauro
Campo
S. Giacomo
all'Orio
Campo
S. Cassiano
C. Companile
Campo
della
Pescaria
Campo
SS. Apostoli
ardini
apadopoli
S. POLO
Campo
S. Paolo
Campo
S. Giacomo
di Rialto
Campo
SS. Giovanni
e Paolo
Campo
dei Frari
Fond. del Vin
Canal Grande
Campo
S. Rocco

0   N   200 m

Santa Maria dei Miracoli, p. 405

Santi Apostoli, p. 392

I Gesuiti (Santa Maria Assunta;
Interior), p. 395

365

San Giobbe

The church of San Giobbe, built in the middle of the 15th century, is one of the few old churches in this district. It was funded by Doge Cristoforo Moro (in office 1462–71) in honor of St. Bernardine of Siena, who had stayed for a short time in the adjacent Franciscan monastery. The building was begun in the Gothic style by Antonio Gambello, but was completed in the Renaissance style by Pietro Solari, known as Il Lombardo. Some visitors to the church may be disappointed by the rather plain sparseness of the interior. Others may enthuse about the clarity of the Early Renaissance architecture. Although the most important decorative piece belonging to the church, the St. Job altarpiece (Pala di San Giobbe), has been in the Accademia since the 19th century, there are still some interesting works of art on the site. The fine *Birth of Christ* (c. 1540), a masterpiece by Girolamo Savoldo from Brescia, is situated in the Contarini Chapel on the right, beside the choir.

Ceiling of the Cappella Martini

On the ceiling of the second side chapel on the left is one of the rarest Early Venetian Renaissance ceiling panels, made of colored terracotta. This was almost certainly made in the Della Robbia workshop in Florence, which specialized in this type of ceramics. The tondi are decorated with reliefs of the Four Evangelists and Christ with angels. This chapel was owned by the Martini family, silk weavers from Lucca. For its construction they commissioned another artist from Tuscany, possibly Antonio Rossellino, to whom the sculpture of John is attributed. The choice of the ceiling decoration, which was otherwise unknown in Venice, as well as the choice of other Tuscan artists for the chapel, was perhaps due not only to the Tuscan origins of the Martini family, but may also aim to demonstrate the superiority of Tuscan art over Venetian. In the 15th century, San Giobbe was one of the most modern buildings in Venice. The interior is pure Renaissance style, which

had long been common in Florence. With its genuine Florentine chapel, the Martinis gave the church a significance that was new. Their example, however, was not copied. Such a ceiling could not compete with the expensive mosaics known to the Venetians from other buildings.

Palazzo Labia

The Labia family was known for its immense wealth, an expression of which was their magnificent palazzo, which they started building in 1685 and extended further in 1720. The originally bourgeois Labia family acquired their wealth as military suppliers. When, in the 17th century, the Republic of Venice faced bankruptcy after the war against the Turks, many bourgeois families had the opportunity of buying patrician status for large sums of money. The external splendor of their palazzo is bettered only by its interior. Several rooms were decorated in 1745–50 by Tiepolo, the most respected Venetian painter, as well as by other artists. Today, the building is used by RAI, the Italian television company. In order to visit, an appointment must be made in advance by telephoning 78 11 11. This small task is worthwhile: the frescoes by Tiepolo in the main hall are the most important examples of Venetian decorative art from the 18th century.

Giovanni Battista Tiepolo:
A Genius on Pegasus Banishing Time
Fresco, diameter: 600 cm

This ceiling painting in the ballroom is Tiepolo's splendidly exuberant climax to the frescoes in this room, in which the architectural painter, Gerolamo Mengozzi Colonna, also played an important part. Colonna painted the room with architectural forms and illusionary columns, pilasters, and other architectural decorative work as a magnificent framework for Tiepolo's scenes from the life of Cleopatra. Tiepolo opened up the ceiling to a sky, where the genius on Pegasus banishes time, while, above, glory and eternity beckon. This is an allegory of the happy, carefree banquets to be celebrated here, and also to the anticipated immortal glory of the family, to which the time motifs on the ceiling refer.

Giovanni Battista Tiepolo:
Cleopatra's Banquet, 1746-47
Fresco, 650 x 300 cm

Giovanni Battista Tiepolo:
Cleopatra's Entourage (detail), 1746-47
Fresco

The important aspects of the picture's composition, and the motif of the balustrade overlooking the garden, were not Tiepolo's own invention. Paolo Veronese had already used similar compositions 200 years earlier.

The Queen of Egypt, who in antiquity was known as a great seductress, is dressed in a magnificent pink brocade dress and a blue silk cape. Her breasts are bare, which is a sign of her lascivious nature and her romantic interest in Mark Antony. In Venice, very low-cut necklines were popular from the 16th century on, and ladies of the night would have their décolletage more or less completely on view. In addition to her beauty, Cleopatra was also known for her immense wealth and exotic displays of splendor with which she entertained her guests. At this moment, she is holding a large and priceless pearl in one hand, and a glass of vinegar in the other, in which she will dissolve the jewel and then drink it. Tiepolo treats this moment as an expression of great luxury. It is also a not so subtle hint that the Labia family could entertain on a similarly lavish scale in their huge room, on account of their enormous wealth.

In the Palazzo Labia, real and painted architectural details are stylishly mixed together. One cannot always tell on first inspection whether these are genuine or painted, and this gives the frescoes a very realistic character. The game of deceiving the eyes requires the viewer to seek out the boundaries between art and reality and draws the viewer into the painted world.

Campo del Ghetto Nuovo

The Jewish Ghetto: protection or prison?

Today, anyone passing through the quiet streets of Venice's former Jewish Ghetto, with the tall, narrow, and crumbling facades of the buildings, can scarcely conceive that this part of Venice was once one of the wealthiest and most vibrant Jewish residential quarters in Italy. The tranquil, solitary *campo* once echoed with the cries of clothing merchants extolling their magnificent garments. This square was filled with the aroma from bakeries and surrounded by Jewish banks lending their money. Today the

word "ghetto," in the aftermath of the atrocities carried out by the Nazis, sends a shiver through all who hear it. What few people realize, however, is that this term was originally coined for the Jewish quarter of Venice and that for centuries it did not evoke terrible images but the exact opposite: the ghetto meant a guarantee of safety and protection.

Even in ancient times, Rome had its own Jewish community. The Venetians, on the other hand, denied permission to Jews who wanted to settle there: they were welcome only as merchants. These Jews were not native to Italy but rather were of oriental or German descent. The way in which these merchants were treated was no different to that of any other merchant from the same area. Jews arriving from the northern countries were assigned to the Fondaco dei Tedeschi, while Jews from the East could move freely through any part of the city. Italian Jews, who were used by the Venetians as money lenders, had to remain on the mainland in Mestre.

After the great plague of 1348–49, Jews all over Europe were accused of poisoning wells and fountains and were thus held responsible for the terrible disease. Many fled to Italy to escape the violence resulting from these accusations. Increasing numbers of German Jews made their way to Venice, which had become known for its tolerance. Bearing in mind the state coffers, which were practically empty after the war with Genoa, in 1382 the Venetians allowed these Jews to settle in the city. This time the authorities made no distinction between Italian Jews and the Ashkenazi Jews coming from Germany and eastern Europe. A *condotta*, or time-limited contract, governing the

rights and obligations of Jews, which was found in similar forms in other Italian cities, specified that they could lend money at an interest rate of 10–12% and that they were exempt from all taxes provided they paid a fixed amount to the authorities. By imposing a time limit on the contracts, it was possible for the authorities to demand ever higher payments. From a very early stage, the Jews themselves

Scuola Levantina, 17th century

requested a permanent, fixed area in which to live, as well as the allocation of a Jewish cemetery. These would have represented some form of guarantee for the Jews that they would be permitted to stay in Venice permanently. The Venetians, however, had no interest whatsoever in this: the Jews were only tolerated for as long as they were of benefit to the Venetian economy. In 1395, as the city began to recover from the aftermath of the war, Jews were denied extensions to the *condotta*. Instead they were assigned two-year permits. The only exception to this rule were doctors, who were specifically chosen because of their outstanding expertise and knowledge, and because they were held in higher regard by Venetians than their Christian colleagues. It was not until 1509 that Jews were once again permitted to come to Venice for extended periods of time in order to escape the advancing troops of the League of Cambrai. The fact that many of the refugees brought with them substantial amounts of money was clearly of assistance in obtaining this permission. The settlement of Jews in the city did not take place without protest and indeed some priests attempted to turn the citizens of Venice against the strangers with different beliefs. They had very little success, however, in the cosmopolitan and, above all, profit-oriented city that was Venice. In 1516 the Jews finally received their own residential quarter. The Senate selected the grounds of an old foundry in Cannaregio. From the Italian word for casting, *gettare*, the settlement received its name, Getto or Ghetto, a word which would one day acquire a chilling resonance.

Entrance to the Ghetto

Only the Ashkenazi and the Italian Jews were granted permission to settle in their own quarter. However, there were also Jews from the East and those who had fled the Iberian Peninsula to escape death and forced conversion to Christianity. Among these refugees were many *conversos*, Jews who were initially forcibly baptized but were then expelled from Spain and Portugal. They brought with them their own traditions, which were often very different from those of the frequently

Giovanni Grevembroch: Gli habiti de' Veneziani, Jew, 18th century, Museo Correr, Venice

Giovanni Grevembroch: Gli habiti de' Veneziani, Levantine Jew, 18th century, Museo Correr, Venice

very devout Ashkenazi and oriental Jews who had settled in the city.

This type of dedicated residential area for a specific ethnic community was in no way thought of as discrimination; on the contrary, it was regarded as a privilege. Even Venetian merchants lived in their own exclusive areas while in the Orient. These areas were locked up at night for their own protection. There they could practice their own religious traditions and they were subject to an independent jurisdiction. All of these advantages were also enjoyed by the Jews in the Ghetto. It was not until 1589 that oriental and Iberian Jews were allowed to settle near the Ghetto on the site of a much older foundry, the Ghetto Vecchio. The Ghetto Nuovo (or new foundry) was, in fact, the much older Jewish quarter.

The attitude of Venetians to the Jews was dominated largely by economic pragmatism. In contrast to the Jews in Germany or Spain, those in Venice were never in danger as a

discriminatory customs such as "Jew races" at Carnival time, in which seminaked and, if possible, fat Jews were forced to take part in races for the amusement of the people. Often these races had to be repeated several times amid claims of cheating, much to the delight of the crowd. It has also been reported that the Venetians were known to use this opportunity to throw rocks at the Jews. Similarly, the living conditions within the Ghetto were extraordinarily poor. The Jewish community was constantly growing. By the end of the 16th century, some 2000 Jews lived in the Ghetto Nuovo, which had been established in the early part of the century for 600 people. As a result, over time, people built their houses higher and higher. Additional ceilings were inserted in what were originally high stories, so that one could barely stand in the low rooms. On many occasions, buildings which had been "expanded" in this way collapsed because the foundations were never intended to bear such loads.

Ark of the Scuola Levantina, attributed to Andrea Brustolon (1662–1732)

result of religious fanaticism. Nevertheless, co-existence with the Venetians was never easy. The Jews had to pay very high taxes and compulsory charges. They were compelled to fund feasts for high-profile dignitaries who visited Venice. The Christian population had

Scuola Grande Tedesca, 16th–18th century

Palazzo Treves, 18th century

Nevertheless, all of these disadvantages were offset by the protection which was afforded to the Jews by the Venetian state. Virtually nowhere else in Europe did Jews feel so safe for such a long period of time nor were they held in such high regard. The occasional Christian infringements were dealt with severely. Jewish doctors were much sought after: they were allowed to study at the Venetian university in Padua, although they had to pay extremely high fees. Despite numerous interventions by the censor, particularly in the 16th century, Venice was the center of Jewish book printing. Jewish music and dance schools were visited by many Christians, and Jewish musicians were invited to perform in the homes of the nobility. Christian and Jewish scholars frequently worked together to translate ancient and Arabic texts. The highly educated and wealthy Iberian Jews, in particular, were in close contact with Venetian families. For these Jews, the Ghetto Nuovissimo (Newest Ghetto) was created in 1633. This ghetto had more comfortable apartments, even palazzi, such as those owned by the Treves family. As the economy of the Republic began to decline, however, so too did the Ghettos. In the 18th century, increasing numbers of liberal Jews left Venice. The Ghetto began to decay: the once rich cultural life was restricted to synagogues with dwindling attendances (the Venetian term for synagogue is *scuola*). When Napoleon burned the doors to the Ghetto in 1797, the fate of the once flourishing quarter was finally sealed. With poor living conditions, there was no reason for anyone to remain there, religion aside. In 1848, Jews finally received full citizenship. They were Italians of Jewish faith by the time the insanity of Nazism began to sweep across Italy. Not all of the Jews in Venice could be saved. This was especially true of those who lived in the vicinity of the synagogues. And so the Ghetto, in which families had sought sanctuary for over 300 years, contributed to their terrible downfall. Some Jews who had survived the terror of Nazism returned to Venice, though its large Jewish community no longer existed. A small focus of Jewish life remains in the vicinity of the synagogues, although it is miniscule in comparison with the former community. Here one can still find a Jewish bakery and butcher. The visitor will hardly notice this, however. Instead, the sad confinement of the Ghetto imposes itself, no longer eased and brightened by joyful and happy lives.

Arbit Blatas: Monument to Victims of the Holocaust (detail), 1980, Campo del Ghetto, Venice

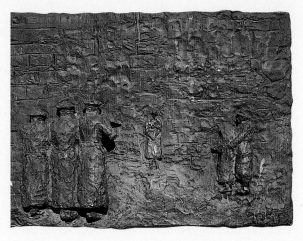

Madonna dell'Orto

In 1377, a statue of the Virgin, believed to have miraculous powers, was found in a garden. The nearby church of St. Christopher, to which the statue was brought, became known as the church of the Madonna of the Garden, or Madonna dell'Orto in Italian. The church belonged to the monastic order known as the Umiliati, which had been dissolved by 1571. Situated in a quiet corner of the city, the Madonna dell'Orto is one of Venice's most beautiful Gothic churches. The building dates back to the mid-14th century and, unusually for a medieval church, we know the name of the architect, a certain Fra Tiberio from Parma. The church was renovated in the 15th century using the original materials. The Twelve Apostles in the niches in the upper part of the facade were previously attributed to Venetian sculptors. Today, however, they are thought to be the work of Tuscan artists.

Sculpture of St. Christopher

The beautiful portal and circular lunette come from the Venetian workshop of the Buon family, though they were not completed until 16 years after Bartolomeo Buon's death. The combination of classical forms (e.g. the columns) with old Gothic forms (such as the ogee arch) is typical of Bartolomeo. Thus it is difficult to tell which parts of the portal come from the Buon workshop, which Bartolomeo managed alone after his father's death, and which were reused elements of the old facade. The sculpture of St. Christopher was also attributed to Bartolomeo, but this is highly disputed and also seems unlikely when compared with the figures which he sculpted for the Porta della Carta at the Doges' Palace. Earlier it was thought to be the work of Matteo Raverti, but research has also disproven this.

Interior

The first surprise is the great brightness filling the interior of the church, which is unusual in Gothic buildings other than in Venice. The columns, which have only to support a light brick wall and, as is common in many Venetian churches, a wooden rather than a brick ceiling, could thus be kept unusually slender. They are made of Greek marble. After complete restoration in the 1970s, which was funded in part by Great Britain, today the Madonna dell'Orto again presents itself as an intact church with many paintings and altars, including impressive works by Giovanni Bellini, Cima da Conegliano, and Jacopo Tintoretto.

Giovanni Bellini:
Madonna, c. 1475 (copy)
Wood, 75 x 50 cm

A copy of Bellini's wonderful Madonna can be seen in the Cappella Valier (the last chapel on the left). The original was stolen in 1993. Fort Worth Museum in the US has an almost identical painting, attributed to either Bellini himself or his studio.

Bellini succeeded in depicting both the vividness of the child and the tender devotion of the Virgin Mary, whose melancholy expression suggests she foresees the child's future Passion.

Jacopo Tintoretto:
Presentation of the Virgin at the Temple (detail)
1552
Oil on canvas, 429 x 480 cm

This painting of the Virgin being presented at the Temple was originally in two halves, as it was for exterior wings used to close the organ when it was not in use. Just when it was fixed in this form is unknown. The organ wings were the first work which Jacopo Tintoretto completed for the church, at the beginning of the 1550s. To the astonishment of onlookers, the three-year-old Mary climbs the high steps to the Temple unaided, as the high priest awaits her. There is a certain menace about the steep, confusing, shimmering steps. The miracle of her managing to complete them is clear to the viewer. A little girl in the lower part of the painting stands with her mother, both of them looking at Mary, who has already reached the high priest. The juxtapositioning of the two little girls, which means that the viewer could easily take the child at the bottom to be Mary, particularly emphasizes the extraordinary achievement of the future Mother of God.

Galleria Giorgio Franchetti in the Ca' d'Oro

The Turin musician and collector Giorgio Franchetti, who bought the Ca' d'Oro in 1894, left the palazzo and his important collection to the city of Venice in 1916 (see p. 47). Since 1927, the house and the collection have both been open to the public. Despite additions to it since then, Franchetti's collection still demonstrates its original high standard. His art collection contains not only paintings and sculptures, but also frescoes, tapestries, faience, and furniture.

Titian: Judith (Justice), 1508–9
Fresco (removed) 213 x 346 cm

Together with Pordenone's frescoes from the cloister of Santo Stefano and a few other wall paintings, the remainder of Titian's famous frescoes for the Fondaco dei Tedeschi (see p. 51) are to be found in the Ca' d'Oro. These were discovered in 1961 during renovation work. With their paintings for the Fondaco dei Tedeschi, the two young artists, Titian and Giorgione suddenly became famous. Until that point, Giorgione's work was little known and Titian's completely unknown. The Venetian government failed to anticipate the enthusiastic response to the paintings. On the contrary, it had forbidden the German trading house from having lavish architectural ornamentation, and chose the simplest and quickest frescoes so that the building would not be too prominent in relation to the other buildings on the Grand Canal. Today, only small traces of these frescoes – which were so admired by Titian's contemporaries – remain. However, even the traces give us some idea of the powerful plasticity of the figures, which was very different from anything painted by Venetian artists previously. Some of the images of these frescoes from the Fondaco dei Tedeschi were preserved in 18th century engravings and as a result are still known to us today.

Jan van Eyck:
Crucifixion of Christ
(copy after Jan van Eyck),
15th century
Wood, 45 x 30 cm

Art historians have long held that this picture is not an original, but a very high-quality work by a painter in the circle of Jan van Eyck (c. 1390–1441). Jan van Eyck was the most celebrated Netherlandish artist of the 15th century. At this time he even had an excellent reputation in Italy. He was one of the few Northern European artists mentioned by the Italian scholar Bartholomaus Facius in his poem in praise of various painters, published in 1456. It is possible that the *Crucifixion of Christ* was already hanging in Italy by the 15th or 16th century, as by this time Netherlandish paintings were sought after by Italian collectors. They were fascinated by the wide, captivating landscapes, the precisely observed, finely painted details, and the intense, radiant colors. Venetian merchants and diplomats, who worked and lived temporarily in the Netherlands, often brought these characteristic paintings back with them.

Giambono (Michele di Taddeo Bono):
Madonna with Child, early 15th century
Tempera on wood

Giambono (documented between c. 1390 – 1462) belongs to the group of early 15th century Venetian painters whose compositional style was still very influenced by the "gentle" look of the late 14th century. One would never suspect that he was a contemporary of the naturalistic artist from the Jan van Eyck school who painted the *Crucifixion of Christ*. On first inspection, there is no trace in Giambono's work of either the central perspective, which developed in the early decades of the 15th century in Florence, or the accompanying attempts to create more plasticity in the portrayal of figures. Nevertheless, the way in which the left foot of the Christ Child is visible by the fold of the Virgin's cape clearly demonstrates that Giambono was interested in plastic values. However, Giambono only includes graphic modeling, visible for example on the left-hand side of the Virgin's cape, in a very sparse way. He models much more with colors, indicating plasticity by their stronger or weaker intensity. An essential aspect of his painting which is particularly attractive is the infinite delicacy of his use of color tones. This can be seen in the Virgin's dress, in the skin tone of both figures, and in the hair of the Christ Child.

Andrea Mantegna:
St. Sebastian, 1504-6
Canvas, 210 x 91 cm

Together with the *Portrait of one Mr. Brignole* by Anthony van Dyck, this painting was the most important work of art in the Franchetti collection, which forms the basis of the Ca' d'Oro gallery. Three paintings of St. Sebastian done by Andrea Mantegna (1431–1506) have survived: a small picture in Vienna, a large altarpiece in Paris, and this canvas at the Ca' d'Oro. It is assumed that this painting was one of those found in Mantegna's workshop after his death in 1506. The extraordinary and what has been described as stone-like plasticity of Mantegna's figures is again very clear in these late paintings of his. The saint, his body riddled with arrows, and his anguished face raised heavenwards, looks as if he

is made of marble. A costly chain of coral and semiprecious stones, which is painted hanging in front of the niche disappearing behind the saint's head, further strengthens the impression that St. Sebastian is standing in front of the niche and not in it.

His arms are tied behind his back with a single rope, cutting deep into his flesh. Mantegna painted the arrows and the blood coming out of the wounds with unbelievable skill. It is almost as if it is meant for the viewer to feel the pain which St. Sebastian is suffering. Towards the bottom right of the picture there is a fading candle, around which a band with a Latin inscription is wound. It reads that only the divine is immortal and that everything else disappears like smoke.

Anthony van Dyck:
Portrait of one Mr. Brignole,
1621–25
Oil on canvas, 205 x 125 cm

Anthony van Dyck (1599–1641) was a great admirer of Venetian art. Titian was always a particular point of reference in his style. From 1621 to 1625, he spent time in Italy, particularly in Genoa. From this period comes his distinguished portrait of an imposing man in the typical black silk costume of his time. Van Dyck has a masterly knowledge of how to reflect the play of light off the thick, dark material. Giorgio Franchetti purchased the painting from the Genoese Brignole family.

Francesco Guardi:
Piazzetta, c. 1755 or 1770–80
Oil on canvas, 45 x 72 cm

Research has given this painting of the Piazzetta two very different dates. This also applies to its pendant or companion piece, a view of the *Piazzetta with the Libreria*, which is also in the Ca' d'Oro. Some writers have placed the painting in the 1750s; others suggest a date of between 1770 and 1780. Although the painting is one of Guardi's real *vedute*, i.e. the paintings in which he portrays real cityscapes and not a mix of imagined images, he does allow himself to take certain liberties for the benefit of the composition. In particular, he strengthened the red tones in the building works. Thus, in conjunction with the color tone of the clouds, he achieves the serene atmosphere of a summer's evening, which he emphasizes with the long shadows of the buildings.

district around Santi Apostoli as early as the 6th century. However, numerous renovations have changed the church. Noteworthy are, among other things, the Renaissance Cornaro Chapel, (Caterina Cornaro was originally interred here in 1510) which is also clearly distinguished on the outside by its dome, as well as the Baroque tower, which was added in the 17th century. This is one of only a few examples of towers from this period in Venice. Made of bricks, as are almost all other campanili in the city, it has a beautiful summit designed by Andrea Tirali, a leading Venetian architect of the late 17th and early 18th centuries.

Ceiling

The church was radically altered in 1575, possibly to a design by Alessandro Vittoria. In the 18th century it was refurbished. In 1748, Fabio Canal and Carlo Gaspari decorated the ceiling with frescoes, which show the Communion of the Apostles and the celebration of the Last Supper.

Santi Apostoli

The church of the Apostles is one of the oldest churches in Venice. The first refugees from the mainland settled in the

Gesuiti Church
(Santa Maria Assunta)

Many Venetians only know the name of the church of Santa Maria Assunta on the northern edge of their city by the name of the order for which it was erected, the *Gesuiti*, or Jesuits. This name was enough to describe the church, which was only permitted to be built, and then only on the edge of the town, after a power struggle with

the Venetian government, which the Jesuits lost. In the struggle for possession of the patriarchate of Venice, which flared up again at the end of the 16th century with the stronger papacy, the Jesuits took the side of the Pope. The Venetians remained steadfast in their protest that they had the right to have the final say in determining high church offices in their city, while the Pope tried to win back this right. In 1606, the Pope excommunicated the entire city of Venice, in order to impose his will, whereupon the Venetians expelled the Jesuits, who acted so vehemently on behalf of the Holy Father. And this was not all: Venice's inhabitants were also forbidden, on pain of death, to send their children to be educated at the famous Jesuit schools. It was not until 1657 that the Jesuits were allowed to return to Venice.

Between 1715 and 1730, the Jesuits built a magnificent Baroque church based on a Roman design. From the outset, the architectural form left no doubt as to the Order's orientation after their loss of the dispute about church offices.

Interior

The interior of the church, with its powerful, single barrel-vaulted nave, is also designed similarly to the Roman churches of the Jesuit Order, such as Il Gesù. Most remarkable is the sumptuous decoration, which was completed to Domenico Rossi's design in 1729. It looks as if the walls are draped with luxurious fabrics but, on closer inspection, it is clear that they are made of marble.

Titian:
Martyrdom of St. Laurence
(and detail), c. 1548–59
Oil on canvas, 493 x 277 cm

Titian probably received his commission to paint an altarpiece for the funerary chapel of the Massolo family by 1546, before he went to Rome. He did not, however, complete the commission immediately. When Lorenzo Massolo, who had wanted a painting of the saint sharing his name to go over his grave, died in 1557, the painting was still not complete. The artist probably delivered the painting the following year. In any event, in 1559 it was hung in the chapel, which at the time was the second on the right hand side.

St. Laurence was the favorite pupil of Pope Sixtus II, who was murdered during the persecution of the Christians under Emperor Valerian (253–260). On the Pope's instructions, Laurence gave away the Church's treasures to the poor, to prevent them from falling into the hands of the emperor. When Laurence was finally apprehended by Valerian's henchmen, he suffered martyrdom by being roasted to death over an iron grid.

Titian tackled this subject in a fascinating way. With the emperor's palace in the background and a heathen idol on a magnificent, embellished pedestal on the left, he conjures up the imperial Rome of antiquity. Here, he uses the experiences of his stay in Rome without using actual antiquities. This is particularly evident in

the statue, which to date has not been identified. In order to accentuate the fire, Titian chose a night scene: the darkness, the flickering light of the fire and the flames give the painting a sinister atmosphere. The outstretched hand of the saint, in earthly light, contrasts with another, heavenly beam of light, which promises him release and salvation into a welcoming heaven.

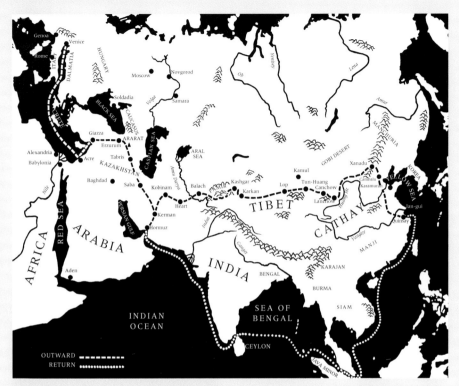

Marco Polo's route to China

Discoverer of an unknown world: Marco Polo (1254–1324)

In the 13th century, it was not uncommon for Venetian families to go for months, even years, without hearing from their loved ones who were trading in distant lands. Twice each year, huge merchant fleets set sail across the sea. Only then was it possible to send letters between Venice and Venetian trading posts in the entire known world. If, however, the merchants were traveling by caravan in the Orient, it could take even longer before they returned to Venice, or at the very least, before they were able to send word home. On the evening in 1269, when someone pounded on the gates of the Polo family's palazzo seeking admission, perhaps no one could have anticipated that it was two long-lost sons of the family returning home after many years. Niccolò Polo and his brother, Matteo, had been missing in the Orient for nine years. Niccolò's wife died shortly after his departure and his small son, Marco had grown into a young man. The tale recounted by Marco is that no one recognized the two figures slumped at the door and that they tried to turn them away as beggars. While on their adventures, Niccolò and Matteo followed a long and tortuous route which was supposed to take them from the Black Sea back to Venice, but which in fact led them to the Mongol emperor of China, Kublai Khan. Eventually they were commissioned by the Khan to ask the Pope to send him 100 priests so that he could compare the Christian

Portulan map of the Adriatic, Museo Storico Navale, Venice. Maps of this type, which include only the coastlines, were used by seafarers until modern times.

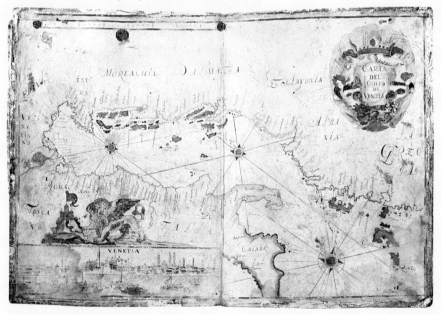

The Polos' Departure from Venice, Livre des Merveilles, Paris, Bibliothèque Nationale Française, 2810, before January 1413, folio 4r

faith with the religions found in his empire. The prospect was that, should the men of God prove to be worthy, the enormous Mongol empire would be converted to Christianity. In addition to this mission of considerable historical significance, the Polo brothers also managed to bring valuable materials, especially jewels, back to their homeland with them.

The Polo brothers had intended to return immediately to China once they had presented Kublai Khan's request to the Pope. Indeed, they were in no doubt that the leader of the Christians would be delighted at this prospect. However, world history thwarted their plans.

The Pope had died and for over a year no one had been able to agree upon his successor. So they continued on their way regardless. This time, Niccolò brought his son Marco with him. For Marco, this was not just an adventure but also a key part of his education – something which all young Venetians from great commercial families experienced. Only very few, however, managed to travel as far as China. The journey to China and the visit to the court of Kublai Khan were to be unforgettable experiences for Marco.

The three, along with some servants, left with the annual *muda*, the huge departure of Venetian merchant ships, and made their way to Acre, a crusader fortress in the Holy Land and one of the most important trade hubs for Venice. Still they awaited news of a decision about the new Pope. Eventually they made their way resignedly to Syria. When they arrived there, they received word that at long last a new Pope, Gregory X, had been elected. Although the new Pope did not provide the requested 100 churchmen, he did send two monks, as well as gifts for Kublai Khan. On the land route, the small caravan made preparations in order to reach Hormuz via Erzurum in Armenia, Tabriz, Saba, and Kerman in what is now known as Persia. From there they hoped to find a boat on which they could secure a passage to China. The boats they found here, however, were built without nails and in places were held together only by ropes. Comparing them to the ships built in their homeland, the Venetians were horrified. The hot, merciless climate in Hormuz made any hope of waiting for a better ship seem pointless, so they decided to take the land route to China. Needless to say, the monks, who were more accustomed to a life of contemplation within the monastery, and certainly not suited to the adventure and strain of such a long journey, had long since left the company of the small group of travelers. Even though Hormuz itself was very far from Venice, the Polos were still in a region which was traveled by European merchants. Now they forged a path which had not been trod by Europeans for a considerable period of time. They crossed the Lut desert and what is now known as Afghanistan, and finally reached the Pamir mountains. It is possible that the Polos had some vague idea of this area of the world from the reports of ancient geographers. Indeed, the kingdom of Alexander the Great extended as far as this point and was known in the Middle Ages. On the far side of the mountains, however, was a world of which nobody could conceive. This was the starting point of the Silk Road which had been forgotten in the West since the fall of the Roman empire.

This picture is frequently presented as the arrival of the Polos in China. In fact it shows how merchants unloaded their goods in the port of Hormuz. Livre des Merveilles, Bibliothèque Nationale Française, Paris, 2810, before January 1413, folio 14v

The king who, instead of wearing jewelry on his clothing, wears it on his bare skin. Livre des Merveilles, Bibliothèque Nationale Française, Paris, 2810, before January 1413, folio 78

Travelers arrive in Madagascar. The illustrator presents the elephants as being very small and with cloven feet. Livre des Merveilles, Bibliothèque Nationale Française, Paris, 2810, before January 1413, folio 88

If, on their journey, the travelers had encountered peoples whose cultures in terms of the achievements of civilization, were equal or inferior to their own, they were now about to enter a land the prosperity and cultural wealth of which must have been inconceivable to Europeans. Traveling along the Taklamakan and Gobi deserts, they finally reached Cambaluc,

the capital city of the fabulous land of Cathay. The Mongols, who had ruled Cathay (or China as it is now known) for just two generations, transferred the seat of power from Quinsai (now known as Shantou) to the north (now Beijing). The Polos were welcomed warmly by Kublai Khan, despite the absence of the priests. While his father and uncle tended to their business, Marco, who was 20 by now, pursued a career at the Chinese court, if we are to believe his reports. As a secret commissioner, he traveled throughout China and a large part of Southeast Asia. His tales of what he saw there must have seemed like pure fiction to his contemporaries in the West. He would just as soon write about an amazing and giant animal like a snake but with two feet like tiger's claws near its head, as of Quinsai, with its population of over five million people, its paved main street over 130 ft (40 m) wide, and the enormous markets, or of the incredible wealth of the Khan. Marco discovered precisely what his fellow Venetians thought of him when he returned to Venice via India in 1298. Nobody believed a word he said. For as long as he continued to relate his stories in oral form, they would be regarded as an old sea dog's tales. After he had written down his story while being held captive by the Genoese, he was mockingly known as Il Milione and his name became synonymous with that of a braggart. His writings were often copied, but more often than not as fairy tales and not as an actual report of the facts. However, a few people believed what this Venetian claimed he had seen. More than 100 years later, it was his book which inspired a young Genoese man to regard not only a sea route to Arabia as possible, but also a sea route to India. His name was Christopher Columbus.

Various kinds of strange people (one-legged, with heads in their chests, and naked savages) whom Marco Polo reported, partly based on the reports of other travelers. Livre des Merveilles, Bibliothèque Nationale Française, Paris, 2810, before January 1413, folio 29v

Santa Maria dei Miracoli

As in many Venetian houses and passageways, a picture of the Virgin Mary was situated in the courtyard of a house neighboring this church no later than 1407. Such pictures were not only devotional, but also had more practical purposes. It was hoped that, in the dark streets, alleys, and courtyards, no one would dare threaten or rob a fellow citizen, or answer a call of nature, under the gaze of the Virgin. This particular picture of the Virgin was regarded as miraculous, and from the late 1570s, was inundated with offerings. It was therefore decided that, in order to honor the picture, a church would be built on the site of the St. Clare convent (which no longer exists). From 1481 to 1489, Pietro Lombardo and his workshop, which included his sons Tullio and Antonio, worked on this little church, which looks more like a charming jewel casket. The Lombardo family were known for their fine stonemasonry work, which they used here to sumptuous effect.

Faber von Ulm, a German traveler, who saw Santa Maria dei Miracoli soon after it was built, suspected that no German ruler could afford such a building. Like the rest of the church, the facade is not only decorated with fine masonry work, but it is also covered with expensive stone slabs. Marble in different colors, green serpentine, and red porphyry, give it its magnificent character. The ornamental reliefs are *all'antica* and in modern Renaissance style. A composition of this abundance is reminiscent of Venetian marble encrustation of the 13th century. The Lombardo family achieved a typical Venetian variant of Early Renaissance architecture, which was milder in effect and less architectonic than in central Italy.

Niccolò di Pietro: Miraculous Picture of the Virgin, early 15th century

Interior

The interior of the church is also sheathed in marble. A richly carved wooden ceiling with painted busts of the Prophets spans the upper space of the church in a barrel-vaulted nave. The ceiling is attributed to Pier Maria and Girolamo Pennacchi, as well as Vincenzo Dalle Destre and Lattanzio da Rimini. Only the small, high apse is given a pendentive dome. The sanctuary, in which the holy picture is situated, is lit by several windows, and is brighter than the nave, so that one's attention is imperceptibly drawn to the altar. Architectonic themes such as pilasters and cornices, which lead the

viewer's gaze to the constructional elements of a building, play an even smaller role in the interior than on the exterior. The decoration of the church with movable works of art is particularly sparse. Two bronze sculptures attributed to Alessandro Leopardi are of Saints Peter and Antony Abbot. Nothing detracts from the holy picture itself. The church looks like an elegant jewel box, and not a heavy building. Marble and gold give the space its celebratory air. It is hardly surprising that Santa Maria dei Miracoli is Venice's most popular church for weddings.

Altar closet (detail)

With infinite and loving attention to detail, even the smallest surfaces are decorated. The altar closet shows not only delicate, highly imaginative reliefs with *all'antica* ornaments and designs, but the main surface of the small pedestal is covered in lace-like filigree work. A delicate lattice made of ever-varying forms has a disk of green stone in the middle. The hardness of the stone, which is so artfully worked, makes it astonishing that this small work of art is nothing more than a piece of decoration.

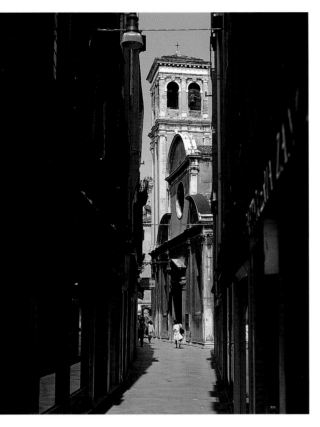

is a cruciform, based on a Greek cross plan. The relatively small, undecorated church demonstrates the harmony of this typical Venetian building design. Characteristic of Codussi, and also of structures by those succeeding him, is the dark gray emphasis on the load-bearing parts.

Sebastiano del Piombo: St. John Chrysostom with Saints Catherine, Mary Magdalene, and Lucia, and John the Evangelist, John the Baptist, and Theodore, 1509–11
Oil on canvas, 200 x 165 cm

The high altar painting of St. John Chrysostom is one of the few examples of the style of Sebastiano Luciani, known as del Piombo (c. 1485–1547), when he was still strongly influenced by Giorgione and Titian. Shortly afterwards, he left his home town of Venice to continue his career in Rome. The powerful figures seem rather inorganic and dreamlike.

San Giovanni Crisostomo

This small church, situated on one of Venice's shopping streets not far from the lively Rialto, was built by Mauro Codussi in 1497–1504 and was the last work of this important Venetian architect. The interior

Giovanni Bellini: Saints Christopher, Jerome, and Louis, 1513
Wood, 300 x 185 cm

In the first side chapel on the right, the altar is decorated with a late painting by Giovanni Bellini. In comparison with the high altar painting, executed at an earlier date by Sebastiano del Piombo (see p. 409), it is clear how well the master, who was 83 years old by this time, was able to compete with his younger colleagues. His point of reference was not, however, del Piombo: both artists were more oriented towards Giorgione. Bellini assumes the naïve expression of the figures. His use of light, however, gives the figures more plasticity and clarity. This particularly applies to the deep colored, heavy garments. The hermit Jerome is separated from the other saints, who are standing under an arch, in front of a balustrade. Jerome is seated in his study, alone and absorbed, on a hill on a wide, barren mountain landscape. Whereas in del Piombo's altar painting the landscape is more or less superfluous, in Bellini's it is a key part of the painting. It conveys not only the isolation, but also the complete peace which is transferred to the saints in the foreground as well as to the viewer.

The Christ Child on the Shoulders of St. Christopher (detail)

This detail shows the great empathy with which the artist portrays the close relationship between adult and child. The child sitting on the shoulders of St. Christopher does not appear to be the one from the legend, who momentarily makes Christopher carry the weight of the entire world on his shoulders as he carries the

Christ Child across the river. Slipping slightly backwards, holding on tightly, with an anxious sideways glance, he comes across more as an unsure and shy, small child. Christopher gazes tenderly upwards towards the infant. In his re-

vealing portrayal of the saint, for whom the Christ Child is also an attribute, Bellini gives a small, inner psychological profile, which is evident only on close inspection.

A question of honor and the Feast of the Twelve Marys

In Santa Maria Formosa, which is one of the oldest churches in Venice, the box makers (or *casselleri* in Venetian dialect) have the altar of their Scuola. Together with the *bombardieri*, or artillery men, who also once had their own altar in the church, they enjoyed the privilege of an annual visit from the doge and his magnificent retinue to their church and altar.

The *casselleri* earned the great favor of a visit from the doge by their bravery during a

Interior view of Santa Maria Formosa

pirate attack in the middle of the 10th century. This series of robberies had damaged the Venetian sensibilities in many ways.

On January 31 or, according to another legend, at Candlemas (the Feast of the Purification of the Virgin) on February 2, Venetian brides went to Olivolo, now Castello, in order to have their marriages blessed by the bishop. For the purposes of this ceremony – and here the *casselleri* come into play – they brought their dowry in a box, or *arcella*, with them. One day, however, according to the legend, the pirates succeeded in mingling with the crowds out to watch the blessing of the brides. In a surprise attack, they abducted the maidens and their money boxes. While the majority stood by, helpless with shock and fright, the powerful *casselleri* immediately went in pursuit. They succeeded in bringing back both the brides and their dowries unharmed. The Venetians were so grateful to the Virgin, on whose feast day – February 2nd – the victory over the pirates occurred, that, from every Candlemas henceforth, they endowed the twelve most beautiful poor maidens, for whom marriage would have otherwise been impossible as they had no dowries, with everything they required, and in particular with a well-filled money casket. Although historians today assume that this story is only a legend, it was so powerful that the Venetians continued to hold one of their most lavish festivals on that date even many centuries later. The visit of the doges to the *casselleri* was only the last, small vestige of incredible and splendid festivals which, during the Middle Ages, lasted for several days at a time. The whole of Venice traveled to see the gifts being given to the twelve brides, who, perhaps because of their beauty and their splendid clothing, were known as the Twelve Marys. At the end of the 10th century, Doge Pietro Orseolo is said to have spent a third of his huge fortune on fitting out the brides. Every noble family, and also the poor inhabitants of a street or a quarter, considered it a particular honor to be allowed to provide for one or more such girls. The rush was so great that those to whom it was entrusted were chosen by lot.

It was not only private funding which was involved. A law of 1303 meant that the immeasurable treasures of San Marco could be used in order to give the maidens an even more magnificent appearance. The whole city would come out to have a look at the twelve beauties. They were paraded through the city in a large procession for an entire day.

The procession began early in the morning with a church service at the episcopal church in Castello. Then, the maidens, accompanied by

Fashionably dressed Venetian ladies from a 13th century mosaic, San Marco, Venice

the bishop and a large retinue of priests and monks, would get into boats, which ferried them across the lagoon to San Marco. There they would be received by the doge and, after another church service, the head of state

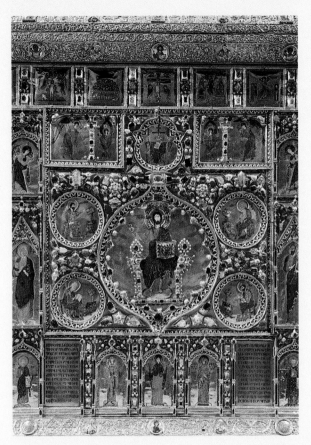

Pearls and jewels on the Pala d'Oro, San Marco, Venice. These are similar to the precious stones from the treasures of San. Marco which adorned the young maidens.

Canal to the Rialto and then over the rio at the Fondaco dei Tedeschi to another mass at Santa Maria Formosa. There, the chapel of the *casselleri* was situated. The Marys would be paraded in the streets in their fine clothes on the following days as well. Festivals in their honor were held not only in noble palazzi, but also in the poorer quarters. A visit from the Marys brought luck. Bitter disputes would arise as to which street they would travel down and which districts would prepare the most lavish reception for them.

A poem, dedicated to Doge Pietro Gradenigo (in office 1289–1311), describes the magnificent sight of the beautiful young women and the huge, happy crowd which came not only from Venice, but also streamed in from the mainland. The poet does not neglect to point out that the Venetian ladies went to every conceivable means to deflect the gazes of the men from the young maidens onto themselves.

would board his glistening golden barge. This would then lead a procession of boats, which brought the Marys along the Grand

The overall romantic theme, that even the poorest of the poor could, solely on the grounds of beauty, be generally admired and achieve prosperity and marriage, must have in no small way contributed to the popularity of the festival. Many a young girl must have dreamed of one day being feted in a similar way before the rejoicing crowds.

Over the course of time, however, the nature of the festival changed. The religious aspect retreated more and more into the background of the parade of young women. Their poverty made them vulnerable. The easiest way for a beautiful young girl to escape this difficult situation was prostitution and not the vague chance of being chosen to be one of the Twelve Marys and gain the possibility of an honorable marriage. Whether there were Marys who earned their living in this way is not known. Through a law of 1349, we know that the government felt obliged to forbid people from abuse or lewdness towards the maidens. Perhaps to prevent such scandals, and perhaps also to curtail the huge amounts of money spent on the maidens and the festival in their honor, dolls were eventually paraded through the town instead of the girls themselves. The financial "pulling power" of these wooden Marys was limited, however, and the economic difficulties faced by the Republic of Venice at the end of the 14th century, due to the Chioggia Wars, finally brought the festival to an end in 1379. The visits of the doges to Santa Maria Formosa, however, continued until the end of the Republic on this happiest and most splendid of medieval feast days.

Pala d'Oro (detail), San Marco, Venice. The richly bejeweled Empress Irene

Sestiere Castello and the Lido

Sestiere Castello

In the Middle Ages, Castello was called Olivolo, after the olive garden found there. The name Castello probably comes from a former, long since gone, defensive building in this district, which is situated on the eastern side of Venice. The quarter extends almost as far as the Piazza San Marco and very much carries the mark of an inner city. Castello is known, among other things, for the arsenal and the worker settlements there, and is a district for ordinary people. Especially in the area with public gardens from Napoleon's time, there is relatively cheap housing in 19th and early 20th century buildings. In any event, in olden times the district was far enough away from the real center of power for the Venetian government to establish the diocesan base there. The comfortable distance from the Doges' Palace and the Basilica di San Marco made it clear that the religious office holder had no authority in the city of Venice.

San Zanipolo (Santi Giovanni e Paolo, interior), p. 471

Andrea del Verocchio: Bartolomeo Colleoni on Horseback, 1481–94, p. 480

Santa Maria Formosa, p. 446

Scuola di San Giorgio degli Schiavoni, Vittore Carpaccio: St Augustine in his Study, 1501–1503, p. 439

Further sights:
1 Palazzo Querini Stampalia
2 San Giovanni in Bragora
3 San Giorgio dei Greci
4 La Pietà
5 Biennale pavilions
6 San Pietro di Castello

San Zaccaria, p. 421

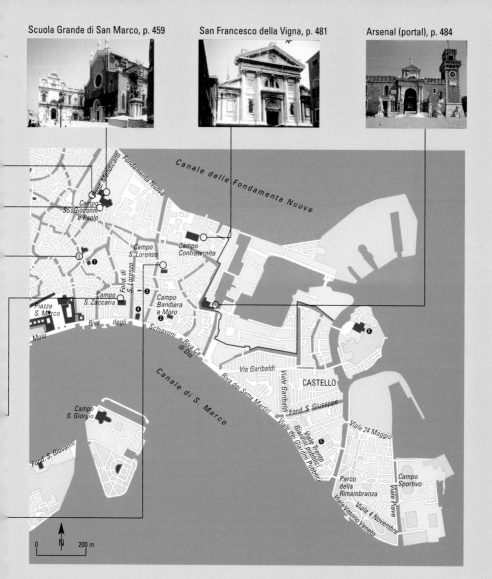

Scuola Grande di San Marco, p. 459

San Francesco della Vigna, p. 481

Arsenal (portal), p. 484

Canale delle Fondamenta Nuove

Fondamenta Nuove

Calle Mendicanti

Campo
SS. Giovanni
e Paolo

Campo
S. Lorenzo

Campo
Confraternita

Fond. di
S. Lorenzo

Piazza
S. Marco

Campo
S. Zaccaria

Campo
Bandiera
e Moro

Molo

Riva   degli

Schiavoni

Riva Ca
di Dio

Canale di S. Marco

Riva dei Sette Martiri

Via Garibaldi

CASTELLO

Fond. S. Giuseppe

Viale Garibaldi

Campo
S. Giorgio

Fond. S. Giovanni

Viale Trento

Viale 24 Maggio

Giardini pubblici

Viale dei Giardini Pubblici

Parco
della
Rimembranza

Viale Vittorio Veneto

Viale 4 Novembre

Viale Piave

Campo
Sportivo

0   200 m
N

419

San Zaccaria

Not far from the Piazza San Marco is the church of San Zaccaria, which, before the dissolution of the majority of the Venetian monasteries in 1810, was one of the most influential convents in the city. Only daughters of the most important noble families in Venice were accepted here. Its ties with the government were very close: the convent was presided over by a sister or close relative of the doge. From its establishment in 829 to the end of the Republic in 1797, the distinguished Benedictine convent was visited once a year by the doge and the entire Signoria. This visit took place on September 13, the consecration date of the church. Later it was postponed to the second day of Easter. Agostina Morosini, an abbess of the convent, is said to have been the first person to give a doge, Pietro Tradonico (836/7–864), the characteristic red cap, known as the *corno ducale*, worn henceforth by every doge as a mark of his office. It did not bring Tradonico any luck. After his annual visit to the convent on September 13, 864, he was murdered by a political opponent.

His successor then took up the tradition of attending a magnificent banquet put on by the nuns for the doge and the city's government after the annual visit to the church. This appears to have also been a sort of Easter celebration among relatives, as the female participants who lived in the convent were always from the leading families. In later, less strictly moral times, the convent was one of the city's leading places of hospitality. The nuns held something akin to a *salon* in their *parlatorio*. Parts of the decoration from the 18th century can be seen in the Ca' Rezzonico today (see p. 69). The convent was a place for educated conversation and exquisite banquets.

The significance of the convent needed to be expressed powerfully in the facade, which the nuns commissioned Antonio Gambello to build in the middle of the 15th century. Before his death in 1481, Gambello was probably able to finish only the first floor. His successor was Mauro Codussi, the leading Venetian architect at the very end of the 15th century and the beginning of the 16th. While Gambello's facade was still predominantly in small, flat forms, Codussi organized the work on the upper stories with a small number of large, arched windows and free-standing columns. The transition from the first floor to the upper stories creates a zone with narrow, very flat shell niches. The difference between a first generation Early Renaissance architect, who was just approaching the new forms, and architects from the second generation, who had clearly mastered the Renaissance repertoire, is clear on this facade.

Giovanni Bellini:
Pala di San Zaccaria (and detail), 1505
Wood covered with canvas, 500 x 235 cm

The interior of the church is richly decorated, reflecting the importance of the building. The best known work of art at San Zaccaria is the altarpiece (*pala*), by Giovanni Bellini, of the Virgin with Saints Peter and Catherine on the left, and Saints Lucia and Jerome on the right. It is a late work by Bellini which demonstrates how successfully the leading 15th century Venetian master met the demands of the new century with greater plasticity. The beautifully colored robes give the figures their great volume. Bellini signed his name on his great altarpiece on a *cartellino* (from the Italian *carta,* meaning paper) at the Virgin's feet. This painted piece of paper with his signature, on which creases can be seen, is typical of Bellini's workshop. Beside it sits a musician angel. The painting is still in its original frame. This is hard to believe given that the painting does not completely fill it. Parts of the canvas were cut away when Napoleon brought the altarpiece to the Louvre after plundering Venice. Once the French were defeated, the painting returned to its original site.

Capella di San Tarasio

Andrea del Castagno:
The Evangelists Luke and John, 1442
Fresco, 176 cm

The large adjacent chapel, which is partly the remainder of the previous church building, bears witness to the great age and prominent position of this former convent church. The San Tarasio Chapel is the Gothic choir of the old church. The vaulting was decorated in the 1540s by

Florentine artists, such as Andrea del Castagno (c. 1421–57), with fresco-style portraits of the Evangelists and God the Father. Why a local artist was not chosen is unclear. Perhaps it was thought doubtful that a local artist could master the difficult technique, requiring one to paint very quickly on wet plaster, since frescoes were not very practical in the salty Venetian air. It was far more probable, however, that the wealthy convent particularly wanted to use modern artists painting in the style of the Tuscan Renaissance.

Andrea del Castagno:
God the Father, 1442
Fresco, 176 cm

Surrounded by clouds, cherubim, and the triangular aureole of the Holy Spirit, God the Father looks down from the vaulting. The Florentine painter manages the view from below and consequent foreshortening of the body masterfully. This is particularly clear with the hands. Through the play of light and shade, which form the folds, the garment also has extraordinary plasticity. No Venetian had managed to do anything similar before the middle of the 15th century. Castagno's frescoes at San Zaccaria were an important starting point for the new direction of Venetian artists around 1450.

In particular, Andrea Mantegna, the painter

from Padua who had married into the Bellini family, must have been deeply influenced by Castagno's frescoes. Mantegna also aimed for a plasticity of form modeled by light and shade. It is not without good reason that he is seen as the designer of the *Death of the Virgin* in the Cappella dei Mascoli in San Marco. The drawing for this mosaic had earlier been attributed to Castagno. Other Venetian artists, however, profited more indirectly from Castagno's style.

A poor violinist, a girls' choir, and the world of the aristocracy: Antonio Vivaldi (1678–1741)

For many, the bright and magnificent music of Vivaldi evokes images of the delicate pastel tones and splendor of the Venetian rococo period. What few realize is that his music was closely linked to the Ospedale della Pietà, one of Venice's largest orphanages. On March 4, 1678, a massive earthquake rocked Venice, causing considerable damage in the community of San Giovanni in Bragadora and surrounding areas. It was on this very day that Camilla Calicchio, wife of the barber Giovanni Battista Vivaldi, gave birth to her first child. The young Antonio Lucio was so weak that the midwives arranged an emergency baptism for him. Later, when he wanted to escape the grueling obligations of the priesthood, Antonio Vivaldi would always recall his poor health as a child. There followed other sons and daughters of which little is known, except that two of the brothers were active as street criminals in nocturnal Venice. These circumstances point to the fact that the family did not belong to the class of prosperous Venetians. This did not change when the father increasingly pursued a career as a musician. Antonio was destined for priesthood, perhaps because of his constitution or because of the dramatic circumstances surrounding his birth, which led his mother to make a vow to that effect. Priests from poor families without connections enjoyed little financial and social security. The musical talent of the young Antonio on the other hand was much more promising.

Anonymous: Portrait of Antonio Vivaldi, 1723, lithograph

Vivaldi's father was also a talented violinist and more than likely taught his genius son. Thanks to his outstanding musical talent, Antonio Vivaldi obtained a position as violin teacher at the girls' orphanage of the Ospedale della Pietà in September 1703, shortly after he was ordained as a priest. This position seemed to have been created specially for him and he immediately gave up his function as a priest.

By today's standards, a position as a violin teacher at an orphanage for girls does not seem particularly enticing. The annual salary of 40 and, eventually, 100 ducats was rather modest. One should not underestimate, however, the musical opportunities of this appointment. A further three institutions maintained this type of girls' choir and orchestra in addition to the Pietà: the Mendicanti, the Incurabili, and the Ospedaletto. They were a permanent and renowned part of the Venetian musical community and competed amongst each other and with the Cappella di San Marco for the favor of the public. From the 16th century onwards, Venice became famous for choral music in which the orphan choirs rose to the highest levels: first the choir at San Marco but, from the early 17th century, also the orphanage choirs. At first it was primarily the girls' choir that made the Pietà famous. However, while Vivaldi was there, there was also the excellent orchestra. Many of the compositions performed by the girls, which have been retained until today, prove that they were outstanding musicians. Vivaldi continued to write new masterpieces for his pupils.

These were primarily religious pieces, but they also included many of his concertos.

The incentive for orphans to distinguish themselves in the choir or as musicians was considerable. Initially, they were divided into

Santa Maria della Pietà. Today, the church is still used for concerts.

Vignes, Orfanelle dictæ, in Hospitalibus Venetiarum ad Musicalia inservientes.

Vincenzo Coronelli: A girl from a Venetian orphanage, engraving, Museo Correr, Venice

elsewhere. Since their family names were often unknown, the girls were known by their first names, together with the name of their voice type or the instrument they played.

Attending a concert at a girls' orphanage was an essential part of any visit to Venice in the 18th century. Their outstanding abilities were also shown off to state visitors, since music was one of Venice's exceptional features. In addition to the incredible musical talent, something which contributed to the popularity of the concerts was the fact that they were performed by very young girls in modest robes, entirely without ornamentation, and wearing flowers in their hair. The eldest of these girls were barely 20. Those who had entered religious life wore red, while the others wore white. More than one listener commented that the girls, with their wonderful music and pure voices, were closer to angels than any creature of this earth. It is difficult to confirm reports that less than convent-like behavior took place behind the walls, so the reputation of the Ospedale remains unsullied. After all, what counted most was the music. Through their concerts, the girls brought considerable sums of money to the Ospedale. In the 18th century, music enthusiasts traveled from all over Europe to Venice to see them. It was not just the Carnival, with its countless new operas, that drew visitors to Venice, but also the chance of hearing brand new instrumental music, perhaps acquiring a valuable instrument, and last but not least, bringing a few notes home as a form of souvenir. Antonio Vivaldi was a favorite focal point for visitors. He was lauded as a great violin virtuoso and his

two groups: the simple, unmusical, or less talented pupils; and the choristers, who also received a first-class musical education. The latter were afforded greater freedom within the convent-like regime of the orphanage, and the best were even allowed to venture outside the Ospedale to hear their art being practiced

name was on the lips of everyone following the publication in Europe of his collection of concertos, entitled *L'estro armonico* (Harmonic Inspiration). After they had heard Vivaldi's compositions at the Pietà, distinguished visitors would be keen to commission specially dedicated concertos by the famous composer. He was never paid a princely amount and his position in the orphanage was anything but secure: in fact, he was once relieved of his post for a short period. Eventually, the opera presented itself as a better source of income for the impoverished priest and consequently he became increasingly active in this genre. For a brief period, Vivaldi even left Venice to work as choirmaster at the court of Mantua. None of these activities, however, brought him much happiness, even though, in the meantime, he had become one of the most highly paid composers. Again and again, Vivaldi returned

Vivaldi's Concerto RV 237, 1717, dedicated to the Dresden court choirmaster, Johann Georg Pisendel

to the apparent security of the Pietà but, as Venice began to look for something new and exciting towards the end of the 1730s, even the Ospedale became less willing to pay him appropriately. After all, the orchestra was intended to earn money for the orphanage and even though distinguished visitors were just as enthusiastic as ever, the people of Venice were no longer happy with him. Vivaldi attempted once more to achieve happiness through one of his distinguished patrons. At the age of 62 he moved to Vienna. The goodwill of Emperor Charles VI provided this happiness, but, at the same time, it made him weary. In fact, the emperor died shortly after Vivaldi's arrival. The composer became seriously ill and died in poverty on July 28, 1741. On the very same day, as a poor priest, he was buried in a pauper's grave at Vienna's Spittaler Gottesacker. The cemetery was closed in the 19th century and the whereabouts of Vivaldi's grave are unknown.

Francesco Guardi: Concert by the Orphan Girls, 1782, oil on canvas, 67.7 x 90.5 cm, Alte Pinakothek, Munich

San Giorgio dei Greci

This church, with its alarmingly tilted campanile, is, as the name implies, a church for the Greek community living in Venice. A large proportion of former Greek territory was under the influence of Venice. It was not surprising, then, that in 1453 after the conquest of Byzantium by the Turks, many Greeks sought refuge in Venice. In 1470, the government of Venice granted them permission to hold official Orthodox services in the city. In 1514, during the rapprochement between the papacy and the Greek Church at the beginning of the 16th century, Pope Leo X also allowed them to build their own church. Work began in 1539 according to a plan by Lombardo. By the time the church was completed, with its dome, in 1571, the Pope's attitude to the Greek Orthodox Church had dramatically changed. In Venice, however, the

Senate had a very tolerant religious policy. Papal bans were not valid here and the Greeks were left alone to worship.

acoustics on account of its musical tradition. Today, the oval-shaped church continues to be used for concerts.

La Pietà (Santa Maria della Visitazione)

Known simply as *La Pietà*, this church belonged to one of the most famous orphanages in Venice, which was housed in the adjacent buildings. It was founded in 1346 as the Ospizio degli Esposti (Home for the Abandoned). It received the particular protection of the Pope and the doges. Every year, on Palm Sunday, the doge and his huge retinue would visit the Pietà's orphanage to listen to the choir of orphan girls who received musical training here. In the 18th century, the famous composer and violinist Antonio Vivaldi (see p. 426) taught here. In 1741, Giorgio Massari began new building work on the church, which needed to have good

San Giovanni in Bragora

This church is so old that no one knows why it has the name "in Bragora". It may go back to earlier Venetian dialect, in which *bragola* meant marketplace and *bragolare,* to sell fish. Perhaps there was once a fish market on the small square in front of the church. This is a typical Venetian Gothic-style parish church from the late 15th century.

Cima da Conegliano:
Baptism of Christ, 1493–94
Wood, 210 x 350 cm

This church has exceptional altarpieces. The finest is at the high altar: the *Baptism of Christ* by Cima da Conegliano (c. 1459–1517), whose theme features St. John the Baptist, the patron saint of the church. The mountains and the castle in the background are reminiscent of Conegliano, Cima's home town.

Scuola di San Giorgio degli Schiavoni

The east coast of the Adriatic was within Venice's sphere of influence. The Venetians conquered the Slavs living there, who, as pirates, had threatened Venetian trade, with armed force and treaties. The Schiavoni, as they were known in Venice, came to the city to work as cheap labor and as traders. When, by the middle of the 15th century, very few locals were willing to work as boatmen, they were replaced by the Schiavoni. Because of prejudice, Slavs were never allowed to row Venetian ships (as had sometimes been the case in antiquity). This was restricted to well-paid teams of men who, in the early days of the city, would be picked from among the local residents. However, as increasing numbers of tradesmen migrated from the mainland, it was difficult to find suitable teams.

The residents of the east Adriatic coast were not only valued for their strength, but also for their great seafaring experience. In 1451, they received permission to join together to form a scuola, for whom they chose Saints George, Tryphon, and Jerome as the patron saints. That the Slavs were not wealthy people is clear from the relatively modest building, which was built at the beginning of the 16th century by Giovanni de Zan, an architect of the Arsenal.

Vittore Carpaccio:
Triumph of St. George, 1502–07
Oil on canvas, 141 x 360 cm

The Scuola degli Schiavoni commissioned Vittore Carpaccio (c. 1455–1525) to paint their meeting house with several scenes from the life of Christ and the legends of their patron saints. When, in the 19th century, collectors began to show interest again in the so-called "primitive" painters of the 13th–15th centuries, Carpaccio was included. His colorful pictures, full of detail, suited the Romantic imagination and are still captivating today.

The *Triumph of St. George* is one of three paintings in which Carpaccio portrays the slaying of the dragon and the story of the saint. According to the legend, a dragon lived in the sea by the town of Silene, Libya, to which animals and people had to be sacrificed. When the beautiful daughter of the king was being offered as a sacrifice, George succeeded in defeating the dragon with the sign of the Cross and then piercing it with a lance. The freed princess put her belt round the monster's neck and George led the animal and the rescued princess in triumph into the town. In gratitude for the rescue, the king and queen were baptized.

In this picture, the center of the scene shows George's triumphant return to the town. He is holding his sword high, ready to finally slay the dragon. On the left are the king and queen and the rescued princess. Behind them on the right, a band plays music in celebration of the happy event. This painting by Carpaccio is typical of his method, with the abundance of exotic figures and the imaginative architecture. Sketches show how precisely he planned the composition, even if the hand of his pupil is discernible in the finished work.

Vittore Carpaccio:
Christ on the Mount of Olives, 1501–03
Oil on canvas, 141 x 107 cm

While, in the portrayal of saints' legends, there is a wealth of detail and creative arrangement in the foreground, the subject of the Mount of Olives does not give much opportunity for embellishment. Carpaccio takes the mountain reference literally. Christ is portrayed praying on a hillside, at the foot of which the disciples are sleeping. In other such paintings, the disciples are mostly shown in a sitting position, having fallen asleep while keeping watch. Here, however, they are shown as if they did not even bother trying to stay awake. Stretched out comfortably, they sleep through the hour of the Lord's greatest need. In this night scene, Carpaccio's great mastery of light is clear. Christ's face, the rocks behind him, and the very tips of the olive tree are illuminated by a divine light.

Vittore Carpaccio:
St. Augustine in his Study,
1501–03
Oil on canvas, 141 x 210 cm

St. Augustine, who was not one of the Scuola's patron saints, is shown at the precise moment he sits down in his study to write a letter to St. Jerome. He is

writing to ask Jerome for help with a treatise about the blessed in paradise. At the same moment, Jerome dies and appears to St. Augustine in a vision. He asks Augustine to abandon his plan, because a mortal is not in a position to make a judgment about paradise. In referring thus to the death of St. Jerome, the painting of St. Augustine is a wonderful conclusion to the scenes from Jerome's life. This story, where the letter replying to Augustine is sometimes shown, was widely known in the 15th and 16th centuries. Carpaccio shows, in fascinating detail, a study from the late Middle Ages. The many books, with their magnificent covers, show that Augustine was a scholar. The small collection of art objects on the left wall is also very interesting. Large candlesticks on both sides of the room allow enough light for reading after dark. Books lie around Augustine's writing desk, and there is a case containing a medley of small objects.

Carnival in Venice

In 1979, young Venetians interested in theater and culture had the idea of reviving the Carnival in Venice, which had lost its color and power vigor since Napoleon banned it at the end of the 18th century. As the new ruler, he feared the subversive power of the masks.

Pietro Longhi: Masked Venetians in the Ridotto, c. 1757, Biblioteca Querini Stampalia, Venice. Members of the nobility could come to the ridotti to meet informally and play games of chance.

Now, in the last week before Ash Wednesday, countless colorful costumes can be found romping around the Piazza San Marco and in the alleyways. The Venetian Carnival of today is different from every other form of carnival, with its magnificent, highly imaginative fancy dress outfits inspired by costumes from centuries gone by, which continually develop ever-new gloriously colorful, fantastic forms. The mild colors of Venice in the winter provide the Carnival with a romantic backdrop. Here, there is neither loud music, naked skin, nor people linking arms in merriment. If one were to speak to the disguised, one would meet very few Venetians. The street carnival is primarily a tourist event. One meets Venetians, perhaps, on the squares not overrun by foreigners, and at private parties. Today's Carnival has little to do with the 18th century festival. Only the masks continue to be modeled on old examples.

In the old Republic, Carnival seemed to carry on almost all year long, or so it must have appeared to the many visitors to the city. Even though in Venice it officially lasted only from December 26 until Ash Wednesday, in the 18th century, the masked game of anonymity was an inseparable part of Venetian daily life and society.

In Venice, certain disguises or masks such as the *bauta* were not costumes, but were worn almost constantly. The *bauta* consisted of a

Gabriel Bella: Ambassadors' Reception at the Collegio, before 1792, oil on canvas, Biblioteca Querini Stampalia, Venice.

black veil, concealing the hair, ears, and neck, worn with a black tricorn hat, and normally a white mask which hid the upper part of the face. The costume was completed by a long cape, known as a *tabarro*. Both men and women, rich and poor, could wear this garment. On special occasions, such as the inauguration of a doge, or receiving distinguished guests from abroad, this garment was actually compulsory. In any event, as a rule, masks were first worn in the evenings, after vespers. In church, they were banned on particular holy days and from December 16 to 26.

The Venetian fashion of wearing masks brought with it many advantages and freedoms which must have seemed close to paradise for many foreigners. Whereas, in other European cities, differences in social standing could be seen clearly from a person's clothing, the masks blurred social boundaries and also the barriers between the sexes. Ordinary citizens dressed in costumes made of expensive fabric could feel like wealthy noblemen. Respected members of the nobility could visit the city's many gaming halls and be entertained there without being recognised. Women had the

Gabriel Bella: Masked Procession on St. Stephen's Day, before 1792, oil on canvas, Biblioteca Querini Stampalia, Venice.

opportunity to move about unhindered (perhaps even in trousers, under a long coat). Romance, valued so highly in the age of Roccoco, expressed itself in undreamed of possibilities. Protected by the mask, one could arrange secret trysts and yet be seen in public. The yearning to stand out, though in the same basic clothing and mask, could be expressed through a *bauta* of fine Burano lace or a *tabarro* of pure

silk. Another mask, not restricted only to Carnival time, was particularly loved by young women: the *moretta* offered more opportunity to show off feminine attractions, as it did not completely cover the skin and hair. It was an oval face mask made of black velvet, which was worn with the help of a button on the inside, which one held in place with the teeth. The consequent forced silence offered considerable scope for flirting, which on the woman's part involved only gestures. Together with this mask, the *zenale* or *zendale* was often worn, a small colorful cape which one could drape over the head. Thus Venetians were used to wearing masks almost all year round, but it was only during Carnival that the traditional costumes unfolded their splendor and diversity.

The first mentions of such fancy dress were recorded in 1268. The Carnival in the old Republic was in no way a quiet affair but, on the contrary, one of noisy gaiety and lively merriment. There were wild men, in animal hides and paper costumes, who charged about the city singing obscene songs; men dressed as women who accosted passers-by; "infants" who stood in groups around the streets discussing politics and current scandals in baby-talk; *mattacini*, who did not talk but who carried with them eggs filled with rose water and other fine scents, which they would throw to pretty girls. For unpopular contemporaries, there would be the odd rotten egg thrown in. In addition, there were also very many masks relating to characters from the commedia dell'arte and costumes caricaturing professions and nationalities: the stiff Englishman, the garrulous woman from Burano, the lunatic syphilis sufferer, the sinister plague doctor, etc.

On certain days, such as December 26, the first day of the Carnival, the masked crowds met at the Campo S. Stefano and from 1647 at the Piazza S. Marco. The wealthy brought out their most valuable costumes and jewelry: on this day, the law which forbade the public display of excess luxury was lifted. People strolled around the square, masked, enjoying the color-

ful costumes, watching and being watched. In the evening, the theater and gaming halls, which had been closed since December 16 for the quiet preparation for Christmas, reopened and a new season of entertainment began. Another high point of the Venetian Carnival was the feast of "Maundy Thursday" on the Piazzetta. In remembrance of the victory over the patriarchs of Aquilea, bulls were

Giovanni Grevembroch: Gli habiti de' Veneziani, 18th century, Museo Correr Venice.

Gabriel Bella: Maundy Thursday on the Piazzetta, before 1792, oil on canvas, Biblioteca Querini Stam

Festie Che Si Solegiono Far
Nella Piazza Di S: Marco
Nel Giorno Del Giovedi Grasso

slaughtered by the smiths' guild. The bulls, representing the patriarchs, would be condemned to death by the doge and the meat distributed to the poor, the Signoria, and prisoners. Every year the new, daring tightrope walks would be set up, which a bold Arsenal worker would cross to present the doge, with a bouquet of flowers on the balcony of the Doges' Palace. The Nicolotti and Castellani, the inhabitants of the feuding districts of San Nicolò and Castello, would show off their skill. The Forze di Ercole (deeds of Hercules) were human pyramids: the two districts would try to outdo each other in courage and strength. Towards the end of the day they would together lead a Morisco dance, a battle dance between Moors and Christians, which would end with fireworks. What was valid the whole year for the *bauta* became the norm during Carnival. Class barriers appeared to be lifted. Rich and poor celebrated together throughout the city and the astute Senate, which recognized this as an escape valve for social unrest, pronounced that no one wearing a mask was superior to any other.

Santa Maria Formosa

Like many squares with old churches, the area around Santa Maria Formosa was one of the earliest areas to be settled in Venice. According to legend, in 639 the Virgin appeared to St. Magnus, Bishop of Oderzo, not in the guise of a young girl, but as an older, "shapely" (*formosa* in Italian) woman. She asked him to build a church at the location where a white cloud floated over the island. In 1492, Mauro Codussi was commissioned to build a new church on the site of a dilapidated church from the 11th century. The architect probably based his conception on the former church, which, in turn, imitated the central section of the Basilica di San Marco with its domes. It is a typical Venetian cruciform-domed church, with three absidal chapels, in a square plan. The clear forms in the interior of the church are echoed on the outside in the smooth, cylindrical forms of the apses.

Facade

The front of the church was built at the expense of the Cappello family. This was a common practice in Venice: wealthy families maintained a public place in memory of famous members of their family for the benefit of the church. This was of particular importance as, with few exceptions, the Republic did not allow statues. In addition, family palazzi could not be as lavish as those in other cities since an unwritten code of honor forbade excessively sumptuous display. Therefore, these family facades on churches, which also often had the function of a memorial stone, were of special significance. In comparison with others, the Cappello family facade is relatively modest. In 1542, the display of an urn and a statue of General Vincenzo Cappello was permitted on the facade overlooking the *rio*. The section facing the *campo* was decorated, from 1604, with busts of different family members. The campanile was also added in the 17th century.

Palazzo Querini Stampalia

Today the Palazzo Querini Stampalia, situated in a small square behind Santa Maria Formosa, houses the foundation of the same name. In 1869, Count Giovanni Querini Stampalia bequeathed the family palazzo, including its furniture, its large collection of paintings, and its extremely valuable library, to the city. Querini added his valuable landholdings in order to finance the foundation and to enlarge the library for the public good. The collection of books on the second floor is open to students and academics. The art collection is open to the public as a museum, with the stipulation that the rooms of the palazzo be maintained in the condition in which they were left to the city by the Count in 1869. At this time his family had lived in this house for more than 350 years.

Entrance

The entrance and first floor of the palazzo were remodeled at the beginning of the 1960s by the leading 20th-century Venetian architect, Carlo Scarpa, (1906–78), one of the founders of Italian postwar architecture. Concrete, bronze, marble, and brick are his preferred materials, with which he achieves surprising contrasts. The juxtaposition of the cold, gray concrete and cool, smooth marble with the warm bronze tones and the soft red of the exposed brick determines the charisma of the rooms. The entire basement has been newly laid out to Scarpa's design: views to the inner rooms entice one into the building. At the same time, the visitor is imperceptibly guided to the exhibition rooms. All of the structural remodeling work had to take account of the fact that the Rio di Santa Maria Formosa, which is separated from the palazzo by only a small square, is often flooded at the basement level by high tides.

Pietro Longhi:
The Marriage, before 1755
Oil on canvas, 62 x 50 cm

The Palazzo Querini Stampalia has an interesting collection of paintings representing all the periods of Venetian art. Its main focus is the 18th century, with works by Gabriel Bella (1730–99), who portrayed Venetian life in a precise historical fashion, and a series of paintings by Pietro Longhi (1702–55). From each of these two significant painters of the Venetian scene, the foundation has a series of the seven sacraments, to which *The Marriage* belongs. The painting shows the moment when the priest blesses the union of the couple. The youthfulness of the main characters (the priest, the server, and the newly weds) contrasts with the elderly person on the left and the person sleeping against a column in the background. The internal space of the church in which the marriage takes place is diffuse except for the column on the right: the scene is focused completely on the sacrament itself. From the light brown and cream tones which dominate the painting, only the bride stands out in her salmon pink dress. The pink tones of her costume seem to reflect the color of her tender cheeks. The presence of the two strange older figures could lead one to speculate that perhaps we are looking at two lovers marrying secretly and against the will of their families.

Jacopo Palma il Vecchio:
Paola Priuli and Francesco Querini, 1528
Oil on wood, 82 x 72 cm and 85 x 73.5 cm

These two paintings show Francesco di Zuan di Niccolò Querini Stampalia and his wife, Paola Priuli di Zan Francesco. It was probably on the occasion of their marriage on April 28, 1528 that the new building work began on the palazzo. Paintings of a future married couple were often completed, or at least started, while the couple were still engaged. However, the painting of the bride remains unfinished, as the few strokes on the arm and hand show. This was because the artist, Jacopo Palma il Vecchio (born Jacobo Negretti,

1480–1528) died on 30 July, just three months after the wedding.

The portraits of Francesco and Paola are both sited before a round niche, behind pilasters with simple capitals. Astonishingly, the figure of the bride is nearer than that of the groom. Whether any significance can be attached to the fact that these pendant portraits do not match (also, the portrait of Paola is slightly higher than that of her spouse), or whether the portrait of Francesco was already in his possession when Palma was painting Paola suggesting that he just approximated the setting, cannot be determined today.

Sebastiano Bombelli:
Full-length portrait of Gerolamo Querini as
Procurator of San Marco, c. 1669
Oil on canvas, 236 x 161 cm

Sebastiano Bombelli:
Full-length portrait of Paolo Querini as
Procurator of San Marco, c. 1684
Oil on canvas, 236 x 161 cm

Sebastiano Bombelli (1635–1719) was one of the best portrait artists of his time. He was summoned from Venice by all of the major Italian ruling houses. The famous portrait of Gerolamo Querini is a typical representational painting from the Baroque period. The young Venetian commands deep respect in his magnificent robe of office.

The Querini were one of the oldest Venetian noble families. The nickname Stampalia came from a Greek island of which the Querini were feudal lords until 1522. Their influence up to the end of the Republic is shown by the many portraits of family members in leading offices of state.

Giovanni Battista Tiepolo:
Portrait of a Procurator and
Admiral from the Dolfin family, 1749–50
Oil on canvas, 235 x 158 cm

In the late 19th century, this painting was taken to be a portrait of Procurator Giovanni Querini. Since it is not listed in old inventories, it probably only came into the Querini collection from the Palazzo Dolfin in the middle of the 19th century, and this is why it is now thought to be a portrait of a member of the Dolfin family. In addition, at the end of the 1820s, Tiepolo had painted ten large scenes from Roman history for this family. In contrast to Bombelli's portraits, Tiepolo's mastery is very clear. The sharper red tones, the architectural background, and the lower viewpoint all command respect. The white glove indicates that it may be a portrait of Daniele IV Dolfin, who injured his left hand during his heroic struggle at Metellino.

Bedroom

The Palazzo Querini Stampalia contains not only a fine art collection but many of the rooms display typical 18th-century interiors for a Venetian city palazzo, providing some idea of life at the time.

This bedroom is furnished with late Rococo decorated and varnished furniture, paintings, and a particularly impressive tapestry. The tapestry shows aristocratic entertainment in the open air, such as that which would be offered during a stay at a villa in the summer months.

Gabriel Bella:
Corpus Christi Procession to the Piazza S. Marco, before 1792(?)
Oil on canvas, 95 x 147.5 cm

The collection features another treasure which shows the viewer something of Venetian life in the 18th century. It owns 67 paintings by Gabriel Bella which portray Venetian festivals, games, and processions, and the life of the nobility and government. His technique could almost be called naive: the architecture is clearly better executed than the figures. This painting shows the Corpus Christi procession. We see that a large, covered, wooden arcade has been erected to protect the many participants in the procession from the heat of the sun.

While Pietro Longhi specialized in intimate portrayals of individual events, often on the inside of noble palazzi, and the great *vedutisti*, such as Guardi and Canaletto, painted the buildings of Venice, Bella provide a detailed depiction of life in the city. His artistic, but not particularly high-quality paintings are nevertheless a first-rate source for the study of Venetian customs and traditions.

Pietro Longhi:
Duck Shoot on the Lagoon, c. 1760
Oil on canvas, 57 x 74 cm

Duck Shoot on the Lagoon is one of Longhi's masterpieces, which he reproduced many times in some of his paintings. The painting here is a portrayal of human types. Especially recognizable is the servant rowing at the back of the boat who has an expressive face and displays a certain individuality. Longhi also succeeds in portraying a foggy day on the lagoon, where the water reflects like glass and the sun lights up the fog into a damp, golden mass. The unusual emptiness of the picture, which Longhi's contemporaries may have seen as a lack of composition, emphasizes the solitariness of the misty autumn morning with the sun just beginning to breaking through.

Giovanni Bellini:
Presentation in the Temple, c. 1460
Wood, 82 x 106 cm

The *Presentation in the Temple* by Giovanni Bellini is one of the greatest Venetian masterpieces of the 15th century. It was the result of a thorough study of the painting on the same theme (now in Berlin) painted by Bellini's brother-in-law, Andrea Mantegna. Following Jewish tradition, Mary brought her firstborn child to the Temple and presented him to the high priest. In addition to the usual people present at this scene – Mary, Simeon the priest, and the prophet Hannah, joined by Joseph and a servant – Bellini shows two further young men on the right. Mantegna's painting already contained an unidentifiable young man, not traditionally found in such a picture.

Scuola Grande di San Marco

The magnificent entrance facade, with its three soaring round gables and sumptuous colored marble incrustation and reliefs, points to the fact that the Scuola Grande di San Marco was one of the six *scuole grande*, i.e. the six most important lay confraternities in Venice. The facade of the church, together with the Dominican church of Santi Giovanni e Paolo and the equestrian statue of Bartolomeo Colleoni, make the Rio dei Mendicanti particularly attractive. On the narrow canal, boats with blue lights pass by from time to time. These are Venice's ambulances. Since the 19th century, the building of the former Scuola has been a hospital.

The Scuola was founded in 1260 and was first based near the church of San Croce. In 1437, an agreement was reached with the Dominican monks from SS. Giovanni e Paolo to obtain a piece of land near their church. Building work began immediately on the Scuola and, including the internal building and decoration, it continued until the 1470s. Those who worked on it included the eminent architects Bartolomeo Buon and Antonio Rizzo. Shortly after the work was finished, the Scuola building was destroyed in a fire, on March 30, 1485. Just a few days later, the Consiglio dei Pregadi (religious authorities) decided to grant the Scuola di San Marco a rebuilding grant of 100 ducats per month for a period of two years. In addition, the Scuola received a loan of 2000 ducats to help finance the new building. Pietro Lombardo and his sons, who had just completed the fine entrance door to the Scuola di San Giovanni Evangelista, received the commission to rebuild the Scuola. The costs of rebuilding increased very quickly and completion of the building was continually delayed. Then the board of the Scuola dismissed the building master and, without further ado, commissioned another leading architect, Mauro Codussi, to finish the work. Codussi was responsible for the three crowned round gables. In 1495, ten years after the terrible fire, the facade was finally completed.

The old confraternity, which had chosen St. Mark, the city's patron, as their own patron saint, was held in the very highest regard. In the Middle Ages and the Renaissance, it had huge influence as it included many of Venice's most respected citizens among its members. Equally high was the expenditure on decorating not only the facade but also the interior of the new building. This work was ongoing from the late 15th century to the early 17th century. The interior contained valuable paintings, including paintings from the Bellini studio and also Tintoretto's St. Mark cycle. Most of these are now in the Gallerie dell'Accademia.

Tullio Lombardo:
Cure of Anianus, 1487–89

Tullio, the most gifted of the Lombardo sons, was given the task of sculpting the perspective reliefs on the lowest level of the facade with scenes from the legend of

St. Mark. On this page, we see the cure of the cobbler Anianus in Alexandria. With a pitiful expression, the cobbler, sitting on the ground, holds the hand which he had injured with an awl up to the saint. The reliefs are like a window into the wall of the Scuola and are reminiscent of the paintings which at the time decorated the inside of many Venetian palazzi. This link would have been evident to the contemporaries of Tullio Lombardo (c. 1455–1532). It is very probable that here he is inviting direct comparison with painted decoration. His relief had the advantage of greater durability, while the quicker process of painting had color on its side. As in painting, Tullio tried to achieve spatial effects with the different depths of his figures. While the two main figures protrude a good deal, those at the back are in very flat, barely noticeable bas-relief. This is how he achieves perspective.

Tullio Lombardo:
Baptism of Anianus, 1487–89

Having been cured, Anianus allowed St. Mark to baptize him. The former cobbler himself then became a missionary and ultimately the first bishop of Alexandria. Both reliefs from the legend of St. Mark and the two lions on either side of the entrance are designed to be viewed from a distance. Only then does their complete perspective and plasticity prove effective. Tullio Lombardo impressed his contemporaries with his ability to express emotions through mimicry and body language. He was also praised for his knowledge of antique sculpture, which influenced his work. Because of the strong classical influences on his style art historians have often suggested that the young Venetian may have

traveled to Rome to study ancient works of art. He could not have developed such a style unless he had extensive knowledge of antique sculptures. It is indeed known that he possessed an antique head, which he studied and often used as a model. In any case, Tullio Lombardo so inspired his contemporaries that the treatise *De Sculptura* (c. 1504) by the Paduan scholar Pomponius Gauricus examined his work in detail.

The Black Death

The plague, one of the most horrific diseases known in ancient times, had largely spared Europe in the Middle Ages. The main areas affected by this animal disease, which was also transmissible to humans, were and are to this day the Steppes of Central Asia. The Venetians and Genoese besieged by a Tartar army in the Black Sea city of Kaffa were unaware of the significance of the blackened bodies which the Tartars flung over the walls of the fortress. On its return, a Venetian galley brought the Black Death from the Orient to Europe in the form of infected black rats and their fleas. These fleas and direct contact with the dead rats caused the bacteria responsible for the disease to be transmitted to humans. Starting in port cities, the Black Death set out on its horrific trail of devastation. Between 1348 and 1352, it had reached virtually all of Europe – even Iceland – and claimed the lives of over 25 million people, approximately one third of the entire population. In Venice, the first assault by the disease claimed more than half the population as its victims. None of the measures taken to stop the spread of the plague were successful. Although it was known that the disease was transmitted from person to person, the exact details of the infection were not understood. It was not until 1894 that the pathogen responsible for the disease (which is now treated with antibiotics), as well as the mode of transmission, were discovered.

Tintoretto: San Roch, 1583-87, Scuola Grande di San Rocco, Venice. There was particular devotion to San Roch during the time of the plague.

The Venetians decided in the early 15th century to implement a strategy which would curtail the disease in the short-term. They stipulated that the crew of every ship arriving into Venice from infected areas had to wait 40 days before they could enter the city. This plan was of limited value, however, as it was not known that the disease could be contracted from animals. From the 14th century, individual areas were repeatedly afflicted by the plague. Areas at particular risk were port towns and cities, as well as areas along the trade routes. Venice, with its enormous volume of trade with the Orient, was at great risk. Between 1348 and 1630, the city succumbed to repeated outbreaks of the plague at regular 20 to 50 year gaps. Nevertheless, it is difficult to establish if indeed it was the plague and if so, of what form, because many serious illnesses were incorrectly attributed to the disease. Often it appeared in several forms, most frequently as tubercular or as bubonic plague. Tubercular plague was principally transmitted from person to person and manifested itself through the appearance of black, bloody sputum, respiratory distress, and a bluish discoloration of the skin. Death usually followed in days. In the case of bubonic plague, the pathogens entered the lymph nodes of people bitten by fleas. These nodes then swelled to painful boils measuring anywhere up to 4 in (10 cm), which

Giovanni Grevembroch: "Gli habiti de' Veneziani." Plague Doctor, 18th century, Museo Correr, Venice.

could rupture, emitting blood and pus. In such cases, or when the lymph nodes were opened artificially, there was a chance of recovery. If, however, the pathogens reached the circula- tory system they caused tuberculosis or exten- sive hemorrhaging in small blood vessels. This hemorrhaging turned the body a black color, which gave the disease its name. In addition,

Hans Makkart: The Plague in Florence (Part II), 1868, oil on canvas, 103 x 204.5 cm), Georg Schäfer Collection, Schweinfurt. Makkart's gruesome vision of people's reaction to the plague was not aimed at portraying Florence, but rather the seven deadly sins or the plague in general.

there were also milder forms of the plague which were not life-threatening. If a person managed to survive, they would generally be immune for a long time afterwards. All of these factors made it difficult for doctors in the past to identify and diagnose a plague-related illness.

This was the case in 1575, when the first cases appeared in Venice. The city's doctors

and the health authorities were unsure as to whether this was another outbreak of the plague. For as long as it remained uncertain, the problem was denied so as not to harm trade. Cases soon began to mount up, however, and this outbreak of bubonic plague was one of the most severe in Venice's history. Since very precise records were kept and more people survived than with other forms of the plague to recount their experiences, we are very well informed about the plague years of 1575–77.

Even before doctors concurred that this was, in fact, the plague, the Proveditori alla Sanità (health authorities) began to isolate the sick. When a full epidemic broke out, plague hospitals were established to which the victims were brought, or they were restricted to their homes. Only doctors or nurses were permitted to enter the plague hospitals. The doctors were provided with protective clothing, which also made an appearance at the Carnival as a sinister reminder of the plague. This clothing consisted of a long coat which covered the entire body. The head was protected with a hat and a type of bird mask with a long beak which was filled with fragrant herbs to block out the stench of the victims. It was also believed that these herbs had disinfectant properties. While there were adequate numbers of doctors available to care for the sick, the case was quite different for nurses. The government ordered all prostitutes to be brought to the plague hospitals. Their male colleagues, the *picegamorti*, who were responsible for burying the dead, burning their remains, and making sure that the sick were kept in isolation in their homes, were recruited from among the city's convicts, who

were promised pardons in return. In addition, fearless paupers were recruited from the mainland with the promise of large amounts of money. They possibly also hoped for the opportunity to steal from some of the dead. One can scarcely imagine the brutal regime of corruption, depravity, and sadism inflicted by these carers, since they themselves would not have expected to outlive their service. On the other hand, there were other people who, in a spirit of true self-sacrifice, provided assistance. Both the sick and those suspected of having contracted the plague were transported to the city's two plague hospitals when the outbreak first occurred. The sick and dying were brought to the old plague hospital; those in whom the disease had not yet taken complete hold went to the new plague hospital. In time it was realized that these facilities were too small and additional facilities were provided on isolation ships. These were surrounded by a guard, and well provided with priests, doctors and food. Here were mainly the wealthy who had fallen prey to the disease. Some described the ships as islands of cheer in the midst of a sea of sickness and death from which hundreds of voices could be heard in the evenings, joined in song and prayer. Relatives came to visit and care for their sick. Those who had recovered gave ecstatic parties to celebrate their departure. In comparison, the old plague hospital, where the dying were confined, must have been a dismal place, characterized by dirt, stench, carers' indifference, appalling suicides and madness,

and, according to sources of the time, close to hell. The new plague hospital, where not all hope was lost, was more like purgatory. The longer the illness lasted, the worse the conditions became. From July 1575 until February 1576, some 3500 people lost their lives. The following year about 46,000 died – approximately one quarter of the population of Venice. Those who could, left the city, leaving behind the poor and the sick as well as a government which was barely in control of the situation. Religion provided the only form of hope and, at the height of the plague, in July 1576, the Signoria publicly vowed that, as soon as the city was free of the clutches of the plague, a votive church would be built. From February 1577 on, fewer and fewer people became ill and by the summer the plague had completely vanished from the lagoon. In recognition of their salvation, Andrea Palladio was retained to build the church, Il Redentore, on the Giudecca, which to this day is the end-point for processions of thanksgiving for deliverance from the plague of 1577. Another magnificent church owes its establishment to a similar vow. Santa Maria della Salute was built after the last wave of the plague, which struck Venice in 1630–31. Many Venetians still visit the church on the annual Festa della Salute on November 21, and thanks are offered up for an entire week. During this last outbreak of the plague, 32 percent of the population died. After this time, Venice was spared further epidemics.

Il Redentore was built as a votive church to mark the end of the plague of 1575.

San Zanipolo
(Santi Giovanni e Paolo)

Almost at the same time as the Franciscans came to Venice, there arrived a second mendicant order founded at the beginning of the 13th century, the Dominicans. They also received a piece of land from Doge Jacopo Tiepolo (1229–49), which was far away enough from the Piazza San Marco, the city's center of power. The land for the Dominican brothers' building was even further away from that of the Franciscans, with whom the order had often found itself in theological disputes over the cen-turies. In addition, the orders were not allowed to woo powerful donors in the same neighborhood. The mendicant orders relied solely on alms from the public. The cruciform Dominican church of San Zanipolo was built at the same time as the Franciscan Frari. Work began in 1234 and finished in 1430. The Venetian name for the Gothic church is "Zanipolo," a typical abbreviation of the long "Santi Giovanni e Paolo." The church was dedi-cated to two Roman martyrs from the 3rd century, Saints John and Paul.

Portal

After a generous bequest in 1458, the Dominican friars were able to commission a magnificent entrance portal. The six Greek marble columns used in the portal came from Torcello. Because the whole facade was to be remodeled, the exposed bricks of the old facade were left. It looks as if it had been prepared to be covered with stone slabs at a later date. The fine portal combines, in an interesting way, Gothic forms, such as the lancet arches, with modern elements of Renaissance building. A striking example of innovation is the highly embellished entablature.

Choir (exterior)

The choir of Santi Giovanni e Paolo is the most beautiful and most important example of Gothic church architecture in Venice, of which there are only a few distinctive examples. (Another is the choir of the Franciscan Frari church). The competition between the two orders would have played a part in the design of their churches. Certainly, the wide geographical bases of the orders and the consequent stylistic influences from other regions would have been significant. The Dominicans retained their own master builder who did not come from Venice, but from Emilia Romagna.

Interior

The Dominicans still had to battle with Venetian conditions, however. They clearly did not want for their church an open roof truss, which was common in Venice, but instead a typical Gothic barrel-vaulted roof, as the Franciscans also had in their church. Although wide, round supports were used, a brick vault, which was common on the mainland, was too heavy for the Dominicans' marshy building site. Therefore, a typical Venetian solution was found: the vaults are equipped with plastered wooden tie beams, creating a basket-like effect, so that from underneath they look like real stone vaults. Great wooden beams give additional stability to the structure. In this way, a very wide distance between the supports is possible, giving the space its expansive character. After the choir seating was removed in 1682, it was not subject to any more building work. Thus the width of the church takes full effect. Like many other churches, today it has a large congregation only on special occasions.

Doges' Tombs in San Zanipolo

The mendicant orders' churches were favorite burial sites. The intercessions and prayers of the monks held out the hope of a better judgment on Doomsday. The virtuousness and voluntary poverty of the brothers were reflected back on the dead, who, having purchased their tombs and requiem masses at a high price from the monks, thereby ensured that the latter could carry out their lives' work.

The Dominicans were, as supporters of the Inquisition, instructed to be on particularly good terms with the State. In other cities, they wanted to maintain the goodwill of the authorities more than the Franciscans, who were mostly popular with ordinary people. In Venice, close connections with the rulers were particularly important, because all church matters ultimately lay in the hands of the government. In nurturing their contacts with the state, the Dominicans combined the financial advantages of a mendicant order with great proximity to power. Santi Giovanni e Paolo thus became one of the most important burial churches for the doges.

Tomb of Doge
Andrea Vendramin († 1478), p. 476

Tomb of Doge
Pietro Mocenigo († 1476), p. 47

Tomb of Doge
Tomaso Mocenigo († 1423), p. 475

The tombs of the doges in Santi Giovanni e Paolo:
1 Tomb of Doge Alvise Mocenigo († 1577)
2 Tomb of Doge Pietro Mocenigo († 1476)
3 Tomb of Doge Bertuccio († 1658) und Silvestro
   († 1700) Valier
4 Tomb of Doge Michele Morosini († 1382)
5 Tomb of Doge Leonardo Loredan († 1521)

6 Tomb of Doge Andrea Vendramin († 1478)
7 Tomb of Doge Marco Corner († 1368)
8 Tomb of Doge Sebastiano Venier († 1578)
9 Tomb of Doge Pasquale Malipiero († 1462)
10 Tomb of Doge Tomaso Mocenigo († 1423)
11 Tomb of Doge Giovanni Mocenigo († 1485)

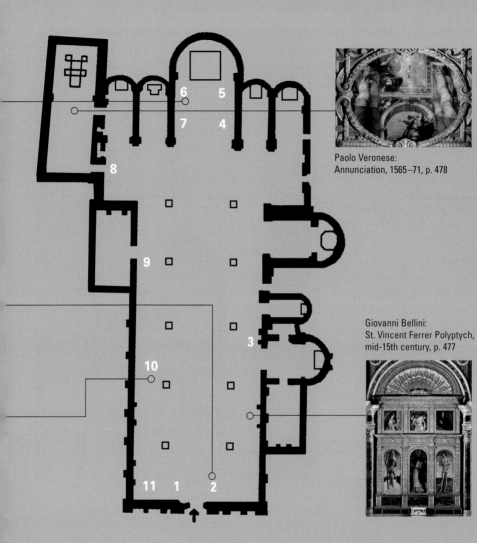

Paolo Veronese:
Annunciation, 1565–71, p. 478

Giovanni Bellini:
St. Vincent Ferrer Polyptych,
mid-15th century, p. 477

Pietro Lombardo: Tomb of Doge Pietro Mocenigo, after 1476

References to the mortality of the body are completely banished in the tomb of Pietro Mocenigo (in office 1474–76) executed by Pietro Lombardo's workshop. A sculpture of the deceased Doge in armour stands proudly on his coffin. Of the two boys at his sides, the one on the left holds a shield with the Mocenigo coat of arms. On the sarcophagus two reliefs depict the greatest political successes of the Doge. On the left, the conquest of Smyrna by Mocenigo himself, and on the right the handover of Famagusta to Queen Caterina Cornaro and thus to the Republic of Venice under the Doge, is depicted. In the side niches, many warriors are conspicuous. It is not clear if these are Christian saints or classical commanders who allude to Mocenigo's military virtues. A bas-relief with sculptures of the three women at the empty tomb of Christ crowns the monument. Above it is a free-standing sculpture of the Redeemer. The belief in the Resurrection and life after death are consequently central themes of this tomb.

Pietro di Nicoló Lamberti and Giovanni di Martino da Fiesole: Tomb of Doge Tomaso Mocenigo, 1423

In 1423, the tomb of another doge from the Mocenigo family was completed. However, it was carried out by Florentine and not Venetian sculptors. The two artists responsible, who signed the monument, were strongly influenced by Donatello, whose style is clearly reflected in their figures. A soldier on the corner mirrors Donatello's celebrated *St. George*, which he sculpted for Or San Michele in Florence. The design of the tomb, however, with the large baldachin and the sarcophagus with the figures of the Virtues, is Venetian. Also, the monument does not show the pure Renaissance forms which one might expect from Florentine sculptors. This typical transitional style between Gothic and Renaissance was common in Venice until the end of the 15th century.

Tullio Lombardo:
Tomb of Doge Andrea Vendramin,
c. 1495

This tomb, which was sculpted around 1495, was not originally intended for the church of San Zanipolo, where it was brought in 1812 from the church of Santa Maria dei Servi. Like the Mocenigo tomb, it is also from the Lombardo workshop. It was largely the work of Tullio Lombardo, the most talented of the Lombardi. When compared with the tomb of Pietro Mocenigo, its special quality becomes clear. The reliefs are more finely cut, the figures softer, but, at the same time, more vibrant. In this late work of the Lombardo workshop, the deceased is once again portrayed lying down. The overall structure of the tomb has the shape of a classical triumphal arch. The grief for the deceased, which is also expressed by the young figures around the bier, contributes to an overall meaning which can be read in diverse ways. The Virtues, which are symbolized by

the figures on the sarcophagus, pray for forgiveness of earthly sins, portrayed in the relief in the roundarch, where the deceased kneels before the Madonna.

Giovanni Bellini: St. Vincent Ferrer Polyptych, c. 1465

This altarpiece was commissioned by the fraternity of St. Vincent Ferrer. Whether or not Giovanni Bellini completed all parts of the polyptych himself is disputed: Lauro Padovano is often mentioned in this connection.

St. Vincent Ferrer was a late 14th-century Spanish Dominican, who tried to put an end to the schism in the Church concerning the election of the popes. He was known for his hard, intransigent preaching for repentance, which inspired many of his followers to accompany him as penitents on his journey of repentance through France and Spain. His unforgiving speeches made Vincent Ferrer many enemies. In 1419, just after his death on a journey through Brittany, a number of confraternities were founded which chose him as their patron saint. They devoted themselves to further extreme acts of penance and were fully committed to his canonization, which took place in 1458. This brought about the installation of an altarpiece with a portrait of the new saint by the Venetian Dominicans in their church.

Paolo Veronese: Annunciation, 1565–71
Oil on canvas, 340 x 435 cm

Originally, the Cappella del Rosario was home to an interesting collection of 16th-century Venetian art. It was the seat of the Scuola del Rosario, which was founded in honor of the Madonna of the Rosary in 1575 to mark the victory at the sea battle of Lepanto, won four years previously on October 7, the feast day of the Madonna. Due to the enormous political significance of this battle for the Venetian Republic, this chapel was given a richly carved and gilded ceiling. In addition to Jacopo Tintoretto's famous *Crucifixion*, works by Domenico Tintoretto, Palma il Giovane, and Francesco Bassano were collected.

In the summer of 1867, in addition to a Madonna by Giovanni Bellini, the church's most important painting, Titian's *Assasination of St. Peter Martyr,* was removed because the left hand choir chapel which normally housed the painting was being renovated. A copy hangs there today.

On August 16, the unthinkable happened. A fire destroyed not only the chapel's art treasures but also Titian's masterpiece. When restoration work began again on the chapel in the late 19th century, Paolo Veronese's ceiling painting was brought here from the former church of the Umiliati.

Thus today important art works from the 16th century and a magnificent chapel ceiling, together with the impressive architecture and the altarpiece by Alessandro Vittoria and Girolamo Campagna, adorn a late 16th century chapel.

Doges' chair, 17th-century

It was on this magnificent chair, covered with sumptuous brocade, that the doge would sit when he attended services at the church of Santi Giovanni e Paolo. This church was the final stage in many of the festive processions trough the city which were led by the doge. San Zanipolo also played a particularly important role after the death of one of these Venetian rulers. The great procession

to honor the dead doge culminated here and the final lying-in-state of the body took place in the church.

Andrea del Verrocchio:
Equestrian Statue of Bartolomeo Colleoni,
1481–94

The *condottiere* Bartolomeo Colleoni requested in his will that an equestrian sculpture of him be placed in front of San Marco in recognition of the many victorious battles he led on behalf of the

Republic of Venice. The Venetians, who did not want to refuse the money, agreed. However, a monument on the Piazza San Marco – and for a foreigner from Bergamo at that – was completely unthinkable. Even doges did not get public statues. After Colleoni's death, the crafty and business-like Venetians showed how they could keep an agreement to the letter and yet turn it to their advantage. Andrea del Verrocchio was commissioned to produce a statue which would be erected in front of the Scuola di San Marco (i.e. rather than the Basilica). The Florentine solved the technically difficult task of a bronze equestrian statue with great style. As Marin Sanusdo, a chronicler of the 16th century, reported, the Venetians came in droves to marvel at this masterpiece. Alessandro Leopardi was responsible for casting and erecting the monument. Even the base, on which he proudly put his name, was made by the Venetian. There is absolutely no doubt, however, that the statue is the work of Verrocchio himself.

San Francesco della Vigna

The name of this church, San Francesco della Vigna, means church of St. Francis in the vineyard; it is so called because the church stands on the site of an old vineyard which existed in the Middle Ages. In 1253, the influential Ziani family made a gift of the land to the Franciscans, who built their second church in Venice here. It was still, however, overshadowed by the Frari church. This did not change when Jacopo Sansovino began work on the new building in 1534. With its brightness and balanced proportions, the church is typical of simple Venetian High Renaissance style. For the facade (the illustration on the right, shows part of it) the elderly, almost 80-year-old Sansovino, was not retained but, instead, the new star who outshone all other Venetian architects, Andrea Palladio. This church, along with San Giorgio Maggiore, was to provide an impressive example of his ability. The facade of S. Francesco della Vigna seems strangely flat and inexpressive when compared with that of San Giorgio. In addition to the more powerful sub-

divisions with architectonic details, the contrast between the two facades results from the fact that the building stands in the middle of other buildings and one cannot view it from a distance. Possibly, Andrea Palladio's flatter structure is a response to this narrow site. The huge temple facade which, here, just as in San Giorgio Maggiore, appears to burst out of a smaller one, does not have such a free effect as the facade of San Giorgio Maggiore seen from a distance.

The Arsenal

Since the Middle Ages, both battleships and merchant ships were built in the huge state dockyard of Venice, the Arsenal. In 1570, when many ships were needed for the sea battle against the Turks, the Arsenal was able to produce 100 galleys within two months, thus displaying a level of productivity which was completely unheard of in pre-industrialized Europe.

The reason why the Venetians were in a position to make so many ships so quickly was due to the development, since the Middle Ages, of highly rationalized work methods. One could almost describe these as being like an assembly line, in which every stage of the work process was carried out in a precise, predetermined sequence in different buildings on the Arsenal site. For all tasks, from the building of the hull over the caulks, the stitching of the sails, the turning of the ropes, to equipping the ships with arms and supplies, the Venetian battleship stayed in the Arsenal. On a surface area of over 60 acres (25 hectares), and with up to 16,000 workers, it was the largest-ever enterprise in Christendom, if not the world. At the beginning of the 14th century, Dante, the great Italian poet, had already compared the hectic bustle, noise, dirt, and heat of this place with that of hell.

of the buildings on the site, however, do not date from this time, but from the 16th–18th centuries. Particularly impressive is the *tana*, the great rope room in which the long ropes are turned.

Watchtowers at the entrance

As protection against attacks, and particularly against agents wanting to spy on the secrets of Venetian shipbuilding and arms manufacture, the Arsenal was surrounded by a high stone wall. The canal entrance from the land side was guarded by high towers built in 1574, which one can see from the Vaporetto. Behind this wall stands an architectural landscape, which to today's visitors from the industrial age looks very much like 19th-century construction. Most

Gateway

In accordance with its huge importance for the city, in 1460 the Arsenal was given a magnificent gateway executed by Antonio Gambello. Its columns are like those of a Roman triumphal arch. It was modeled on the antique arch in Pola (from the 1st century), which belonged to Istria, then under Venetian rule. The gateway to the Arsenal is thus one of the first structures in Venice which is clearly modeled on the antique and thus fulfils the main Renaissance requirement of being close to antiquity. Over the course of time, sculptures recalling Venetian victories at sea were added to the gateway, which increasingly became a monument to the military strength of Venice. The winged Lion of St. Mark over the door was erected during the building stage. The comparison with its antique companions, which stand by the door and were placed here in the 17th and 18th centuries, would not necessarily be in its favor.

San Pietro di Castello

Even today, it is clear that Castello is far removed from the real center of power in the city. Neither trade nor bustle nor vast palazzi affect the appearance of the district around San Pietro, but instead simple residential quarters and, by Venetian standards, a surprising amount of green. The church of the Venetian bishop has been located here since about 1091 and, from 1451, the seat of the patriarch of Venice, who had, in practical terms, lost his entire church authority to the doges. What a contrast between the splendid Basilica di San Marco and this large but rather barren-looking church, which was completed between 1594 and 1596 by an architect of no particular significance, Francesco Smeraldi, possibly from some preliminary plans made by Andrea Palladio.

Biennale exhibition center

An international exhibition of modern art has taken place in Venice every two years since 1895. Since 1907, the exhibition has been held in pavilions in the far-easterly Giardini Pubblici (public gardens). These gardens, which can be described today as a town park, were laid out in 1810 at Napoleon's behest. Several churches, monasteries, and even a hospital for poor sailors were demolished to make way for the gardens. Here, in the extreme eastern corner of the main Venetian island, lacemakers, fishermen, and ordinary sailors had lived from time immemorial. The park to which residential quarters had to give way is like a foreign body in Venice. Only when the Biennale opens its doors every two years does it attract tourists. The national pavilions stand along the various sides so that here (even if only during the Biennale), one can also experience a piece of architectural history. Of particular interest is the Dutch building of 1954 by Gerrit Rietveld, as well as the wooden pavilion designed by Alvar Alto the same year for Finland. The most important Venetian architect of the 20th century, Carlo Scarpa, built the pavilion for Venezuela. The German pavilion erected in the late 1930s is a striking example of Nazi representational architecture.

National pavilions at the Biennale center:

1 Spain
2 Belgium
3 The Netherlands
4 Italy
5 Finland
6 Hungary
7 Brazil
8 Austria
9 Poland
10 Egypt
11 Former Yugoslavia
12 Romania
13 Greece
14 Israel
15 USA
16 Nordic countries
17 Denmark
18 Czech Republic and Slovakia
19 France
20 Great Britain
21 Canada
22 Germany
23 Japan
24 Russia
25 Venezuela
26 Switzerland
27 Ruins from 1950 of the Book Pavilion built by Carlo Scarpa

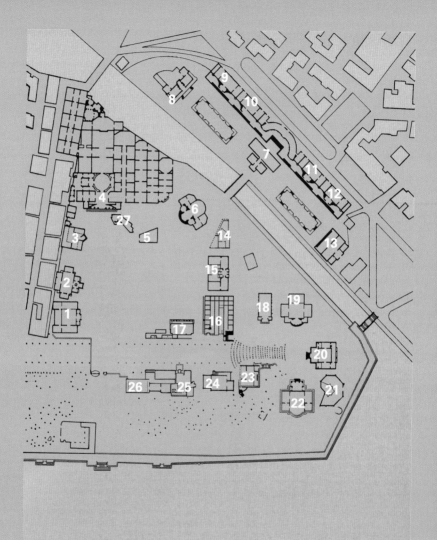

The Lido

The narrow sand bank across the lagoon from Venice was one of the first fashionable seaside resorts in Italy. Since 1860, the wealthy and beautiful of Europe and America have been coming here to enjoy summer vacations. Today, the elegant *belle époque* hotels built along the promenade around 1900, such as *Des Bains* and *The Excelsior*, continue to reflect this magnificence. The 7 mile (12 km) long Venetian beach became a symbol of fashionable seaside living, so much so that, in Italian, the word "lido" is now synonymous with *spiaggia* (beach). Even today, the fine white sand still surprises visitors. In summer, the area thrives even if there are only fleeting glimpses of the international jet set, and the Venetian casino relocates to the Lido from the Palazzo Vendramin-Calergi.

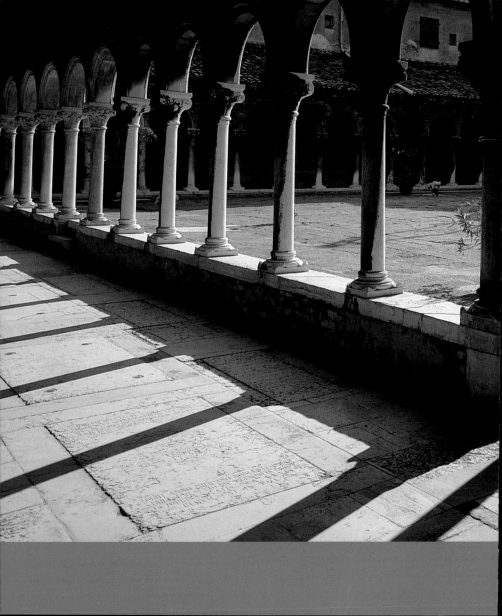

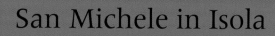

San Michele in Isola

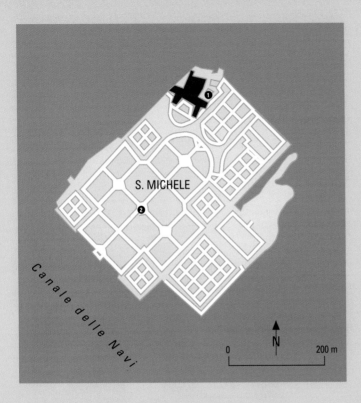

S. MICHELE

Canale delle Navi

0   N   200 m

1 S. Michele in Isola
2 Cemetry of San Michele

San Michele in Isola

Even from far away, the pristine white front of San Michele in Isola shines across to the visitor. The church, with its distinguished, simple facade made of Istrian limestone, was the first Renaissance building in Venice. Erected for the Camaldolese monks, it was begun by Mauro Codussi in 1469, as his first work. The lavish decoration of the hexagonal Cappella Emiliana, built from 1530, appears to be trying to outdo the plain facade of the church.

Cemetery of San Michele

Today, San Michele is no longer a monastery. Like many others, it was closed by Napoleon. He also ordered the Venetians to give up their inner city cemeteries and bury their dead on the island of San Cristoforo della Pace, next to San Michele. Burying the dead around the churches within the city was, in fact, not very hygienic. Because of the water, deep graves could not be dug and some visitors to Venice reported on the terrible odour from the cemeteries. In addition, there were often fountains in the open church squares which, particularly if they were not properly sealed or during high tides, could be polluted by those buried. When San Cristoforo became full, the canal between the two islands was filled in so the land of San Michele could also be used as a graveyard. The cemetery is laid out in typical Italian form: walls of memorials, places for interment, and a park-like section with some very expensive mausoleums which appear to follow the Venetian burial culture of the past using modern means. Since Venice has only this one graveyard, non-Catholics may also be buried here. Among those interred in San Michele are some important artists and writers who regarded the lagoon city as their second home.

as they are in later Renaissance architecture, but are decorated with soft plant and geometric motifs. The load-bearing parts of the structure are formed in contrasting colors and materials to the rest of the building. Codussi also made all of the walls extraordinarily thin, which gives the building a light and filigreed appearance, a typical feature of the architect's work. On this island, Codussi's church design is particularly justified since the terrain is extremely soft and could not support a heavy structure.

Interior and choir

At first sight, the interior of the church comes across as being rather somber. A deeply recessed gallery hinders the view and extensive water damage indicates that renovation would certainly be beneficial. On closer inspection, one can see the fine early Renaissance motifs in the architecture. The capitals of the columns are still not modeled on classical examples,

Capella Emiliana

The Emiliana Chapel is a good example of the still very pretty and richly decorated Venetian architecture from the early 16th century, although it is the only round building in Venice from this period. With the turned columns and the embellished mock doors, the hexagonal chapel has the same jewel box character of some other Renaissance buildings in Venice. For this type of building, architects from Bergamo were especially valued. They used Renaissance forms, but linked so many motifs together that their buildings are more reminiscent of Venetian Gothic architecture. Just 30 years after the architect Guglielmo Bergamasco had completed the building in 1530, Jacopo Sansovino had to undertake the complete renovation. The hexagonal chapel which Margherita Vetturi, the widow of Giovanni Emiliana, had built, was threatening collapse. The chapel's stone cupola is far too heavy for the delicate site. Thus, to this day, serious damage continues to occur. In the church, Codussi used a trick which was common in Venice for light and magnificent domes: the internal cupola is flat. The exterior shows a much higher cupola made of thin lead over a wooden frame.

Murano, Burano, Torcello

Murano

Murano is one of the islands in the Venetian lagoon which was settled by refugees from the mainland at the same time as the main island was settled. With the rise of Venice, the fate of Murano as a dependent island was sealed. It was here that Venetians established their industrial sites for glass production and built their summer houses with extensive gardens. The island enjoyed a certain degree of political freedom under the rule of Venice, however. It had its own head of government and councils as well as its own Golden Book of the oldest families, who enjoyed similar privileges to those of the Venetian nobility. Murano's economic strength, which was closely tied to that of Venice, came from its glassworks, one of Venice's most important industries. Perhaps the art of glassmaking was brought to Murano by the Romans. In any case, the many kinds of Murano glass were an important export through the centuries. Today, one can still see the difficult art of glassblowing in some of the glassworks. Many glassworks produce copies of traditional shapes and there are also a number of world-famous companies which continually produce new, modern (and very expensive) designs by artists and designers. The glass museum is well worth visiting.

Santi Maria e Donato, p. 506

Palazzo da Mula, p. 505

San Pietro Martire, p. 503

Further sights:
1 Museo dell'Arte Vetraria (glass museum)
2 Palazzo Trevisan

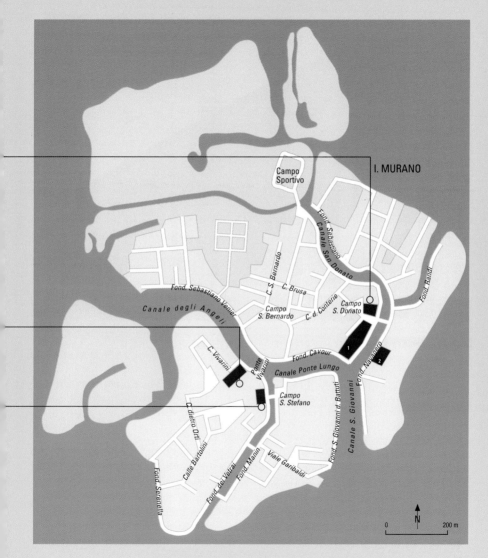

I. MURANO

Campo Sportivo

Fond. Sebastiano
Canale San Donato

Fond. Sebastiano Venier

Canale degli Angeli

C. S. Bernardo

C. Brusa

Campo
S. Bernardo

C. d. Conterie

Campo
S. Donato

Fond. Randi

Fond. Cavour

1

Fond. Navanero

2

C. Vivarini

Ponte
Vivarini

Canale Ponte Lungo

Campo
S. Stefano

C. dietro Orti

Fond. S. Giovanni d. Battuti

Canale S. Giovanni

Calle Bartolini

Fond. dei Vetrai

Fond. Manin

Viale Garibaldi

Fond. Serenella

N

0   200 m

San Pietro Martire

Interior and Choir

Today's parish church on the island was founded in 1348 as the church for a Dominican monastery. After a terrible fire, the monastery's church was almost completely rebuilt, which took until 1511. The exterior, with its bricks and the few, sparse details accented in white, shows the typical features of a Venetian mendicant order church. Under Napoleon's rule, in 1808, both the church and the monastery were closed down and their art treasures were stolen.

The interior of the church is surprising, particularly because of its bright space. Large windows allow daylight to stream in, illuminating the three wide naves. When the church was reopened in 1813, works of art were brought to San Pietro Martire from other churches which had also been closed down. Despite this, the church still seems rather empty: it is very clear that a large proportion of its once rich decoration is missing. Particularly conspicuous are the many white crystal chandeliers. These hang in the choir area on beautiful wrought iron chains from wooden beams which link the columns in the central nave. The wooden beams were erected in order to balance the thrust of the wall higher up; the arches have to bridge a relatively large gap between the columns. In the sacristy, there is a tapestry with scenes from the life of John the Baptist. In the right aisle, there is a painting of the *Baptism of Christ* by Jacopo Tintoretto.

Giovanni Bellini:
Pala Barbarigo, 1488
Oil on canvas, 200 x 320 cm

During the lifetime of Doge Agostino Barbarigo (1486–1501), this painting by Giovanni Bellini hung in his palace. After the doge's death, it was bequeathed to the church of Santa Maria degli Angeli and was brought from there to hang in San Pietro Martire.

Doge Barbarigo is kneeling in prayer in front of the Virgin. St. Mark places his right hand gently on the dog's shoulder and appears to be commending Barbarigo to the Virgin and her Child. While Mary gazes dreamily into the distance, perhaps listening to the music of the two angels, the Christ Child blesses the aging doge. Standing opposite Agostino Barbarigo is St. Augustine. Unusually, it is not his namesake who introduces the believer to the Virgin, but St. Mark. The painting clearly presents the doge in his office as state ruler lower than that of the patron saint of the republic. The doge's personal patron saint, St. Augustine, also visually recedes in comparison to St. Mark. Thus, discreet reference is made to the duty and position of the doge's office being of higher value than that of an ordinary individual.

The composition of the painting is very balanced. The emphasis of the action and

also the colors lie on the left side, where the doge kneels; the colors of the enthroned Virgin are repeated in the colors of St. Mark.

On the right side, St. Augustine stands in light-colored robes. Next to him, the view opens up onto a landscape of the foothills of the Alps. The left side is different: there, the scene is of thick trees. The denseness of the left contrasts with the wide open view of the landscape on the right. The artist signed and dated the painting with pride.

Palazzo da Mula

This 15th-century palazzo was a summer dwelling for a Venetian family. Despite some remodeling in the 16th century, with its beautifully framed lancet windows this is a good example of a Gothic palazzo. Compared with a villa on the mainland, a palazzo in Murano had the advantage of being very accessible. Here, there was space for large gardens, which were rare in Venice.

Santi Maria e Donato

At the Campo di San Donato there once
stood a row of 14th-century palazzi, which
were demolished in 1815. Luckily, however, the church was spared. It is one of
the oldest in the lagoon, dating back to the
major settlements which took place in the
7th century. It was then dedicated to the
Blessed Virgin. But, in 1125, it was given a
second patron saint, when the relics of the
body of St. Donatus of Sicily were brought
here. The building was begun in its present
form shortly after the Basilica di San
Marco and is, therefore, an important
example of the varied Veneto-Byzantine
style. Despite massive restoration in the
19th century, the unusual apse is particularly worth seeing. It is built to a hexagonal plan on two levels, the upper one
being a gallery. On the inside of the
church, only a few pieces of the original
decoration which evolved over centuries
have survived. The church has a lavish
floor mosaic, dated 1140, which is made of
marble and colored glass paste. Among a
rich treasure of ornamentation, animals
are portrayed as allegories of the Virtues.
The badly worn mosaic was restored in the
1970s mainly with American funding.

Burano

With its small, colorful houses, Burano has retained its character as a charming fishing village. At weekends it is a favorite destination for Venetian daytrippers, who go walking here and enjoy freshly caught fish in the local restaurants. During the week, however, Burano is quiet and peaceful. At one time the fishing village of Burano was famous throughout Europe for the lace it produced.

Burano's lace was once as important an export as glass from Murano. In the 18th century, however, cheaper goods from France gained dominance. It was not until this century, when a lacemaking school was established, that the old craft was revived in Burano. The first teacher was a 70-year-old woman who had learned the craft from her mother and grand-mother. Genuine Burano lace is still made entirely by hand and is as precious as it is expensive.

Torcello

Santa Maria Assunta

Long before Venice began its climb to the most powerful trading city in the Mediterranean, the island of Torcello, in the north of the lagoon, was already a center of civilization. It is especially worth a visit because of the important evidence of the earliest settlements. The cathedral of Santi Maria Assunta, as a valuable inscription testifies to this day, was built in 639 under the Byzantine Emperor Heraclius, after which the island became a diocesan district.

The present building which dates back to the 9th–11th centuries, is the oldest in the lagoon. The facade was constructed in the 9th century and heightened in the 11th century. Alongside the cathedral are the remains of an 11th-century oratory, which was restored in the 18th century. According to legend, it was here that the body of St. Mark first touched Venetian soil, after he had caused an unbelievably quick crossing of the Mediterranean through a miracle while his rescuers were sleeping.

Interior

The austerity of the interior architecture, which has lasted down through the centuries, is striking. The open roof truss, the splendid marble columns, and the 11th-century mosaic floor combine to give this impression. The choir, with the main apse, is separated from the nave by an 11th-century iconostasis. This screen is made of Byzantine marble panels with animal reliefs (peacocks, lions, birds) placed between the slender marble columns in the lower part. Over the iconostasis there is a series of paintings of the Virgin and the Twelve Apostles, which are the work of a 15th-century Venetian artist. The curve of the apse is surrounded by marble steps, on which the priest stands. The bishop's throne is on the right hand side. The design of the mosaics, which also show the Mother of God and the Twelve Apostles, may well stem from the 7th century, though the actual mosaics which today decorate the upper part of the apse date from the 13th century, and the Apostles are from the 12th century. Here, in the apse, there is also an inscription relating to the founding of the church in the 7th century. The mosaics in the right-hand choir chapel are also noteworthy. From the late 12th or early 13th century, they show Christ giving a blessing, between the archangels Gabriel and Michael; above, the saints Augustine, Ambrose, Martin and Gregory. Like the other mosaics from this period, these would have been made by artists from Ravenna. There is also an impressive mosaic of the Last Judgment and Salvation on the wall situated inside the entrance from the same period.

Santa Fosca

The cathedral in Torcello was part of an extended complex of religious buildings. The island was settled in the 5th and 6th

centuries, at the same time as the islands which would later make up Venice. At that time, however, it appeared as if Torcello would be more successful as the magnificent buildings testify. Although the slow decline of the area was already apparent in the 9th century, it only sank into complete insignificance over the following three centuries with the rise of Venice. As a result, important buildings from the early Middle Ages remain here unchanged. On the right of the cathedral stands the church of Santa Fosca, built to a centralized plan in the 11th–12th centuries, probably replacing an earlier 7th-century building. With the oratory of St. Mark and the baptistery, it completed the architectonic surrounds of the cathedral. The exterior of the apse is decorated with narrow double columns and elaborately arranged brickwork, as well as various decorative friezes. This beautifully proportioned small church, built on a Greek cross plan, with an extended choir, was built to house the relics of the martyred St. Fosca from Ravenna.

Devil's Bridge

In Torcello there is a low bridge without any railings spanning a small canal. The inhabitants of the city find it so eerie that they call it the Ponte del Diavolo (Devil's Bridge). Formerly, such bridges were quite common in Venice. A traditional game, which the residents of various quarters would often play, was a fist-fight in which the opposing teams would try to throw each other off this type of bridge into the water. Over time, however, the bridge without railings disappeared from the Venetian cityscape.

Picture and map acknowledgements

The majority of the illustrations originate from the Scala Group S.p.A. in Florence. The publishers would like to thank all the museums, collections, archives, and photographers for granting rights of reproduction and for their kind assistance in the production of this book.

Archiv für Kunst und Geschichte, Berlin (191, 239, 280, 281, 400, 401, 402, 403, 426); Artothek, Peisenberg: photo: Joachim Blauel (430/431); Bildarchiv Preussischer Kulturbesitz, Berlin (283); Osvaldo Böhm, Venice (4/5, 6/7); © Cameraphoto — Arte, Venice (2, 22/23, 66, 96/97, 104, 109, 114, 120, 131, 139, 147, 153, 168, 172/173, 175, 178, 183, 199, 202 right, 206, 207, 208, 210, 211, 214/215, 219, 224, 225, 235, 250, 253, 256, 260, 254/265, 268 left, 271, 288, 340/341, 362/363, 376, 377, 378, 379, 408, 412, 435, 490/491, 498/499, 514/515); Astrid Fischer-Leitl, Munich (85, 217, 267, 342/343, 364/365, 419, 492, 501); Foto Flash di Zennaro Elisabetta, Venice (351 right, 463); Gemäldegalerie Alte Meister, Dresden (56/57); Giovetti Fotografia & Communicazioni Visive, Mantua (241); Herzog August Bibliothek, Wolfenbüttel (58); © Markus Hilbich, Berlin (24/25, 32/33, 36, 40, 47, 48, 52/53, 59, 61, 63 below, 67, 82/83, 92, 94, 95, 98, 100, 101, 112, 118, 119, 129, 130, 145 below, 176, 186, 187, 198, 218, 222/223, 247, 251, 263, 272, 282, 296, 297, 300, 334, 354/355, 367, 374, 381, 382, 383, 384, 392, 393, 394, 395, 416/417, 447, 468, 485, 494/495, 497, 502, 510, 513); Rolf Krause, Essen (26—31, 103, 146, 148, 156, 224 right, 232/233, 315, 398, 473, 487, 517, 518, 519, 522, 523, 524, 526, 528 below, 530, 531, 534, 535, 564—69); Magnus Edizioni, Fagagna (132, 174, 177, 373); Ministero per i Beni e le Attività Culturali, Milan (350); Museo Correr, Venice — photo: Fotoflash (16 left, 190, 197, 351 left, 375, 428, 443); Eduard Noak, Cologne (237); © The National Gallery, London (16 right); © Raccolta Teatrale del Burcardo, Rome (307); © Sammlung Georg Schäfer, Schweinfurt (464/465).